FASHION, MEDIA, PROMOTION
the new black magic

FASHION, MEDIA, PROMOTION
the new black magic

Jayne Sheridan

WILEY-BLACKWELL

A John Wiley & Sons, Ltd., Publication

This edition first published 2010
©2010 Jayne Sheridan

Blackwell Publishing was acquired by John Wiley & Sons in February 2007. Blackwell's publishing programme has been merged with Wiley's global Scientific, Technical, and Medical business to form Wiley-Blackwell.

Registered office
John Wiley & Sons Ltd, The Atrium, Southern Gate, Chichester, West Sussex, PO19 8SQ, United Kingdom

Editorial offices
9600 Garsington Road, Oxford, OX4 2DQ, United Kingdom
2121 State Avenue, Ames, Iowa 50014-8300, USA

For details of our global editorial offices, for customer services and for information about how to apply for permission to reuse the copyright material in this book please see our website at www.wiley.com/wiley-blackwell.

Library of Congress Cataloging-in-Publication Data

Sheridan, Jayne.
   Fashion, media, promotion : the new black magic / Jayne Sheridan.
       p. cm.
   Includes bibliographical references and index.
   ISBN 978-1-4051-9421-1 (pbk. : alk. paper)
1. Advertising–Fashion.   2. Fashion design.   3. Fashion designers.
   4. Clothing trade.   I. Title.
   HF6161.C44S54 2010
   659.19′74692–dc22

                                        2009038725

A catalogue record for this book is available from the British Library.

Set in 13 on 15pt Garamond by Toppan Best-set Premedia Limited
Printed and bound in Malaysia by Vivar Printing Sdn Bhd

1   2010

CONTENTS

ACKNOWLEDGEMENTS

Many people have taken an interest in this book and offered encouragement. I would especially like to thank the following for their cooperation and timely responses: Madeleine Metcalfe, Hilary Hollingworth, Lynne Franks, Anita and Maurice Clarke, Martin Dawber, Sonia Land, Frances Tempest, Hilary Alexander, Susan Marling, Richard Williams, Dilys E. Blum, Hannah Shakespeare, Matthew Frost, Wally Olins, Claire Wilcox, Eleri Lynn, Valerie Steele, Amy Glover, James Sowden, Ann Sparks, Suzy Menkes, Leila Dewji, Andy Stafford, Douglas Smith, Rachel Moseley, Alisa Richardson, Eric Hildrew, Louise Pullen, Anna Fletcher, Jane Arnold, David Wheeler, Kevin Almond, Georgia Vuletic, Claire Allen, Louise Stocks-Young, Ann and Howard Westwood, who have the 'Bolly' on ice, Christine Browett, Kathryn Brennand, Louise Parkinson, Irene Spink, Ruth Scanlan, Jan and Natalia Wdowczyk, Penny Macbeth, Judith Farnell, Lucy Stride, Jemma Crooks, Leonie Cowton, Wendy Toole, Stephen Brook, Rosemary Dunnage, Pauline Hawkins, Diane Crabtree, Ernest Hall, Fran, Lyn and Robert Crabtree, *Circle of Friends*, Hebden Bridge, Sonia Maud, John and Veca Wilson, Ian and Jean Moodie, *Gymophobics,* Halifax Minster, William Naylor, Michael Poole, Sue and Nigel Bamford, Christopher Bailey, Colin McDowell, Joyce Thornton, Vanessa Denza, Sylvia Ayton, Christian Gardiner, John Rooney, Fiona MacDonald, Emma Brockes, Judy Berger, Louise Peel, Jane Ritchie, Emma Hunt, Martin Wanless, Shelia Rowbotham, Alison Nick, Cath Varley, Rosemary Varley, Joanna Beale, Lyn Joseph, Paul Davies, Jan Hamling, Duncan Morris, Chris Hodgkiss, Pip Bishop. Thanks particularly to Simon Warner, for his kind and skilful interventions, and to Sally for her wise suggestions.

All images throughout the book and on the cover are by Anton Storey and are protected by copyright.

DEDICATION

For Sally, Kate, Eve and Jo (Jonathan) Sheridan, with love, and for those students whose enthusiasm, for Fashion and Film, inspires *The New Black Magic*.

INTRODUCTION

Fashion, Media, Promotion: *the new black magic*

Modern democratic society has made Fashion into a sort of cross-subsidising organism, destined to establish an automatic equilibrium between the demand for singularity and the right for all to have it.

Roland Barthes, *Dandyism and Fashion*

When Joanna Lumley told listeners to *Desert Island Discs* that the Fashion set loved *Absolutely Fabulous* because it was *'so right'*, she was acknowledging that, without revealing any of Fashion's secrets, *Ab Fab* had recreated much of its mystique.[1] The Fashion world could enjoy parody. However, the exposé in *The Devil Wears Prada,* by entréist Lauren Weisberger, was seen as suspect by those at the centre of this universe in the offices of *Vogue* at Condé Nast. Fashion's pervasive and persuasive power will be explored here by examining the tropes employed in Fashion's promotion and central to *TDWP*'s narrative. In it, the quixotic links between the industry, publicity and journalism, the inner workings of Fashion's coterie, its apologists, assorted slaves and stars feeding the machine are disclosed. This early 21st-century novella, in its attempt to decipher Fashion's enigma, revives ideas of the intellectual challenge taken on by Roland Barthes when he began theorizing Fashion in the late 1950s and 1960s. In [An Early Preface to] *The Fashion System,*[2] Barthes noted he would capitalize the word *Fashion* to 'distinguish clothing, cosmetics, shoes, hair and jewellery, Fashion from fashion in general; in the sense of vogue or obsession; *fad* not *fashion*'. In this I am taking my style from him, and, from his rhetoric, guiding principles.

Image-clothing and written garments

Before the 1968 *événements* in France, which would advance the democratization of Fashion, as well as providing a *point de capiton* for movements such as feminism and racial and gender equality, Barthes discovered a way to explain Fashion's potent communication techniques. His insight was discerning. He thought that within Fashion magazines there is always image accompanied by text. He realized that the illustrations or photographs, flat and one-dimensional, with writing, exist in relation to what can be seen as 'real clothing', and the real clothing, promoted in this imaginary, asks to be acquired and worn. Barthes also suggested that each of these objects is known through a different Fashion code or system. In the case of 'real clothing', he understood that it must be known not by sight, because its visual image does not reveal all its intricacies. He thought it must be known through the mechanical process of its production: the seams, the pleats, as they are manufactured. The 'image-clothing', we see from designers' drawings, translated through the makers' skills, is made material through significant structures with a vocabulary of their own – seams, hems, buttons and so on. The written garment is made by curators, publicists and journalists; created through words.

Hardly disguised as fiction, *The Devil Wears Prada* charts the year when Weisberger acted as assistant to Anna Wintour, editor-in-chief at *Vogue* US, said to be the model for the 'devil' of the title. It tells of the triumphs and pitfalls of college-educated, but terrified, assistant, the totally stressed-out Andrea Sachs. We learn that a prima donna editor-in-chief on a magazine, with the authority and influence of *Runway* (the fictional *Vogue*), can rule her empire as total despot. Everyone associated with her world needs to be savvy to each and every nuance to survive the fracas. *The Devil Wears Prada* shows Fashion operating in a segregated community where arcane information is deciphered by eager acolytes. Weisberger gives us clues to the factual world of Fashion before it has been mythologized by the wizardry of its writers, stylists and photographers: the journalists who use the language of Fashion to describe *real* clothing. Although Weisberger's book begs questions about power structures, skills hierarchies, zeitgeist and trend movements, global shifts and political interventions, it stimulates the notion that Fashion journalism is unlike any other form of writing because those promoting Fashion, and those commenting on it, speak in code to each other. Barthes, in *The Fashion System*, his semiological and structuralist critique on Fashion and Fashion journalism, says:

> It is clear that Fashion utterances are entirely derived not from a style but a writing; by describing an item of clothing, or how it is worn, the writer/journalist invests in his words nothing of himself [*sic*] nor of his psychology; he simply conforms to a certain conventional and regulated style (we might say an ethos), which furthermore announces immediately that it is from a Fashion magazine.[3]

Industry overview

When Jean Muir visited the galleries I promoted in Yorkshire in 1994, a year before she died, she was sweet and frail and very charming to me. Nevertheless, she had asked one of her assistants to send for an example of my writing ahead of our meeting for the RSA exhibition she was opening before she agreed to be interviewed for our in-house newspaper. This experience gave me a hint of the imperious ways employed by Fashion's divas and the desire to find out why Fashion needs them. Andrea Sachs, *TDWP*'s heroine, portrayed as a naïf, wants to become a serious journalist, preferably with the *New Yorker*, as did the real-life Weisberger. She has no thoughts of how she might need to deal with internal politics or creative temperaments. She has to endure a baptism of fire in the quite specific field of Fashion journalism, believing it will be key to writing success. She finds herself in an all-consuming, powerfully controlled and controlling world. Whether writing inventive case study or complete fiction, Weisberger in *TDWP* describes the strange responsibility she felt, learning from the main arbiter in a world-beating industry:

> Your first job out of college and you're working with the most important woman at the most profitable magazine at the biggest magazine publishing company in the entire world. You'll get to watch it all happen, from the top down. If you just keep your eyes open and your priorities in order, you'll learn more in one year than most people in the industry will see in their entire careers.[4]

David Denby, writing in the *New Yorker* in 2006, describes the compelling personality of the magazine editor characterized by Weisberger, film scriptwriter Aline Brosh McKenna and film actor Meryl Streep:

> Streep's every gesture says that fashion is a multibillion-dollar business in which civility (except when directed at the famous) has become a disposable luxury ... she understands her role in fashion so acutely that you can't make fun of her. He observes that '*Miranda Priestly* is powerful because she makes definitive judgments that are meant to hold sway no longer than a season or two'.[5]

In so saying, Denby defines and maps the limits of Fashion's authority. Recognizing that *TDWP* is a Fashion text with valuable insights subtly embedded in the romantic narrative, he writes, '*Runway* is the engine of desire – not the desire for sex, which the movie regards as relatively unimportant, but for power and for very beautiful things.' The film script by Brosh Mckenna, expressing ideas not included in the novel, explains how Fashion is made and sold. It is expressed in what Denby describes as a:

> nasty but brilliant speech in which she [*Miranda Priestley*] explains the structural connection between a sample from a fashion house – a cerulean belt – that Andy laughs at, and the frumpy sweater that Andy is wearing. It's startling to hear the entire fashion world tied together as an economic unit – Adam Smith couldn't have done better.[6]

It is the industry overview, contained in both book and film, which prompts the proposition that the world-beating Fashion process deserves a story that focuses on its propaganda.

When Barthes writes of dress being 'the sum of individual pieces linked to the development of Fashion's commercial myth-making',[7] it prefigures what Weisberger sets up for Brosh McKenna and Streep, who define the editor's brilliance, identified by colleagues at *Vogue*, as in the style of Anna Wintour. Weisberger describes Sachs's early days working at *Runway* as occupying a world 'only two hours away geographically but ... really in a different solar system',[8] reflecting on how

The Devil Wears Prada *shows Fashion operating in a segregated community where arcane information is deciphered by eager acolytes.*

we might see what could be called 'planet Fashion': the designers, the writers, their assistants, the directors, the stylists, the PRs, the photographers who exist in a rarefied space. In the course of the narrative she reveals a series of intricate, interrelated webs run by those who liaise and conspire to sell Fashion. She says, 'it was all too foreign, too absolutely strange sounding and different to make any sense'.[9] Her world of Fashion has been constructed through a series of intellectual and technological developments, begun in the mid-twentieth century when mass production led to the conspicuous consumption which marked out the new bourgeoisie, and when beneficiaries of expanded educational opportunities had the means to buy status symbols and objects of desire.

Angela McRobbie, writing on Fashion's relationship to Art, explains how fine artists are drawn into the academic fold through the use of 'professional vocabularies' employed by the critics. In contrast, Fashion writers are sometimes sniggered at by fellow journalists, with Polly Vernon writing in *The Observer* in September 2006:

> The industry's most inventive, most debauched and most sneeringly superior will descend upon the city, where they will indulge in an orgy of catwalk shows, competitive canapé under-eating and exchanging of dagger-type looks. Everyone will call each other 'Gorge' (as in –*eous*) or 'Hon' (as in Honey), and wear their very best frocks, and it'll be too fabulous for words. Inevitably, you, outsider, will want to infiltrate this glittering scene. It won't be easy. Even if you do somehow inveigle your way into a show or two, you'll almost certainly find that the shallow glamour, corruption and back-stabbing you uncover will plunge you into a deep pit of nihilistic despair from which you many never emerge.[10]

Nevertheless, Christopher Breward believes that 'Fashion now occupies the centre ground in popular understandings of modern culture',[11] and he and others have turned the Cinderella's slipper of popular discourse into the diamond tiara of cultural theory. Their dialogues are the product of both Modernist and post-Modernist studies, marked by writers and taken as a given by Weisberger and the colleagues she observed. Condé Nast closed ranks to defend itself against any damage done by *The Devil Wears Prada,* said to be based on Weisberger's days as one of Anna Wintour's assistants at *Vogue* US. Emma Brockes, the *Guardian* profile writer, answering an email from me about bitchy comments on *TDWP,* recalls that they were from the *New Yorker*:

> It called it 'trivially self-regarding' and the *New York Times*, which, if I remember rightly, employed a former loyal colleague of Wintour's to review the book, said she was very snotty about it. It seemed to me to get a much tougher time than, say, Plum Sykes's debut novel, which was indulgently received as 'social satire', where *TDWP* was just regarded as bad manners. There was a definite sense that Weisberger had broken some unwritten code about ratting on your former employers, and it obviously irritated the higher-end writing world that she, in her novel, made herself out to be too intelligent for the fashion industry and yet had written this really quite trashy book. I thought they were too hard on her … she was

pretty young when she wrote it and it obviously annoyed a lot of people that it did so well.[12]

At British *Vogue*, Alexandra Shulman and her editorial team decided to review neither book nor film. As an afterthought or compromise, obliging if not terrified assistant Sacha Forbes was commissioned to write a blog based on her role as Shulman's right-hand woman for a *Daily Telegraph* spread previewing the film. Anna Wintour's team in New York were rather more sniffy. I spoke to Phyllis Rifefield, Readers' Queries Desk (Thursday, 16 November 2006), to ask whether they had reviewed *TDWP*. One of her colleagues, in a lovely Manhattan accent, had remarked, 'I can't remember, really.' Rifefield, who confided that she had known Weisberger during her internship in the magazine's editorial offices, said, 'We thought, what was the point of popularising this thing?' She agreed with the idea that the screen version of *TDWP* showed the fictional editor, in Meryl Streep's finely judged performance, as a talented, inspirational Fashion guru. 'Just as a *Vogue* editor must, surely, be?' I ventured. 'Especially *the* editor,' Rifefield pointed out, making a direct reference, I confirmed, to the already legendary Wintour. Their concerns about the revelations of an interloper reflect the general unease felt around fields of promotion and publishing. If inside the system, there is a need to preserve its mystery, and if outside, there is the fear of being taken in by its artifice. This is the paranoia which gives rise to the terror inspired by the concept of 'spin', less feared by students of Barthes and Ed Bernays than by others. The treatment of Fashion in film has invariably been celebratory and there was little anxiety, among the Fashion crowd over the cinema version of *TDWP*, in 2006. Film theory points to important movies playing their roles in engaging audiences of millions. *Gone with the Wind* and *Breakfast at Tiffany's*, both modern in filmic style and narrative themes, and *The Devil Wears Prada*, a self-reflexive post-Modern ironic take on the Fashion industry, have brought Fashion ideas and inspirations to generations of women cinema-goers.

Avant-garde selling techniques

Since Christian Dior's 'New Look' in 1947, Fashion has become a universal delight; transmitted through inspired practitioners, legendary figures, designers and artists who have masterminded myths and created moving image texts to progress Fashion's cause. *Gone with the Wind* and its role in bringing Dior's 'flower woman' to the post-bellum world fascinates 21st-century Feminists and Fashion lovers. The take-up of his designs by manufacturers and consumers, as fabrics were no longer rationed, began a revolution which now sees millionaires, and the unemployed, flashing identical checks and à la mode sportswear branding. Shoehorned in after two world wars and before global warming, Fashion, as an international force, is a pleasure embedded in our lives through subtle and seductive means. At the cutting edge in the 20th century, as a powerful ingenious industry using computerized technologies to reach waiting markets, it is now avant-garde in the way it sells itself universally while remaining idiomatic, exclusive and mysterious.

If 'fashion now occupies the centre ground in popular understandings of modern culture',[13] as Breward believes, here it will be suggested that Fashion has achieved this status, above other Design or Art forms, by being able to adapt to shifting means of promotion and to the changing media: magazines, newspapers, websites, advertising, film, music and radio. The alchemy to achieve this magic is created by Fashion houses in ceaseless competition from one season to the next, supported in their quest for supremacy by a symbiotic Press. In a post-Modern world, where haute couture copies are sold cheaply from out-of-town outlets within days of catwalk appearances, appropriately nuanced messages, created by brand-aware corporate strategists, have to appear in the Media just as speedily. Manipulating the Media, Fashion has achieved pre-eminence; employing millions worldwide, inspiring architecture, buying up real estate, hiring tycoons and inspirational gurus, controlling intellectual property, brokering a hunger for change as accountants might guard the bottom line. Even for the truly talented, it is not just a matter of zeitgeist and being part of the machine. The industry's all-conquering zeal comes from diverse energies and resources. Christian Dior, Elsa Schiaparelli, Mary Quant, Audrey Hepburn, David Bailey, Vivienne Westwood, Paul Smith: how have they played their parts in bringing Fashion, as an accessible Art form, to the world, and who were their paradigms, accomplices and allies? As movers and shakers, are they dedicated retailers, dynamic geniuses or just clever crowd-pleasers?

'*It is obvious that the new Citroën has fallen from the sky in as much as it appears at first sight as a superlative object.*' *Barthes brought his signature revelations to the understandings of Hollywood, Wrestling and the Auto industry for* Mythologies *to become advertising's key text.*

When Jon and Dan Snow teamed up as father and son double act to bring us serious pie charts on the state of the British economy (*Who Makes Britain Rich?*, BBC2, 5 January 2007), they revealed that Fashion plays a major part in creating Britain's contemporary wealth and drew on the history of Viyella as an example. The Derbyshire-based cloth manufacturer's progress reads like a 'How to succeed in business for two hundred years' manual. Using branding before 19th-century, American plainsmen had taken hot irons to their cattle, and taking on the most current manufacturing skills and technologies before competitors, Viyella thrived and prospered. As an international retailer, it survived into the 21st century, as a microcosm of the Fashion industry as a whole, using its legend to promote stores and websites. The UK designer Fashion industry is the fourth largest in the world after the USA, Italy and France. It has a reputation for innovative, and original, approaches to promotion and marketing. David Wynne Morgan, who took Mary Quant's clothes abroad in 1960, and who headed up the international PR company Hill and Knowlton in the 1980s, found himself *selling* British Fashion franchises across the globe through his London-based financial PR house in the first decade of this century.

Beyond his wildest dreams

At the heart of Fashion's success is its instinct for corporate, designer and product branding, and the rapid take-up of new production and distribution systems. My particular interest in how Fashion uses technology towards its inexorable progress began when I was writing about the computerized handling system Eton for the Fashion trade press in the 1980s. The system was developed in the mid 1960s, when the Swedish apparel industry was experiencing a number of cost-related problems. Throughput times were too high and, as a result, demands for quicker delivery times could not be met. In addition, garment workers were forced to waste time handling and transporting material instead of sewing, and capital was needlessly tied up in work-in-progress. In the 20th century, the Fashion industry embraced product handling and computerized technologies to help in the making of garments. One of these systems, with global take-up, is the invention by self-trained technician, and co-owner of the Eton Shirt Factory, Inge Davidson. With its flexible addressing capabilities, it produced benefits *beyond his wildest dreams*. The website which tells the story states that 'the most recent incarnation of the original Eton UPS concept is now gaining recognition as the industry standard for precise, and comprehensive, production control by leading global manufacturers'.[14] In October 2001, the Youngor Group, one of Eton systems' customers opened, a 300,000 square metre manufacturing base in Ningbo, China. It houses some of the world's most advanced garment technologies, including computer-controlled assembly lines from Eton Systems. The Hempel Group has installed the Eton system, among other technologies, to meet orders from international Fashion stores Zara, Liz Claiborne, Jones New York, C&A, Etam, Guess and other high street Fashion leaders.

By end of the 20th century, eminent sociologists had begun to write about the Italian clothing company Benetton, a phenomenon which began as a cottage industry and then spread across the globe. Professor Paolo Perulli, writing about Fordism in 1999, explained how industry had once employed the principles of *'flexible specialization'*, with economies of scale, which had then been replaced by *'economies of scope'*:

> A good example is Benetton, the highly successful Italian clothing company. Benetton is a family firm with 2,500 national and international outlets (all of them franchised). Specially designed electronic cash registers in these outlets constantly transmit on-line full data about sales – type of article, colour, size, etc. This information is centrally received and forms the basis for decisions about design and production.[15]

Although it seemed to fit awkwardly with other Italian industrial models of the time, Perulli acknowledged its advances and its influence:

> In the 1980s Benetton became a huge multinational operation. It dominated its 'artisanal' subcontractors at home and its franchised retail outlets abroad. By 1990 it was said to open a new store somewhere in the world every day of the year. In a new move, it had also begun to open factories outside Italy, with different locations specializing in the production of one or more types of products. It did so for the familiar reason of taking advantage of cheaper labour costs outside Italy. Benetton hence came ever closer to the 'world car' model.[16]

In spotting the similarities between the strategies of Benetton and those of leading car companies, Perulli comments on 'the globalization, increased automation, adaptation of just-in-time procedures and the intensified use of the computer for design, production and stock control', revelling in the way Fashion is able to emulate trading techniques used by the car industry. 'Benetton's development and dominance of a network of suppliers seems little different from that used by Japanese car firms,' he suggests, asking, 'Is the Benetton economy a world of flexible specialization or Japanese-led revitalized Fordism?'[17] If cars led the economy of the mid 20th century then it is through companies like Benetton that Fashion finds itself in its current pole position. Benetton's controversial advertising campaigns in the 1980s and 1990s continued to promote the brand, and it is in the vanguard again, developing innovative and diverse 21st-century ways to stay in the race.

Fashion always adapts to change. In taking on new manufacturing technologies, it kept pace with constantly evolving means of production in the 20th century. Ahead of millennial communication and information transformations, Benetton introduced Fabrica (Latin for 'workshop') in 1994. Conceived by Oliviero Toscani, it is located in the Villa Pastega complex in Villorba, Treviso, recreated by architect Tadao Ando. As Benetton's communication headquarters, it is also a production site for media innovation. There are no courses or seminars held there and no teachers or final degrees. At Fabrica inventions are given form. It is a communication centre made available to 20 students from around the world. These artists-designers-researchers learn by making. Artists and researchers work on communication; on global issues such as racism, fear, famine. Hoping not to be pigeonholed as a cultural hothouse, Fabrica aims at non-elitist audiences via the Media. Graphics, photography, sound, video, design and cinema projects are developed. A bimonthly magazine, *Colors*, is currently distributed in six bilingual editions in Europe, the United States, Latin America and Asia. Describing Fabrica in 2000, Luciano Benetton said:

> I'm often asked why the Benetton Group founded Fabrica. I like to reply by saying that doing business is not just a question of running an enterprise but of being enterprising; of being receptive to everything that experience and our interaction with the world can teach us. So Fabrica's and Benetton's activities are not so far apart. Indeed, concepts of cultural planning and organisation, of communication, of artistic creativity are vital to a global group who operates over 360 degrees in the clothing sector, therefore closely allied to taste, style, quality of life. I consider Fabrica the bridgehead of our corporate culture, where the continuous quest for new points of reference serves to remind us that we must bring not only our resolve to our work, but also our wealth of imagination and creativity.[18]

> Villorba, 9 September 2000

The Fashion entrepreneur Tom Ford announced future plans for global expansion to Milan, London, Los Angeles and Hawaii in June 2007, having opened his first store in April in Madison Avenue, New York. His plans included franchises with Bergdorf Goodman, Neiman Marcus in the States and with Harrods in London, Daslu in Sao Paolo, Brazil, and shop-in-shops in Tokyo and Osaka, Japan. He claimed at the time that their brand's 'tighter distribution' with 'quality, and service' should be 'strong in a world of decreasing standards'.

When he took over at Gucci he was credited 'with putting the glamour back into fashion, introducing Halston-style velvet hipsters, skinny satin shirts and car-finish metallic patent boots. In 1995, he had brought in French stylist Carine Roitfeld and photographer Mario

Ahead of millennial communication and information transformations Benetton, introduced Fabrica (Latin for 'workshop') in 1994. Conceived by Oliviero Toscani, it is located in the Villa Pastega complex in Villorba, Treviso, recreated by architect Tadao Ando.

Testino to create a series of new, modern ad campaigns for the company. By 1999, the house of Gucci, which had been almost bankrupt when Ford joined, was valued at about $4.3 billion. 'We didn't even have a photocopier at one stage,' he admits. 'We didn't have any paper.' In 2000, Ford was named Best International Designer at the first VH1/*Vogue* Awards in New York. He sees his success coming from sleeping little, writing ideas in the middle of the night on Post-it notes, and having the sort of taste which appeals to the general public. *Vogue* believes people feel that 'Ford's secret is the combination of a fine commercial sensibility and a genuine feel for fashion'. In his former role at Gucci, he designed shoes, watches, luggage and men's and women's wear as well as planning the company's advertising campaigns.

In 2009, an additional 12 stores opened, including a directly operated flagship store in London, a franchised flagship store in Shanghai and a second store in Beijing. In 2010, directly operated stores are to open in LA and Hawaii with 15 franchised stores scheduled to open in Asia including a flagship store in Tokyo. Over the next 10 years, a minimum of 87 franchised Tom Ford stores will open throughout Asia in partnership with the Lane Crawford Joyce Group, including but not limited to Japan, Hong Kong, China, Taiwan, Macau, Singapore, Indonesia, Malaysia and Australia. Tom Ford's personality-based marketing is driving this operation, and whether or not his empire will challenge more politically and philosophically motivated brands like Benetton will be assessed through observing Fashion movements under the global spotlight.

Communication power bases

Fashion does not only promote itself through individual dynamic organizations; it also establishes itself through its own information and communication power bases. Providing online research, trend analysis and news to the fashion, design and style industries, Worth Global Style Network is the leading global service, launched in early 1998 by Julian and Marc Worth. It is admired in the industry as a model of online excellence. Its success is based on its global perspective. A hundred-strong team of creative and editorial staff works with a network of experienced writers, photographers, researchers, analysts and trend-spotters in cities around the world, tracking the latest stores, designers, brands, trends and business innovations. Funded by major companies and regarded as the source of international style intelligence, WGSN is essential to other related industries needing to stay in touch with research, analysis and news on emerging trends. Based in London with offices in New York, Hong Kong, Seoul, Los Angeles, Melbourne and Tokyo, Worth Global Style Network won a Queen's Award for Enterprise in 2003, and in 2004 founders Julian and Marc Worth were named Ernst & Young's London Technology & Communication Entrepreneurs of the Year. The *Financial Times* charts its influence: 'WGSN had a good idea to start with. Bad decisions can cost retailers and suppliers millions. Subscribers logging on to the website see more than 500,000 pages devoted entirely to trends in visual style.'[19] The *Wall Street Journal* confirms its value:

> Worth Global Style Network subscribers can watch runway shows around the world, view store-window displays for 20 cities and get a peek at which neutral shade is packed on the shelves at Banana Republics across the US. They can also read about the marketing strategies at H&M, the cheap-but-chic fashion chain from Sweden, and see candid photos of cool kids in Los Angeles wearing the new '*waisted denim*' trend (jeans with the waistband torn off). Designers can even check out fabrics by clicking on an extensive textile section that shows swatches, along with vendors and phone numbers.[20]

Beginning with Abercrombie & Fitch, through Giorgio Armani, Levi Strauss, L'Oreal, Procter & Gamble, Saks Fifth Avenue and Tommy Hilfiger to Zara, WGSN's subscription list is full of established and rising stars. Becoming a dominant Fashion figure without intelligence online from WGSN is an increasingly impossible task, so those missing from its list are interestingly vulnerable and their progress might usefully be monitored.

Retail universe

Fashion is always at the mercy of the communication industry and the limiting measures, which were part of World War II, continued to dog its progress into the middle of the last century. Freed from newsprint rationing in the late 1950s, in 1962 the *Sunday Times* became the first newspaper to publish colour supplements. This was also the year that Bradford-born David Hockney wore a gold lamé suit to collect his gold medal from the Royal College of Art. Art schools, universities, editorial offices and museums – opening doors were beginning to democratize Art and the Fashion industry. With grammar-school talent able to mix with the haute bourgeoisie in colleges and offices, the Fashion industry seems to have needed a secret code to protect its exclusivity. Whether Mary Quant, Terence Conran, Sylvia Ayton, Vivienne Westwood or Wendy Dagworthy, this new breed of art school and college-educated talent began the rise, and rise, of the image industry in Britain, and its practitioners have spread their empires abroad. They have seen department stores, crucial to designer businesses, become less dominant in the retail universe. They have seen international chains come and go from British high streets. They have taken designs and retail strategies overseas and brought marketing and promotional techniques back with them. They have drawn on international Art and images to sell more clothes and recognized the need for ever more imaginative communication strategies to support their trend-driven industry.

In 1981, as a features writer on the *Chester Observer*, a bi-weekly bought out by the Thomson group, I travelled with Alexander Plunket Greene and his wife, Mary Quant, from Chester to Manchester airport, about 60 miles, in a black cab. The Plunket Greenes had absolutely no need to answer my eager questions, nor even agree to have me along. Mary Quant had been an international fashion success since the late 1950s. When I read her autobiography *Quant on Quant* in 2006, I realized I had come across one of Fashion's most passionate salespeople and a woman who hated disappointing anyone. These qualities, which she brought to the promotion of a new kind of Fashion in the fifties and sixties, when she danced to the tune composed by her beloved 'Dolly Birds', will be explored.

As Christian Dior and the fall-out from *Gone with the Wind* began democratizing Fashion in the late forties and fifties, it was then that the next Hollywood sensation saw women, on both sides of the Atlantic, developing a desire for haute couture looks at Singer sewing machine prices. Audrey Hepburn, the androgynous waif, became a symbol of freedom and style for the second half of the 20th century through movies *Sabrina* and *Breakfast at Tiffany's*. For a Condé Nast publication, in 1987, Audrey Hepburn wrote:

> I remember the Fifties as a time of renewal and of regained security. Postwar austerity was fading and although the heartbreak remained, wounds were healing. There was a rebirth of opportunity, vitality and enthusiasm. The big American musicals came to London; people packed the theatres to see the twice-nightly shows of *High Button Shoes*, *South Pacific* and *Guys and Dolls*.[21]

Her interest in clothes, theatre, her sense of nostalgia, and her relationship with the French designer Hubert de Givenchy created the legend that she and her films became.

By being highly visible through its promotional strategies, Fashion succeeds in being seen as an egalitarian industry, attracting professionals from different classes and backgrounds while supplying the emerging and haute bourgeoisie with opportunities to dress as stylish peasants.

The codes, manners and mores – walking the catwalk, talking the shop-talk and joining the in-crowd, too rich, too thin – it's always style never content. Fashion has become seriously fashionable because everyone wants to be in on its secrets. We talk of keeping things up our sleeves, of not letting cats out of bags. But we want to know what colour, texture and length of sleeve we'll be wearing and whether the bag will be Vuitton, Prada or Chanel – how to pose to be en vogue. Here will be told how Fashion keeps its fans entranced, informed and ready to invest. Whether it's *Vogue*, with innovators Anna Piaggi, Diana Vreeland or Anna Wintour, *The Observer*, *Daily Telegraph*, *New York Times* or *The Scotsman*, each has its ways of making readers swoon, salivate and shop. Fashion is about owning new objects of desire, every season, but it is also about how we represent ourselves to the 'other'. Here lies the novelty Freud identified as being essential to inspire eroticism. Many interpellations from other cultures distinguish how fashion is seen and consumed across the globe. Meeting Jacques Derrida at a conference to launch his book *The Politics of Friendship* in 1998, I recognized that his clothes were distinctively tailored, and more fashionable, than those of American or British academics.

How we consume Fashion, across different cultures, has been researched and developed by Paul Smith, whose empire-building career is part of a global fervour, assuaged by building cathedrals and Art galleries in which to shop. It was Marx who decided it is consumption and not production that is at the basis of the social order. If, as his follower Baudrillard says, 'Capital accumulates till it becomes image', it is the Fashion industry which is able to achieve this conversion. Barthes, Baudrillard and Bourdieu have made Fashion reading a reputable pastime for intellectuals. Freud wrote of erotic longings in a Vienna painted by Klimt, and as we continue to desire ever more trappings of seduction, the Fashion industry feeds the need. In 1967, Roland Barthes turning his attention to Fashion photographers, deciding that they used the world as décor, background or theatre, picking on themes to reflect, say, Scotland, medieval times or misty and cold climates. He described photographers as practising a rather 'rudimentary process' with '*association of ideas*', giving as examples, 'the sun evokes cactuses, dark night evokes bronze statues, mohair evokes sheep, fur evokes wild beasts and wild beasts evoke a cage: we'll show a woman in fur behind heavy bars'.[22] The tropes identified by Barthes have become part of an innovative practice, which is exciting, surprising, contradictory and extraordinary. Fashion photography today is an innovative profession in a realm of converging media. It is where ideas and images from Art and Fashion collide. In photography, exchanges and overlaps between the two intensify and merge. Designers create their own artistic statements around clothes and catwalk shows, and artists work with designers to shift the boundaries of traditional fashion photography and film.

Selling dreams

David Bailey, known as the photographers' photographer, is a collector, commentator and instigator of new ways of seeing. I first wrote about him in June 1983, when his show Shots of Style was on at the National Museum of Photography, Film and Television, now the National Media Museum, in Bradford:

> As the free-ranging, fashion-sharp teenagers of the fifties reached for new standards of self-expression, the only important style magazine of the time, *Vogue*, refused to acknowledge the existence of the bikini. Just how far we have come in accepting overt sensuality, and minimalist clothing, as part of our common culture is shown in the first major exhibition of fashion photography, Shots of Style. Social changes from the early years of fashion photography were charted in an imaginative selection made by David Bailey, together with a smaller view of late 20th-century British Women's Magazines. The hotchpotch of period references in today's fashions [the 1980s] is explained as one decade makes allusions to earlier times and as Bailey's discerning eye directs ours to analyse influences. He is not lavish in his praise of colleagues. He describes his selection as lucky survivors from the past, the good ones being rare. Bailey himself was one of the new wave of photographers, from the fifties, when magazines were launched such as *Nova*, aimed at younger post New Look readers. All the photographs were originally commissioned for magazines, and Bailey makes another plea – to note the role of photographers such as Irving Penn of *Vogue*, who were 'selling dreams not clothes'. Fashion became more available to the woman in the street at the same time as the rise of the 35mm camera in the late fifties. Subsequently photographs served as a social document [highlighting] signifying fashion's democratizing power. The process has led to a greater freedom to ignore commercial images. 'Now [in the eighties], fashion can be what you want. A fashion magazine does not have the power to say you wear pink or a mini.

Magazines show what is available, and 'he or she chooses how to look', says Bailey. In the twenties the models were bolder, smiling from between paste jewellery, flashing shapely ankles from below the sequinned glitter. The first glimmer of relaxed freedom in fashion comes in a 1939 Toni Frissell picture for a Saks 5th Avenue promotion. The model leaning over the bonnet of a car is wearing a gored, two-piece, sundress, with a little midriff showing. Flat child-like sandals, made sophisticated by seamed-stockinged legs, complete the whole curvy, languid feel. It was not however until Dior, with the famed New Look in 1947, decided, at the same time as lengthening skirts, to give women some freedom of movement, that the real changes began to appear and in 1949 American *Harpers* saw the last of the little local seamstress tailoring. In 1957 models were seen leaping from steps wearing huge collared coats, carrying decorative umbrellas. Cardin's haute couture was pictured in the same year, in the sleazy backstage setting of the Follies for the international magazine market. The rise of the sensational picture, in the 1960s, climaxed with Richard Avedon's memorable composition of Penelope Tree, in Dior's black strapless evening dress and white sash, frail and supple, holding back a herd of charging elephants. The visual impact shook the world of fashion photography. An interesting pointer in each decade from the twenties through to the seventies is the permanent inclusion of the steadily smoking cigarette. Not only was the slim, white, phallic symbol the model's most constant prop, it was certainly her most familiar accessory. Whether it can be described as greater honesty or merely greater 'turn-on', the next development certainly sees sultry sensuality brought to the fore. The split skirt, black bustier top, and bare midriff worn with classy diamonds, for Yves St Laurent and photographed for French *Vogue* in 1979, may be full of chic but it is also full of sexual overtones.[23]

When Christian Dior's collections referenced a time before World War II which was 'gone with the wind', he was not only paying tribute to his mother's love of the belle époque but was interpreting the zeitgeist with all the focus of a marketing-team leader. When Mary Quant watched her beloved 'Dolly Birds' altering the lines of dresses in her late fifties dressing rooms, she was working ahead of customer-led marketing strategies, widely used by most industries today. Her role in the promotion of Fashion is not underestimated. In the 90th anniversary edition of *Vogue*, successful designer Luella Bartley describes Quant as her continuing Muse. David Wynne Morgan, who helped launch her clothes in Europe in the late 1950s, describes her as a 'genius' and her insight into how Fashion needs to employ many strategies is entrenched in her autobiography:

> Creative talent on its own is just not enough. To be able to work with other people is terribly important; so is the ability to adapt an idea for mass production without losing 'the look'.[24]

One of the ways Quant made her designs available to women more widely was to license her designs to pattern producers. In her biography she compliments other designers who used this technique, mentioning Jean Muir as a colleague. When the pattern-making people at *Vogue* and Butterick brought out designs, based on *Breakfast at Tiffany's* or *Sabrina,* they were gladly feeding the romantic aspirations of 1960s home dressmakers. In the 1990s, and since then, Audrey Hepburn has

The Arts and Crafts flagship headquarters in the heart of Regent Street, developed towards the end of the 19th century, has had its ground floor restored and re-vamped to launch its Liberty of London range.

been seen as a signifier of style, vulnerability and aspiration by succeeding generations of adoring voyeurs.

Highly visible

In the late 1950s, Roland Barthes was concerned that the history of dress was not being considered as a sociological object by academics. My belief is that in the way masculinity retains its power by not being analysed, and being invisible, Fashion avoids being subjected to certain Marxist critiques by using reverse tactics. By being highly visible through its promotional strategies, it has succeeded in being seen as an egalitarian industry, attracting professionals from different classes and backgrounds while supplying the emerging and haute bourgeoisie with opportunities to dress as stylish peasants. By the 1960s, Barthes had come to terms with this 'mass phenomenon', describing it as the 'collective imitation of regular novelty' and adding:

> Fashion has today become everybody's business as shown by the extraordinary growth of women's publications specializing in this area. Fashion is an institution and today nobody believes any more that it distinguishes; only unfashionable is a notion of distinction; in other words, in terms of the masses Fashion is only ever perceived via its opposite: Fashion is health, it is a moral code of which the unfashionable is nothing but illness or perversion.[25]

In its campaign to sustain Fashion's health, Liberty's of London has launched a series of franchises, across the world, by redesigning its own shop and gently rebranding its products. The Arts and Crafts flagship headquarters in the heart of Regent Street, developed towards the end of the 19th century, has had its ground floor restored and revamped. In an extraordinary sleight of hand, Communications Director Jan Hamling succeeded in drawing together the Oriental charms of Empire, part of Liberty's inception, with the idea of London, the democratization of shopping and the glitter of international celebrity. A press release in February 2007 headed 'Liberty of London launches New Boutique' included the following seductive copy:

> 'Liberty of London is a decadent mix of beautiful products created from the softest leathers, velvets and luxurious fabrics, each echoing Liberty's opulent past,' Tamara Salman, the brand's Creative Director, explains. 'Now for the first time, Liberty of London will

have its own dedicated space within the store, providing a stunning showcase for its leather accessories, scarves, swimwear, home, jewellery and new men's collections.'

To get the space 'pitch perfect' for the luxury brand, Liberty brought on board Universal Design Studio. Other Universal Design Studio projects have included retail concepts for Stella McCartney and ongoing work for the redevelopment of the Lotte department stores in Korea.

> Working in harmony with Salman's vision for Liberty of London, Universal has looked to the spirit of the store at the turn of the 20th Century while giving it a contemporary twist, embracing the traditional core values of the brand in a modern way. Thus patterns and textures synonymous with Liberty – such as the iconic Ianthe print or the Tudor rose carvings found throughout the building – form key starting points while modern techniques such as three-dimensional screens created from liquid metal and high sheen surfaces combine to create a very contemporary, luxe environment.

Distributed in the Book Antigua typeface, the release in itself was *pitch perfect,* down to the appropriation of the French word *luxe,* instead of the more common form *luxury* or *luxurious.* Later in 2007, Liberty announced its international expansion under the guidance of a new chief executive Geoffroy de La Bourdonnaye. Former Disney and Christian Lacroix decision maker, he succeeded Iain Renwickas. Saying 'the name Liberty is known all around the world, and has not been given justice in terms of its presence in countries like the US and Japan', he confirmed his mission to take the brand to new markets.

Venture capital

Fashion continues its global domination by moving into new territories under the guidance of international operators. Biba, the quintessentially British fashion label, made popular in the sixties, found a new stakeholder in 2007. Manny Mashouf, chairman and founder of the fashion retailer Bebe, has taken a 60 per cent stake, making it an Anglo-American company like Burberry. Biba had faced a confused season after creative director Bella Freud left the company. According to *Women's Wear Daily,* the online Fashion bible, the investment is a personal one for Mashouf, and Biba will remain separate from the Bebe business. In a statement he alluded to Biba's history saying, he was 'proud to be involved in a brand with such a unique and authentic heritage'. A snap-shot of Fashion's unstoppable progression is recorded everyday on line. Every edition of *WWD* carries stories of major change and development. It was announced in online *Vogue* in March 2007 that Jane Shepherdson, Topshop's former brand director, was launching a venture capital fund for young designers in a joint endeavour with Jaeger owner Harold Tillman. An industry first, it was set up to split profits between design-ers, investors and the London College of Fashion. The goal of the enter-prise is to establish London as a major international player on the Fashion scene. 'Investors find it notoriously difficult to place a value on a young creative brand,' Tillman told *Vogue*. 'Britain is a hotbed of creativity but starved of funds, leading to home grown talent deciding to fly the nest. We will do all we can to prevent this.'[26] He explained that it was an example of the industry's dedication to competition and innovation; a response to British talents like Alexander McQueen and John Galliano transferring their business and talent to Paris.

As Biba was firming up its management tier and Fashion gurus were developing ways to protect talent, Paul Smith was adding to his reputa-tion by launching a book by *GQ* editor Dylan Jones. He hosted the launch of the book, *Mr Jones' 'Rules'*, a guide for young men in the 21st century, at his Floral Street shop. Twenty-two thousand Fashion stu-dents embark on courses related to the industry, in art schools and universities each year, in Britain alone, with every possibility of being employed to devise and run events and opportunities like these. The creative energies of those who have established this thriving world are, here, waiting to be wondered at and for their creations to be drawn on for inspiration.

Two real-life interlopers who wove magic around Fashion are Anna Piaggi and Isabella Blow. Neither originally practised as a Fashion jour-nalist; they both became Muses for Fashion designers and worked on American, English and Italian *Vogue* as innovators. Piaggi who began her Fashion career as a stylist for her photographer husband was the subject of a V&A exhibition, Fashion-ology, sponsored by Topshop in 2006:

> During her journalistic career she contributed to *La Settimana Incom*, *Epoca*, *Linea Italiana*, *Annabella*, *Panorama*, *L'Espresso* and *Arianna* – where she was fashion editor and stylist with her husband Alfa Castaldi, himself a well-known fashion photographer. Through her work with Italian *Vogue* she often collaborated with him as well as

with Chris von Wangenheim, Bob Richardson, Gian Paolo Barbieri, Justin de Villeneuve and Oliviero Toscani. Piaggi was editor-in-chief of Conde Nast's *Vanity* from 1980 until 1983, where she collaborated closely with Antonio Lopez. She has had a long relationship with *Vogue*, as a freelance fashion editor for Italian *Vogue* (starting in 1969), as reporter of trends (*Box*) and as creator of her famous Doppie Pagine from 1988 to the present day. These double-page spreads were the subject of *Fashion Algebra*, published in 1998 to celebrate their first ten years in *Vogue*. Her flair for the styling and anachronistic mixing of vintage couture, fashion and costume was drawn by Karl Lagerfeld during the '70s and '80s and collected into the publication *A Fashion Journal.*[27]

Suzy Menkes, Fashion editor of the *New York Herald Tribune*, took the opportunity, while reviewing the show, to explain Piaggi's fascination:

> Looking at a wall of images of Piaggi and her theatrical get-ups, it is easy to imagine her as some exotic bird perched on the outpost of fashion. In fact, she has been at its epicentre for nearly 50 years, as a *Vogue* fashion editor; as editor of *Vanity*, the avant-garde magazine in which she worked with the illustrator Antonio Lopez in the 1980s; and for the last 18 years in her '*Doppie Pagine*' or double pages, for Italian *Vogue.* They are a collage of visual and cultural references sweeping around a current trend.[28]

Rather more shocking, to me, than anything made known about the Fashion profession in *TDWP* was the revelation of a surprisingly unethical approach taken by Piaggi, the Italian trendsetter, uncovered in the exhibition. She had happily written press releases for Missoni while working as a journalist for Italian *Vogue* in the 1980s, an activity the well-regulated Public Relations profession in Britain and America would have regarded as rather unethical at the time. However, with Machiavelli's dictum 'the ends justify the means' as part of the Italian psyche, and Piaggi's flair for creation, her double life, simultaneously as both publicist and critic, will not have damaged her reputation nor astonished her flocks of fans.

Piaggi and the English aristocrat Isabella Blow, who died in June 2007, were the champions of hatter Philip Treacy and designer Vivienne Westwood, and Blow was an actual assistant to Anna Wintour at *Vogue* US. When she died, Isabella Blow's extraordinary life story appeared

Two real-life interlopers who wove magic around Fashion are Isabella Blow and Anna Piaggi. Neither originally practised as a Fashion journalist; they both became Muses for Fashion designers and worked on American, English and Italian Vogue *as innovators.*

everywhere in the Fashion and style press and on radio and television. She had moved to New York in 1979 to study Ancient Chinese Art at Columbia University and a year later abandoned her studies to move to West Texas, working in Fashion with Guy Laroche. In 1981, her big break came when Bryan and Lucy Ferry introduced her to the director of *Vogue* US, Anna Wintour. She was hired first as Wintour's assistant and then to organize fashion shoots under the discerning eye of André Leon Talley, then *Vogue* US's Editor-at-large, and was soon befriending the likes of Warhol and Basquiat. In 1986, Blow returned to London to become assistant to Michael Roberts, then Fashion director of both *Tatler* and the *Sunday Times* and later as Style editor at *Tatler.*

In a feature-length piece in *New York* magazine in 2007, Issie Blow's meeting with Anna Wintour is described:

On Wintour's desk, there was a biography of Vita Sackville-West. 'I've read that three times, and it always makes me cry,' she told Wintour. 'Issie,' Wintour responded with her signature sangfroid, 'there's nothing to cry about.' But they were a match. 'I loved coming to the office,' Wintour says, 'because I never knew what to expect. One day she'd be a maharaja, the next day a punk, and then she'd turn up as a corporate secretary in a proper little suit and gloves.'[29]

Seen mostly as a muse, her role in the Fashion industry was hard to define but she had an unerring sense for spotting talent. In 1989, Philip Treacy, still a student, arrived at *Tatler* bringing with him a green crocodile hat. Blow knew immediately that he would be worth supporting and asked him to make her a hat for her wedding. He came up with a gold lace headdress, over a flesh-coloured wimple, which she wore with a purple velvet dress to achieve a splendidly Gothic, medieval effect. She was so pleased with his designs that she invited him to come to live, and work, with her and her husband, Detmar Blow, in their house, which he did. Three years later she spotted Alexander McQueen's collection at his senior year show at Central St Martin's Art School and said, 'I know this sounds weird, but I'd like to buy the whole thing.' Blow spotted the potential of models like Sophie Dahl when others, such as Plum Sykes, missed the point. 'We all just thought she was a fat teenager,' she has said. Of Blow, Anna Wintour recalled:

> No one had an eye like Issie. The more corporate of us look at everything differently than someone like Issie, so whenever I got that phone call that Issie said I should see something, I would go.[30]

Fashion mavericks, Anna Piaggi and Isabella Blow are as essential to the Fashion industry as original designers and artists, inventors like Elsa Schiaparelli and Andy Warhol. They prepare Fashion for the worlds of marketing and manufacturing by moving from the real to the imaginary in extreme directions. They introduce novel ways to dress, and look, to take the industry on to its next reinvention. These innovators need supporting; otherwise we lose out to those who simply sell clothes while neglecting joy and pleasure.

Writing of Elsa Schiaparelli after World War II, Christopher Breward explains:

> She found it difficult to compete with the retrogressive and con-
> servative trends introduced by Christian Dior, even though much
> of the dramatic power of the New Look owed a clear debt to
> Schiaparelli's challenging pre-war innovations.[31]

Evidently regretting her financial collapse, he describes her importance to the progression of the art of Fashion:

> Her significance as a designer, however, lay not in her ability to
> accommodate or predict commercial trends, which by the end was
> clearly failing, but in her determination to follow through an idi-
> osyncratic and eclectic personal vision which resided in the field of
> avant-garde creativity and an understanding of the fragility of the
> fashion psyche.[32]

Between the post-war New Look and the arrival of Punk, it was up
to designers and journalists to make clothes fit our fables and for innovators like Piaggi, and Blow, to move the Fashion myth along.
After Schiaparelli, since Vivienne Westwood, and now Hussein Chalayan,
the reliance of the Fashion industry on the collision of Art and Design
is confirmed. How Fashion uses this alchemy, as the early 21st century's
pre-eminent industry, is examined through Hollywood movies and the
lives of important style leaders. The stage will be set to ask whether
Fashion is equipped to maintain its place in tomorrow's simulated
world. Just as lipstick was seen as an essential piece of morale-boosting
equipment in WWII, now, in an image-obsessed, object-of-desire-
hungry world, Fashion will be regarded as the main escape route, from
enforced conservation to imaginary consumption. Virtual consumers
will dress lifelike images on screens, as children unable to afford three-
dimensional dolls dress cardboard manikins in paper clothes. To satisfy
fantasies, we are already supplied by the Fashion industry with more
and more exotic, exceptional, mythical images to generate our longings
and inspire our borrowings. Whatever trend spotters predict, there is
no doubt that passionate practitioners will find ways to make us see, and
be ready to feed, our Fashion fanaticism. As well as using sites and
virtual web spaces as means of spreading its empire, Fashion is able to
build on the inventions, and reputations, from its recent past. Those
shifts and revolutions brought about by the gifted, and the determined,
are examined through the impact they made on their promoters and
critics.

Notes

1 *Absolutely Fabulous*, the 1980s situation comedy mentioned on Joanna Lumley's *Desert Island Discs*, BBC Radio 4, May 2007, was written by and starred the comedian Jennifer Saunders as an erstwhile Fashion PR, with Lumley as a Fashion editor. Lumley's character was usually too drunk to even recall the word 'accessories', and in one toe-curling moment, during a drama-tised television interview, struggled with the concept.

2 Based on a note from '[An Early Preface to] *The Fashion System*' by Roland Barthes, published [*VWA*] 25 (spring), 1998 [1963?]. 'Le Cabinet des manu-scripts', in *The Language of Fashion* by Roland Barthes, trans. Andy Stafford (Oxford and New York: Berg, 2006), p. 81.

3 Roland Barthes, *The Fashion System*, trans. Matthew Ward and Richard Howard (New York: Hill and Wang, 1983).

4 Lauren Weisberger, *The Devil Wears Prada* (London: HarperCollins, 2003), p. 81.

5 David Denby, 'Dressed to kill', *The New Yorker*, 26 July 2006.

6 Ibid.

7 Barthes, *The Language of Fashion*, p.3.

8 Weisberger, p. 77.

9 Ibid.

10 Polly Vernon, *Observer Magazine*, September 2006.

11 Christopher Breward, *Fashion* (Oxford: Oxford University Press), p. 9.

12 Emma Brockes, *The Guardian*, e-mail to author, 24 September 2006.

13 Breward, *Fashion*, p. 9.

14 See Eton website, www.eton.se (accessed 7 April 2009).

15 Paolo Perulli, 'More global and more local: Network enterprises and the Benetton case re-visited' www.sase.org/oldsite/conf1999/papers/Paolo_Perulli.pdf (accessed 7 April 2009).

16 Ibid.

17 Ibid.

18 Luciano Benetton quoted at the Fabrica website, http://2005to2007.fabrica.it/opening/fabrican (accessed 7 April 2009).

19 See Worth Global Style Network website, www.wgsn.com/public/pdf/wgsn_en.pdf (accessed 7 April 2009).

20 Ibid.

21 Audrey Hepburn, 'Foreword' to *The Fifties in Vogue* by Nicholas Drake (London: Heinemann, 1987).

22 Barthes, *The Fashion System*, p. 301.

23 Jayne Sheridan, 'Pictures selling dreams', *Liverpool Daily Post*, June 1983.

24 Mary Quant, *Quant by Quant* (London: Pan, 1967), p.173.

25 Barthes, *The Language of Fashion*, p. 68.

26 Quoted in 'Jane's reign' by Louise Roe, *Vogue* online, www.vogue.com, 6 March 2007 (accessed 7 April 2009).

27   From V&A press release promoting Anna Piaggi – Fashion-ology exhibition, 2 February to 23April 2006.

28   Suzy Menkes, 'Anna Piaggi: An editor with h-attitude', *International Herald Tribune*, 5 April 2006.

29   Amy Larocca, 'The sad hatter', *New York* magazine online, www.nymag.com/news/features/34732/index1.html, 16 July 2007.

30   Ibid.

31   Breward, *Fashion*, p. 75.

32   Ibid.

CHAPTER ONE

Scarlett O'Hara and the post-bellum New Look

First, because the mythology of woman has changed: in the novel, in films, woman is less and less the femme fatale, no longer the destroyer of men; she can no longer be essentialised, stopped from existing or made into a precious and dangerous object; she has rejoined the human race.

Roland Barthes, *Jardin des Arts*, 1961

Millions of women watch movies and fantasize; gazing at stars acting as seductive style guides. We depend on Hollywood, alone in the Fashion firmament, to keep our imaginings alive, and its allure persists. Big screen Fashion legends influence the way women want to look: Joan Crawford in *Mildred Pierce*, Bette Davis in *The Great Lie*, Lauren Bacall in *To Have and Have Not,* Audrey Hepburn in *Roman Holiday,* Kirsten Dunce in *Marie Antoinette.* Through these and other compelling moving image texts, we see ourselves as business gurus, sex goddesses, queens, criminals, mothers, beats, wives and lovers. These roles, and the way stars appear in them, pick up on the mesmerizing model set in motion by Vivien Leigh as Scarlett O'Hara in *Gone with the Wind.* This is *the* movie which began Hollywood's love affair with Fashion and established a pre-post-Feminist ambience which became a potent marketing force. Roland Barthes, recognizing how film was playing its part in changing the way women were seen, and saw themselves, wrote of women as wearers of jewels as status symbols. *Gone with the Wind* is a model for his idea, a paradigm for his hypothesis. In it, Scarlett O'Hara begins as a precious and dangerous object and a destroyer of men; then, seen as a member of the human race, she becomes both Fashion and role model. Her obsession with the way she looked led to her downfall, but it was the way the film looked that entranced her followers. These were the millions of women fans ready to buy into the designs which most reminded them of the film and of Scarlett's doomed love affair with the devastatingly debonair Rhett Butler. Hollywood's make was scorched onto *Gone with the Wind*, its magic conjured by the costumes for the cast, and in particular five of the dresses made for Vivien Leigh. Our seduction was assured as we fell in love with Rhett dressed in superbly draped clothes, commissioned by Clark Gable from his own tailor. In 2007, using new computerized lip-reading technology, footage from silent German wartime movies was released, showing Hitler speaking to one of his loyal countrywomen. She had been invited to visit Hitler's mountain residence, the Berghof in Obersalzberg, bought by the Nazis in the 1920s as a retreat for privileged members of the Party. Eva Braun's home movies, recording meetings with top conspirators, were on offer. 'I know you would rather be watching *Gone with the Wind*,' the mass murderer was filmed saying to the credulous loyalist. Even though Hitler censored Hollywood's output, in both Germany and occupied France, he did not forbid costume dramas; so everyone had *GWTW* to feed their unsafe anti-modernism and even more dangerous nostalgia:

> There was a land of Cavaliers and Cotton Fields called the Old South. Here in this pretty world, Gallantry took its last bow. Here was the last ever to be seen of Knights and their Ladies Fair, of Master and of Slave. Look for it only in books, for it is no more than a dream remembered, a Civilization gone with the wind ...[1]

Margaret Mitchell, who wrote the American Civil War novel in 1936, was awarded the Pulitzer Prize for her book in 1937. By this time, work on filming the transatlantic bestseller was under way and a search for an actor to play the heroine had begun. It was released in 1939, just months before the outbreak of World War II. The film's prologue sets the tone for post-war women to want to return to the looks and settings of the belle époque adored by Christian Dior's mother. For Dior, there was the opportunity for him to start a reactionary revolution, designing dresses for hausfrauen across the developed world, and costumes for parties in Paris celebrating the Ancien Régime without fear of tumbrils or the guillotine.

Scarlett O'Hara begins as a precious and dangerous object and a destroyer of men; then, seen as a member of the human race, she becomes both Fashion and role model.

In *GWTW* David O. Selznick was making a costume epic. He was making it in colour, still a new process at that time. It became a phenomenon, with more tickets sold for it than any other film to the end of the 20th century. Women watching the movie say of Scarlett O'Hara that she is 'powerful' first and 'beautiful' second. She is determined to save Tara, her family's cotton-growing estate in Georgia and, like American pioneers, prepared to kill to defend her property. To succeed she has to take on male values and use her femininity to negotiate a power base while ceaselessly seeking the sexual fulfilment at the heart of the film's romance. Regarded as a feminist role model by film critics in 1974, yet castigated by anti-male feminists for being obsessed by men, the control her glamorous character exerts as a woman interests gay men, and her business acumen is seen by career women as a positive endorsement of their choices. Evidence for audiences to see Scarlett as a post-Feminist role model is found in her behaviour in the scene where she rips down her mother's green velvet curtains. Having remodelled it as a sumptuous day dress for visiting the prison-bound Rhett Butler, she tries to negotiate a loan to pay the taxes on war-ravaged Tara. When Selznick made the movie he could not have realized how many women would be influenced by its story. Research carried out by Helen Taylor, the Exeter-based academic, for her book *Scarlett's Women* (1989), revealed:

> ambivalence towards Scarlett, either because they think they ought to despise her for her outrageous behaviour or because she expresses herself in a way they are reluctant to acknowledge as valid for themselves. 'She's such a con – but also a very clever woman,' says one, and another: 'You can't help admiring her gumption in spite of her faults.' Adjectives with negative connotations, like 'ruthless', 'greed', 'go-getting,' 'flighty', and 'strong-willed,' are juxtaposed with positive attributes such as 'strong,' 'powerful', 'courageous', and 'having zest'.[2]

Investigating the meaning of *Gone with the Wind* as a cultural phenomenon playing a significant part in the lives of audiences, Professor Taylor came to conclusions about its reach and influence across the globe, saying:

> *GWTW* lives in the imaginations, memories and experiences of individuals and groups – that is, through the eyes of its fans, who, to judge by the statistics of book sales, film and television viewing figures and a wealth of memorabilia and popular references, come from many nations, classes, races, generations and life experiences.[3]

The women taking part in Helen Taylor's survey are some of the many millions to have influenced the politics of Feminism, and Fashion, since the middle of the 20th century. Vivien Leigh's portrayal of Scarlett O'Hara in the film offers the view of the dissenting woman forced into a man's world who learns, perhaps too late, that her sexuality does not have to be submerged under veils of propriety. It is Clark Gable's portrayal of Rhett Butler, with his understanding of the compromise involved in dealing with human sexuality, which places Scarlett in this liberating position. Looking back to the time before World War ll, film critic Molly Haskell places Scarlett as the 'ante-bellum version of the flapper, the woman who defies all conventions except the sexual ones'.[4] At this time it was 'a woman's only job to withhold favours, to be the eternal virgin, not all that difficult, really, since her repressive conditioning had so buried the urge in the first place'.[5] During the 20th century, women were involved with much more than these sexual politics. Recognizing that *GWTW* was in tune with the spirit of the age, Haskell describes Scarlett as being:

> unfairly lambasted for her wily flirtatious and waist-pinching femininity, but she was, in many ways a forerunner of the career woman, with her profession (the land), her business acumen, and her energy that accumulated steam from sexual repression.[6]

For Scarlett to become the prototype for post-war woman, she first has to become a popular icon: a guide through lost dreams, a fantasy to enable the re-enactment of our enduring desires. In *Gone with the Wind*, as Cinema weaves its *mise en scène* myths, audiences are seduced by the film's displays of delayed desire and constructed fetishism, its Oedipal quests and repressed sexual lust.

Close-ups

Opening frames show Scarlett in close-up, a technique used sparingly throughout the film. One is used in establishing shots for its opening moments as she is introduced in flirtatious finery, attended by two attractive young southern gentleman beaux. They are excited at the idea of joining the military because they have been thrown out of college; fighting for a cause seems a thrilling adventure to them. She is pictured wearing a white and green, tightly sashed, sprigged cotton dress under a wide-brimmed sun hat, in one of the few close-ups, saying, 'War, war, war. This war talk's spoiling the fun at every party there's been.' In *Fashioning Film Stars*, Drake Stutesman (cited by Rachel Moseley) writes of the hat designer, John Frederics. She explains the hat-and-face illusion at the heart of a contradiction inherent in costume design, hiding to expose, tempting the audience in:

> The milliner, making the look, must also prevent the hat from
> showing off, because if the woman disappears so will the look. As
> Vivien Leigh said when she met John [Frederics] to discuss *Gone
> with the Wind's* costumes – 'all I ask is – don't let them see the hat
> before they see my face'.[7]

Moseley added that various hats like Garbo's jewelled, triangular
helmet in *Mata Hari* (George Fitzmaurice, 1932), Leigh's wheel hat in
Gone with the Wind (Victor Fleming, 1939), were wrongly attributed to
the costume designer and were in fact all made by John Frederics, who as
well as working with Adrian, also worked with Walter Plunkett for *Gone
with the Wind.*[7]

In a later scene, and after Scarlett is seen being tightly laced into a
corset by her devoted Mammy, she poses the rhetorical question, 'Why
does a girl have to be so silly to catch a husband?' At that moment she
is forcing down a mouthful of food to acquire a socially acceptable
appetite for the Wilkes' barbecue. In so saying, the naïve southern-belle
heroine touches on the crucial dilemma of modern woman. She is victim
of the pressures put on women by the modes of the day, not able to
operate as a free-wheeling entrepreneur and sexually fulfilled wife
because she believes to be desirable she must be virginally slim.

Leigh stage-managed the occasion

Vivien Leigh was a Fashion favourite in the mid 1930s even before she
landed the role of Scarlett O'Hara. Cecil Beaton, the London photographer, often took her picture for *Vogue.* They were particularly keen to
have models on their pages with the green eyes associated with heroines
from novels. Vivien Leigh followed the progress of David Selznick's
hunt for Scarlett through the pages of *The Times.* Bronwyn Cosgrave,
in *Made for Each Other*, believes Leigh was obsessed with the fictional
character from Mitchell's novel. Writing of Oscar-winning glories,
Cosgrave says, 'She acquired the necessary characteristic to clinch the
part – blind ambition.'[8] The actor Laurence Olivier, Leigh's lover,
arranged a meeting for Vivien with David Selznick through his agent,
the director's brother Myron. Leigh stage-managed the occasion on the
first day of shooting, moving into view from the glowing embers of the
'burning of Atlanta' set, her eyes made up to emphasize their greenness
and shape, which were Scarlett's from the novel, and wearing a silk

dress which clung to her sylph-like figure. The 36-year-old Selznick, known to be a snob, was completely swept off his feet by the vision. In a published memo he reveals that he knew from Leigh's screen tests, authorized by him that day, that she could act the part, but added, 'I'll never recover from that first look.'[9] There seems to have been no arguing with the rightness of choice of actress except for an embarrassing discrepancy related to Leigh's body shape. Scarlett is not ever seen as a victim figure, but Vivien Leigh suffered for her art and her aspiration. Victor Fleming, the director Selznick appointed after Cukor, and Selznick himself thought Leigh's small breasts were wrong for the costumes. Things became even tougher for her when Selznick suddenly fired George Cukor. He had seen his Scarlett as a more delicate character than the tough cookie, femme fatale his successor, Victor Fleming, wished to create. Fleming and Selznick agreed a 'heaving cleavage' would be necessary for Leigh. They were obviously out of tune with the more relaxed, less tortured, lines of thirties Fashion which Plunkett's unconscious imagination included in his designs. Cosgrave records:

> Trouble was, Leigh's flat chest had gone undetected during her screen test and preproduction. But before Fleming's cameras, the top of Scarlett's antebellum gown caved in, most especially the long burgundy velvet dress her husband, Rhett Butler, in a jealous rage, forces her to wear to the birthday celebration of her beloved Ashley Wilkes. 'Wear that!' Rhett orders Scarlett, removing it from her bedroom wardrobe and tossing it at her. 'For Christ's sake let's get a good look at the girl's boobs!' bellowed Fleming from behind the camera when Leigh appeared in it on set.[10]

Vivien Leigh had to endure the ignominy of having her breasts bound together with tape to create a more luscious effect. Other stresses for the actress were having to suffer tobacco-sodden breath, from fellow actors, and temperamental outbursts from Fleming and Selznick. Even after delivering lines perfectly, but with a not-so-spectacular sunrise, she and her colleagues were forced into 2.30 a.m. re-shoots for the 'I'll never go hungry again' scene. Curiously in character, Olivia de Havilland, who plays the saintly Melanie Wilkes in *GWTW*, noticed changes in Leigh. From *Love Scene* by Jesse Lasky, cited in *Made for Each Other*, we learn that on the final day of shooting Leigh seems not to have recognized her co-star:

'She looked so diminished by overwork,' remembered de Havilland. 'Her whole atmosphere had changed. She gave something to that film which I don't think she ever got back.'[11]

Leigh loved flowers and spent time on precious Sundays recovering from the pressures of filming in the garden belonging to George Cukor, the more humane original director, who had cast her in the role. For the 12th Academy Awards night, when the film won Oscars in nine categories, Leigh wore the *Red Poppy* dress designed by Irene Gibbons from her spring 1940 collection. Fashion gave something back in the uncorseted, gently flowing dress, with its softly floating flowers, which delighted Leigh.

Scarlett O'Hara is seen as a role model when, in Hollywood's most notorious act of bricolage, she rips down her mother's green velvet curtains to be remodelled as a sumptuous day dress for visiting prison-bound Rhett Butler.

During key scenes in which Ashley Wilkes, the honourable land-owning war hero, is introduced, along with the gun-running pragmatic, Rhett Butler, the camera is directed to give us clues to their status in the film. The sequence opens with a shot of Scarlett's back, the first opportunity to show off bustles of every kind. Moving from the carriage to the Wilkes's 'Twelve Oaks' mansion, we watch as Scarlett, with her wavy brown curls covered by the enormous, green-velvet-tied sun hat, holds our attention in the middle of the screen. As she turns to greet India Wilkes, saying, 'What a lovely dress, I just can't take my eyes off it!', the camera reveals the compliment as a lie. Scarlett is not even looking at the dress as she says it; her eyes are glancing around to see who's there. The camera continues to stay focused on Scarlett, her dazzling white dress and green sash in contrast to the muted shades around her. Everything is balanced: the pillars on either side of the doorway she walks through, the staircase running up on each side of the screen framing her; even the figures evenly distributed about room. The iniquitous old order is about to be destroyed and Scarlett is at the centre of the action.

The relationship between Rhett and Scarlett is based on a marriage of equals. They are two materialistic pragmatists. Their love-making in the film matches the ideal vision of sexual bliss imagined by Sigmund Freud, the author of modern sexual theory, who was analysing, and writing, at around the same time that Margaret Mitchell was penning her classic work of fiction. Rhett is able to see Scarlett as a suitable object for masculine sexuality: a synthesis between two feminine sexual types, the idealized chaste wife and the despised, but sexy, prostitute. He advises her on fashionable underclothes, buys her trousseau, although she, even after committing murder and twice marrying for advantage, is still concerned that people should not know about these intimacies. The script might make us think she is being too bold, asking for large diamonds, wanting to make everyone jealous but, in fact, we want her to win because of her gutsy invasions of patriarchal territory, her interest in money, her shoot to kill tactics. As the movie authors Lapsley and Westlake write:

> The constitution of the subject typically takes the form of an iden-
> tification with a character who is lacking – Scarlett in *Gone with the*

Wind seeking fulfilment; spectators identify not solely with ideal-
ised figures, but with those who lack, and they do so in order to
have fantasy organise desire.[12]

Still using *GWTW* as a case in point, they say that Rhett is the
object, constituted at the same time as he is introduced in the film,
which will, apparently, make good the lack. Casting Clark Gable as
Rhett did not alone lead to besotted fans saying 'Everyone wants a Rhett
Butler in their lives'.[13] Gable was Hollywood's biggest star; no one else
could have played the part. Even though Selznick had paid dearly to
get Gable for the film, and went to great lengths to make sure that
nothing would detract from his performance, he did not take on Gable's
tailor. Gable's agent came to his aid and in a note (4 April 1939) to
the directors explained:

> Since Schmidt has been Gable's tailor all through his career, from
> the time he started as an obscure actor to the time he became
> the biggest star in the world, this was an insane order to begin with.
> I would like to know why, in the first place, the one tailor who
> should have outfitted Gable was ruled out? As for the future, and
> in the hope that we will do a decent job with him and not have a
> repetition of what we have had in the past, I am in hopes that you
> will sit down with Gable, determine exactly how he has worked in
> the past, and make sure this is the way he works in the future on
> his clothes. This should be so organized that, if possible, I see
> all the sketches for Gable's clothes for the rest of the picture at
> one time – but not until and unless Gable has personally approved
> them all.[14]

Monitoring crowd scenes

Having searched across the globe for an actress to play Scarlett O'Hara,
it was thought that although Walter Plunkett's meticulous research
and careful design processes were fine for the smaller roles and for the
hundreds of extras, he was not producing the 'sensational' costumes
Selznick wanted for her. Muriel King, a designer in the frame, wanted
screen credit and $750 a week, and she would do only Scarlett's
costumes. Other designers were asking for similar arrangements.
Shooting had started with the burning of Atlanta scene, and Vivien

Leigh had been cast in the important lead role. The production had shifted into a high gear, and Plunkett came through. During the production he had to contend with the difficult Selznick, changes in directors and unreasonable Technicolor advisors. He created more than five thousand separate items of clothing for more than 50 major characters and thousands of extras, as well as monitoring crowd scenes for the proportion of men to women, and the number of women in mourning to reflect the ravages of war. Not a fan of the film, Frances Tempest, the costume designer responsible for *A Room with a View*, *Calendar Girls, Bertie and Elizabeth* and *The Cazelets,* who kindly spent time watching *GWTW*, now offers her thoughts on the clothes Plunkett created:

A film always reflects the time when it is made regardless of when the story is set. This is unconscious and only becomes apparent after, say, ten years hindsight. Even when creating a faithful, historically accurate, reproduction of a particular era, after a few years the film will obviously belong to the 1970s, 1980s or whenever it was made. So *GWTW* belongs to 1939 and is in the tradition of other 30s historical dramas such as *Little Women*. To our eyes these films look 'very 1930s'. I am sure the film-makers thought they were accurately reproducing 19th-century society. With Europe on the brink of war *GWTW* creates a fantasy Deep South. Walter Plunkett has tapped into the zeitgeist, and mined a rich vein of nostalgia, to a world that never actually existed. This is a romantic world of crinolines, ruffles and bows. The men in this world are merely foils for the elaborately dressed women. It is only Rhett Butler, dressed in black, who has any strength or individuality. The Simplicity and Butterick pattern books of 1939 were filled with paper patterns for these full-skirted, puff-sleeved fantasy dresses with ribbon sashes encircling tiny waists, and large picture hats. This is a look also popularised in Walt Disney's *Snow White*. It was a fashion created by the movies, glamorous but not sophisticated. Think of the dresses of Mae West and Ginger Rogers. World War II brought this style to a standstill with its fabric restrictions and military silhouette, only to emerge triumphant as the New Look when the war was over. The dresses in *GWTW* are firmly part of this moment in fashion. The ultra feminine fashions reinforce the idea of women as helpless decorative creatures. The corset scene where Scarlett's waist is whittled down to 18 inches must surely have inspired Peter Weir's *Picnic at Hanging Rock*![15]

Paris

Scarlett, as a model for post-feminist woman, is able to have it all while remaining highly desirable; not cooking brown rice or wearing dull clothes with sandals. Unlike feminists of the 20th century, who marched alone and pitched up tents, Scarlett was helped by Rhett Butler, played by Clark Gable as a 'new man', who lent her horses and chose her lingerie, her dresses and her hats. During the American Civil War, Rhett Butler was a gun-runner and international traveller. After rescuing Scarlett from the boredom of enforced mourning for her duped young husband, he bid a large amount of money for a dance with her during a charity auction to raise funds for the Confederacy. He later returned to Atlanta with the gift of a hat, from Paris, which Scarlett did not know how to wear. Turning it the right way round, and watching her experiment with a sideways angle, he said he thought the war had gone on for too long when women like Scarlett were no longer in touch with French Fashions.

> RHETT BUTLER: ... And those pantalettes, I don't know a woman in Paris who wears pantalettes.
> SCARLETT: Oh Rhett, what do they – you shouldn't talk about such things.
> RHETT BUTLER: You little hypocrite. You don't mind my knowing about them, just my talking about it.
> SCARLETT: But really Rhett, I can't go on accepting these gifts although you are awfully kind.
> RHETT BUTLER: I'm not kind, I'm just tempting you.
> SCARLETT: Well if you think I'll marry you just to pay for the bonnet I won't.
> RHETT BUTLER: Don't flatter yourself. I'm not a marrying man.

This can be seen as the seminal dialogue from *Gone with the Wind* which planted the idea of Paris in the minds of ordinary women all over the USA and Europe, positioning it back at the heart of Fashion after WWII. The city, a Fashion centre over centuries, is considered by Agnès Rocamora in *Fashion's World Cities*:

> Today the Parisian model is no longer conveyed through the principle of patterns to reproduce, but it is no less overt. In the French media, fashion still means Paris. Regularly anchoring fashion to the

Parisian territory, the media have long naturalized the signifying relation between the French capital and *la mode.* The centrality of Paris in all things cultural is consecrated, as it has been since the seventeenth century with the Parisian academies' leading role in the definition of culture, the split between court society and the provinces being replaced by the opposition between Paris and provinces in the eighteenth century.[16]

David Gilbert knows Paris has been 'promoted with great vigour from outside France, particularly in Hollywood's construction of the city and in the international Fashion press',[17] with 'metropolitan centres of style such as New York, Paris and Milan ... routinely incorporated into the advertising of designer brands and retail outlets'. Agnès

Dior's New Look, in 1947, made every other dress look outmoded. There was an electric tension – 'wasp waist of jacket, weight of skirt barely worn by human beings, real old-fashioned corsets to create shape', in direct contrast to the forties look.

Rocamora, who researches in Cultural Studies and whose interests are in Fashion journalism and Fashion consumption, is insightful in her understanding of how Fashion journalism participates in the production of Paris as a Fashion capital:

> The media discourse on *la mode,* then, is also a discourse on Paris, and in the same way that the process of symbolic production of fashion entails the production of the value of designers and their creations, it also entails the production of the symbolic value of Paris. Absorbed, like its derivative 'Parisian', into the Fashion rhetoric, the word 'Paris' no longer simply refers to a geographical origin. Rather it is turned into a fashion signifier whose value resides in its power to evoke the world of fashion, with the word 'Paris' now a synonym for 'chic' and 'elegance', the latter being a 'recurring spiel of French fashion', as Remaury observes in Paris *Vogue,* October 2004.[18]

Half a century before the internet, in the late 1940s Christian Dior, who had spent much of the war dressing the wives of Nazi officers and French collaborators, revived pre-war looks for post-war customers targeted at *GWTW*'s worldwide audience. He created feminized 'flower women', happy to turn their backs on careers and military uniforms. Christopher Breward writes regretting the passing of the exclusiveness of Paris, believing the 'look' represented a disruption of Fashion's inherent inventiveness:

> In February 1947 the evocative imagery of the first couture collection to be presented under the name of the designer Christian Dior imprinted an indelible suggestion of the Parisienne on the consciousness of the fashion world ... the articulation of these themes through the extraordinary architecture came to be termed the New Look engineered a beautiful but flawed marriage between ideas of place and body. It resulted in the mass consumption of versions of the style in every city of the developed world whilst also announcing the decline of the very notion of Paris which had informed its genesis and guaranteed its popularity.[19]

To celebrate the 60th anniversary of the Paris launch of Christian Dior's 'New Look' in 2007, radio producer Susan Marling invited Dior scholar and Paris resident Malcolm McLaren to present a programme for BBC Radio 4 profiling the man whose reactionary revolution enchanted and outraged women in Europe and America.[20] McLaren described the anniversary bash in the orangerie at Versailles, where the House of Dior's 2007 collection was being shown, as the most fabulous Fashion event of the year, to which they had 'all been invited'. He said the $2 million worth of flamboyance, flamenco dancers and fireworks would have 'amused the Sun King himself'. The collection, celebrating Art from Michelangelo to Cocteau, had John Galliano, Dior's chief designer, taking inspiration from Goya's Spanish dancers, Picasso's harlequins and the Muses of the Impressionist and Modern painters, 'many of whom were friends of Christian Dior, himself'.

The atmosphere at Versailles that night was very different from the climate into which the House of Dior had emerged. After four years of Nazi rule the 'city of lights' was dim, but after liberation by the American forces and discovery of bebop, which swept Paris, black Americans stayed on rather than return to the segregated USA. On the streets the cult of cool was about to be born, and women wanted a designer to help them shake off the 'horrible overalls' and the boxy shapes of wartime clothes. They wanted to look sexy and feminine. It was then, in February 1947, that 30 Avenue Montaigne would become the world headquarters of Fashion. Claire Wilcox, who curated The Golden Age of Couture exhibition at London's Victoria and Albert Museum, was interviewed for the programme and recounted the story of Dior's clever launch of the New Look. She explained how he had packed his salon with little gilt chairs; perfume everywhere, curtains drawn, crammed to capacity, creating a 'hot-house atmosphere'. The most important person there was Carmel Snow, influential editor of *Harper's Bazaar*, with American buyers and the Press. As Dior showed late in the season, some were about to leave when Snow started reporting. They all turned round, and it was the beginning of a new era. She witnessed ashtrays being knocked over by the 'vast skirts', and later named the collection the New Look. Lady Antonia Fraser, who translated Dior's biography into English, remembered being a schoolgirl at the time when everything was about shortages. Her mother did manage to buy a full-skirted turquoise coat, for Antonia, which used up all her clothing coupons and was impracticable as it caught in her bicycle wheels. 'We wanted to be ourselves, be women with curves, and tiny waists,' like English model Princess George Galitzine who, as Jean Dawnay, modelled Dior's clothes. Bronwyn Cosgrave described the rebirth of Paris through haute couture. With its fine tailoring, lace-making and fabric production, it produced a glamour and a 'particular sense of excess, which a new generation craved'.

French bourgeoisie

Explaining how the New Look was very good for fabric manufacturers, and especially good for Dior's sponsor, Marcel Boussac, Claire Wilcox talked of the 'Bar' suit, famously photographed by Willy Maywald. With its padded, static jacket and its heavy 80-pound long black wool pleated skirt, it depended for its sculptural form on the 19th-century skills of the corset maker. Coco Chanel said of her rival: 'Christian Dior doesn't dress women. He upholsters them.' Antonia Fraser interpreted his raison d'être, saying: 'All he wanted was to dress the French bourgeoisie.' He was not quite the romantic hero from her imagination, which, perhaps, had been inspired, on some unconscious level, by the work of Clark Gable's tailor. While Harold Wilson was decrying the senselessness of long skirts in Britain, and the UK faced continuing cuts and shortages, Feminists were decrying corsets and long skirts on other grounds. They protested outside Bergdorf Goodman in New York with the slogan 'Monsieur Dior, we abhor dresses to the floor'. Nevertheless, so strong was the urge to return to the feminized romanticism of earlier decades that most women in New York, Hollywood, Toronto and Boston were improvising to achieve the New Look. 'Scarlett O' Hara-style, these women were ripping down curtains to make their voluminous skirts,' Bronwyn Cosgrave revealed. Christian Dior realized that the new silhouette, which was instantly recognizable, caught on with Fashion journalists, making the designs immediately attractive to the public. Even so, Dior seemed perplexed by the level of his success. His designs made up 75 per cent of French Fashion exports, which must have seemed extraordinary, knowing the flow of the political tide in America and Britain.

Before, and during, World War II, New York was poised to become a world-beating Fashion centre. Numbers of American women were being employed away from the home, taking up a diverse range of work and leisure activities. This gave them less time to be involved with having clothes made; for the sourcing of fabrics, the dressmakers' fittings. There was an opportunity for the rise of ready-to-wear and more especially, within that market, for the emergence of sportswear. Norma Rantisi, in *Fashion's World Cities* on the status of American Fashion in the 1930s, writes:

> Claire McCardell, who was trained at the Parsons School of Design, has been credited as one of the first sportswear designers, redefining American fashion, by introducing beautiful yet comfortable garments, which were *not* inspired by Paris. These simple, wearable styles gained broad acceptance because they resonated with new social roles but also, more generally, with values of democracy and with a view of dress as a means of blurring rather than marking social distinctions. However, the broader recognition and acceptance of this burgeoning New York talent demanded the support of local buyers, fashion editors and journalists, who mediated consumption trends.[21]

Important movers and shakers in the New York Fashion industry came through with this backing. Rantisi records:

> Social ties were forged between key actors in the Garment District. In February 1931, a group of leading women in the industry, including *Vogue* editor Edna Woolman Chase, Helena Rubinstein, Elizabeth Arden, Dorothy Shaver and Eleanor Lambert, held the first meeting of the Fashion Group (later known as Fashion Group International.) The stated objectives of the group were to promote the exchange of information and to enhance the careers of women in the industry. Shortly after its establishment, group members acted on these objectives. The association sponsored lectures on merchandising and advertising. By 1932, prominent group member Dorothy Shaver started naming American designers, such as McCardell, in her store advertisements. Local talent also benefited from the annual openings at the Costume Institute, which became the industry's biggest social event, linking designers with style promoters and other cultural elites.[22]

Harnessing America's innate talent for marketing and promotion was only part of the story. After Paris was occupied by the Nazis in 1940, it could no longer be turned to for inspiration and models for replication. There was a need for America to concentrate on native resources. The American Fashion industry had to step up, and have its efforts encouraged by the powerful and energetic Fashion Group International. America's influence through Hollywood was a continuing force in the battle for supremacy. Drake Stutesman, the editor of *Framework: The Journal of Cinema and Media*, records:

> American style as a world competitor was the first to outstrip the French, who dominated fashion commercially and artistically. By the 1910s, stars were photographed in cinema clothes for fashion magazines and Sears-Roebuck catalogues, and the word 'film' was used as an advertising lure. But the public's desire for these clothes is ironic, as many are impossible to wear. Jean Harlow's form-fitting satin gowns were glued to her body and steamed off. Mae West was sewn into two identical garments for a scene, one for sitting, one for standing, because each was so tight she could not do both in either of them. Glenn Close also was unable to sit in Anthony Powell's sexy costumes for her role in *101 Dalmations* (1996). The pink gown Marilyn Monroe wore to sing 'Diamonds Are a Girl's Best Friend' in *How to Marry a Millionaire* (1953) was made from upholstery satin and lined with felt. Given this, it is astounding how many fashion firsts emerged from the bizarre necessities of a film set: padded shoulders (Adrian in the 1930s for Joan Crawford), the cling dress (Rambova for *Salome*), the strapless bodice (Jean Louis in 1946 for *Gilda*, anticipating Christian Dior's New Look of 1947), the pillbox hat (John Frederics and Adrian for Greta Garbo in 1932) and many others.[23]

Linda M. Scott, in *Fresh Lipstick*, redresses the balance between Fashion and Feminism. She raises issues surrounding the power of Fashion itself, the influence of advertising and journalism on women; dealing with ideas of sexualization and objectification. Giving women the opportunity to think beyond looks, and focus on the challenge of achieving equality, she examines evidence of subjugation and stereotyping, exploring ideas of domination, myth, popular culture

During WWII there was the fear that American design would take over. So the Paris group Chambre Syndicale put together Théâtre de la Mode, a collection of dolls on display during the V&A exhibition in London in 2007. Said to have been designed to raise funds for war victims, they were really commissioned to raise the profile of haute couture.

and commercialism. She observes the incarnation of the American Girl:

> In the decades [since], the American girl has appeared in many incarnations. She is Holly Golightly, Scarlett O'Hara and Nancy Drew, we find her in the TV series *That Girl* and *Clueless*. She is Patty Duke's American twin. She is Cyndi Lauper singing 'Girls Just Want to Have Fun'. From these characters, even though they differ, we draw a broad outline of the American girl prototype ... the American girl is a flirt. She likes to dress up and go to parties, but she would rather be staked to an anthill than go to Sunday school. She is neither stuffy nor self-righteous. Like Huck Finn or Tom Sawyer, the American girl is disobedient ... She may seem, at

once, outrageously materialistic and truly heroic, like Scarlett O'Hara driving a mill wagon while pregnant.[24]

Fashion consumption

It is this new woman, from the New World, who became part of a wider narrative, through women's understanding of Hollywood and the experience of Fashion consumption. If European women were conventional, and followed the rules dictated by their mothers or their nannies, before World War II, they wanted to be à la mode after the conflict was over. Scott believes that the American Girl had been encouraged to feel like this from earlier on in the century. The American Girl, she asserts:

> Always dresses in a way that is both the height of fashion and the edge of fashion. Her look, shocking in its own Fashion time, becomes the cliché of an era.[25]

Speaking at the Unravelling Couture Culture conference held at the V&A in November 2007, Alexandra Palmer of the Royal Ontario Museum asked the question, 'How did "Corolle" get onto the streets?' Considered revolutionary by the fashion press, the New Look was actually called 'Corolle Line' by Christian Dior himself. Asking, 'Why here? Why now?', Professor Palmer suggested that the flower petal collection contained 'romantic symbols of a lost world of the elite when women had no need to mend'. This is in almost direct contrast to what was happening in America; here, Fashion customers were being encouraged to buy ready-mades, created by women designers for department stores. She went on to explain the importance of French designers' marketing strategies. The collections were first shown to buyers and the Press and then shown in boutiques and salons twice a day. Saying 'If the House relied on models to show haute couture without the Press it was like weddings without the bride,' she described how essential Carmel Snow was to that Dior 'Corolle' collection. Dior became the 'master of marketing', selling perfumes, and realizing the 'importance of the public identifying with the designer'. Dior had his personal and business journeys mapped and followed by the Media, becoming the first popular celebrity couturier. Recognizing the importance of trade between the House and buyers, by 1948 he and his team include Cuba, Finland, Holland, Mexico and Sweden in their contact lists. When Bettina

With its padded, static jacket and its heavy 80-pound long black wool pleated skirt, it depended for its sculptural form on the 19th-century skills of the corset maker. Coco Chanel said of her rival: 'Christian Dior doesn't dress women. He upholsters them.'

Ballard, the journalist who was Editor-in-chief of *Vogue* US in the 1950s, heard that designs were being geared towards department store owners' wives, she said, 'I would not put it past Dior!' She would not have been surprised also to learn that both Dior and Andrew Goodman of the New York department store Bergdorf Goodman received the *Légion d'honneur*, France's highest accolade for services to the country.[26]

Between 1947 and 1957 all eyes were turned to Paris. So when Paul Gallico wrote *Mrs 'Arris Goes to Paris*, about Ada Harris, a London charwoman in the 1950s, who sees a Dior dress and decides she's going to own one, he conjured a fairy tale which half the world could identify with. First, she scrimps and saves her money, but when she has enough and takes a trip to Paris, she learns that buying an original couture creation is a little harder than simply paying up. Gallico, a first-generation Italian immigrant to America, created a legend which had very little realism, either magical or otherwise. His experience of the lives of British cleaners seems to have been sketchy, but his evocation of Dior's headquarters captures all the hectic commercialism of an international Fashion destination.

> The great gray building that is the House of Christian Dior occupies an entire corner of the spacious Avenue Montaigne leading off the Rond-Point of the Champs-Elysées. It has two entrances, one off the avenue proper which leads through to a Boutique, where knick-knacks and accessories are sold at prices ranging from five to several hundreds of dollars, and another more demure and exclusive one.[27]

Claire Wilcox, Fashion curator at the V&A, told conference delegates that research from 'publications, press and publicity' began a panoramic view when designing an exhibition. Unravelling couture culture after WWII she had discovered that the recovery of the French Fashion industry had been in the hands of Dior, who saved haute couture in the face of a 'growing market of ready to wear, especially in the United States'. Paris was put into a position where it was also able to set the template for London couture and Fashion training. During the war there was the fear that American design would take over. So the Paris group Chambre Syndicale put together Théâtre de la Mode, a collection of dolls which were on display during the V&A exhibition in London. Said to have been designed to raise funds for war victims, they were really commissioned to raise the profile of haute couture.

Dior's New Look, in 1947, made every other dress look outmoded. There was an electric tension – 'wasp waist of jacket, weight of skirt barely worn by human beings, real old-fashioned corsets to create shape', in direct contrast to the forties look. Journalist Alison Settle reported that Harold Wilson had said it was 'unstoppable' in spite of his warnings against extravagance. London was part of the excitement. In 1947 the V&A decided it had to have a Fashion department and Dior himself visited the capital to be fitted for Savile Row suits. The renaissance of haute couture was central to the exhibition, two to five years in preparation, and to its continuing education and research projects. 'The construction of haute couture has been the cipher for the whole exhibition,' Claire Wilcox told delegates. She talked of the Queen wearing Hartnell in 1950 for a visit to Paris: 'couture as diplomatic weapon'. This crucial sector of the Fashion industry, used as a yardstick and guiding principle today, is reflected in the extraordinary number of hits to the V&A timeline, tracking the history of couture from Worth to John Galliano, for the 2007 Couture Culture exhibition. There were 100,000 hits in the first six weeks; this was into tens of millions before the end of the show. The writer and broadcaster Drusilla Beyfus talked about haute couture to Claire Wilcox for the *Daily Telegraph* at the time of the exhibition and came to this conclusion:

> [I]t is natural to speculate on the future of haute couture as it rep-resents such an impenitent display of personal consumption; addi-tionally the exhibition is likely to be viewed against a dicey stock market and a go-green attitude to our glad rags. The metier survives today in a handful of fashion houses, where once there were hun-dreds. When held, the collections are 'often extreme and extravagant … Their role is to garner publicity and provide inspiration … I hope couture doesn't die. It's very important to retain the craft of couture. These skills once lost become extinct – the tailoring, the embroidery, the weaving, the quality.[28]

Dior's part in the revival of this fascinating industry after WWII is considered by Valerie Steele, director and chief curator of the museum at the Fashion Institute of Technology in New York:

> The post-war era would indeed be characterised by an extravagantly romantic and ultra feminine fashion that differed dramatically from wartime attire. Yet it is also true that the fashionable silhouette epitomized by Dior's New Look actually began before the war. During the war years this image of lush femininity was essentially 'put on ice'; it was only after the war that the freeze melted and the rhythm of fashion burst out again in the work of many designers of whom Dior was only the most famous.[29]

It was Christian Dior himself who said, 'A golden age seemed to have come again.' He wanted women to be feminine, describing his intention to create 'clothes for flower-like women, with rounded shoulders, full feminine busts and hand-span waists above enormous spreading skirts'. Eleri Lynn, assistant curator of The Golden Age of Couture: Paris and London 1947–57, writing the preface for their 2008 diary, says, 'Given the austerity of the post-war years, the swathes of fabric required for these flowing designs were an extravagant luxury, attracting a great deal of admiration and controversy.'[30] So how did Dior do it?

Inventive motorist

Originally a student of politics who also studied music, Dior was born in Granville, Normandy, and until 1935 ran an art gallery and spent time travelling. He began earning a living in Paris selling fashion sketches to newspapers, and in 1938 worked at the house of the French/Swiss designer Robert Piguet. Joining Lelong in 1942 alongside Pierre Balmain, he was spotted by the cotton magnate Marcel Boussac, who became his patron and helped him open his own couture house. The success of his first collection gave rise to the return to health of the Paris couture industry, with its thousands of specialist workers supporting hundreds of ancillary trades such as embroiderers and featherers, producing hand-made garments.

Writing in *The Fifties in Vogue*, Nicholas Drake recounts the story of this turnaround:

> Fashion in the fifties had never been more feminine. The success of Christian Dior's extravagantly romantic *New Look* of 1947 with its waspy waists and billowing full skirts reasserted the dominance of Paris fashion and established Dior as its dictator until his death in 1957.[31]

Christian Dior's publicity machine was so effective that in a *Vogue* feature, proposing numerous routes through Europe by car by inventive motorists, Dior was featured by the magazine rather in the way Victoria Beckham was written about by Alexandra Shulman for British *Vogue,* April 2008. We are taken behind the scenes to view the superstar at play. Nicholas Drake's 1950s piece would work just as well today in *Vogue* or *Wallpaper*:

> The difference between Christian Dior's two homes was as great as that between his tweed sports suits and his embroidered ball dresses. In his old mill house at Milly, near Fontainebleau – white stone walls, stone and red-tiled floors, great blackened beams. His Paris house, by contrast, was rich and elaborate, 'reflecting the times of Madame Bovary, Whistler, Louis XVI and the Austrian Empire'.

Precious *objets* were everywhere – particularly Persian and early Chinese, but despite the echoes of many epochs the house had unity. Various shades of red, white and green followed through the rooms which repeated the use of textured fabrics for wall hangings and of ormolu and silver for highlights.[32]

His activities as a designer and guest at charity balls were recorded:

Christian Dior a jovial moustachioed *garçon* and the Comtesse de Beaumont an enigmatic Egyptian mummy swathed in gold lamé. For the Baronne de Cabrol's Circus Ball, in aid of underprivileged children, the flower of the French aristocracy rode into the ring cracking whips and performing dressage, in period costumes especially created by Dior, Givenchy and Lanvin-Castello.[33]

Georgina Howell, looking back over 40 years in *In Vogue: 75 Years of Style*, comments on the contrast between Dior's models and the women in the audience at a show:

His models looked absolutely different from the women in the audience. Dior's newly designed woman had soft neat shoulders, a wasp waist, a bosom padded for extra curve, and hips that swelled over the shells of cambric or taffeta worked into the lining: the dressmaking techniques were immensely complicated, some Victorian, some newly evolved. She walked leaning backward to make the hips more prominent, and her skirt burst into pleats, sometimes stitched over the hips or blossoming out under the stiff curved peplum of her jacket. Her hem bustled around some twelve inches from the floor, from which it was divided by the sheerest of silk stockings and the highest of pointed shoes. She was delicious, and she made all other women green with envy.[34]

Her overview includes comment on the worldwide take-up of the Dior phenomenon. British and American companies, using licences, provided the look for women on home territory:

Women no sooner saw the New Look, but they had to have it. Dereta was one of the first off the mark in producing a grey flannel copy, and was taken aback to see 700 of them vanish from the rails of one West End shop within a fortnight. Naturally, because of the amount of fabric needed, the New Look could only appear in non-Utility clothes, of which production was limited. Yet manu-facturers caught with large stocks of Utility 'man-tailored' suits lost money hand over fist: no one wanted them. Sir Stafford Cripps summed up outraged official reaction: fury at the thwarting of fabric restrictions. He called a meeting of the British Guild of Creative Designers and suggested that they would be helping the national effort considerably if they would co-operate in keeping the short skirt popular – and the Guild obediently agreed to try. He then called in a committee of fashion journalists and, with the help of Harold Wilson, President of the Board of Trade, tried to persuade them to ignore Paris. They pointed out that their job was to report.[35]

And Christopher Breward, writing *Fashion* for the Oxford History of Art series in 2003, takes an even wider view of the French return to Fashion prominence:

> After the war, designers associated with the revived French couture industry like Dior, Balmain, and Givenchy also found Hollywood to be an important source of patronage and a key marketing proposition.[36]

He lists among the most influential fashion films *Gone with the Wind*, from which:

> Walter Plunkett's designs prefigured the New Look and influenced a generation of brides.[37]

Quoting Valerie Steele, Breward explains how Dior himself knew his designs were part of the zeitgeist by saying:

> No one person can change fashion – a big fashion change imposes itself. It was because women longed to look like women again that they adopted the New Look.[38]

Dior was correct in assuming that people wanted something new after years of war, brutality and hardship. His New Look was reminis-cent of the belle époque ideal of long skirts, tiny waists and beautiful fabrics that his mother had worn in the early 1900s. In the post-war period, the avant-garde Elsa Schiaparelli found it difficult to compete with Christian Dior's 'retrogressive and conservative trends'.[39]

It is the revealing, crimson, be-feathered number, not unlike the red dress image drawn by David Downton for Golden Age *publicity texts, which gave Leigh such agonies of embarrassment. It was this Walter Plunkett creation which caused the despotic Fleming and Selznick to cruelly deride her small breasts.*

The website Fashion-Era (fashion-era.com) places Dior in his historical context. In the words of Pauline Weston-Thomas:

> Dior's timing made his name in fashion history. After the war women longed for frivolity in dress and desired feminine clothes that did not look like a civilian version of a military uniform.[40]

Such a traditional concept of femininity also suited the political agenda. Women had been recruited during the war to work on farms and in factories while men were away fighting. In peacetime, those women were expected to return to passive roles as housewives and mothers, leaving their jobs free for the returning soldiers. The official model of post-war womanhood was a capable, caring housewife who created a happy home for her husband and children. Dior's flower women fitted the bill perfectly. Didier Ludot, in his book *The Little Black Dress*, captured the atmosphere of the times in which Dior made his mark:

> After five years of hardship, opulence and hyper-femininity made a comeback in a positive riot of fabrics that Christian Dior brought to life with genius in his first post-war collection: The New Look of 1947 made history. In the next year's season, the Diorama dress took up 29 yards of black wool crepe with a 51-inch width.[41]

Coco Chanel made a surprise return to couture in 1954. She had moved into obscurity, keeping a low profile after the war, so as not to cause distress as a result of her alleged associations with the Nazis during the occupation of Paris. She had seen Dior's New Look as a retrograde Fashion, which would not help women to feel free. Her sleek and stylish bouclé suits and signature handbags took off in the American market.

With post-war Fashion, a new photography emerged which seems to have emphasized the belle époch climate Dior adored. Christopher Breward writes of visions of the 'atmospheric parks and hotels of Paris' where:

> Dior's creations suggested the romance of the 18th and 19th centuries. There complex constructions relying on supportive undergarments and dramatic cutting similarly emphasised an idea of femininity that harked back to the decorative roles played by aristocratic women in decades past.

Breward, again in regretful mood, echoing some of Coco Chanel's feelings, concludes:

> In the immediate post-war period, the closely related mediums of fashion and film lost much of their sharp relevance to modern life in the face of an onslaught of vaguely historical and socially conservative set pieces which revived the glamour and gender politics of the Second Empire and the belle époque.[42]

Christian Dior is seen by industry watchers as a merchant as much as a designer. He knew there were hordes of glamour and waist-obsessed women hooked on Scarlett O'Hara, the devastating flirt from *Gone with the Wind*, waiting to swish around in full skirts, in post-bellum party mood. In 1947, they were ready to fall for his New Look and he needed little help in identifying and attracting consumers. In 1945 he was designing for the textile tycoon Marcel Boussac, a man who had made his fortune from fabric and was interested in Dior's new idea that involved using layers of extravagant fabrics.

The four-hour epic *Gone with the Wind* closed a chapter on four decades of change and transformation for women across the globe as Scarlett became the prototype for the post-Feminist woman; someone who would wear Paris hats to deal with death and defeat, become the pioneering head of house, grow crops, and trade to feed the family while still searching for romance. As we cannot return to the goddess-worshipping matriarchies of ancient Celtic, Grecian, Roman or African times, we have to make do with the post-Feminist compromise summed

Christian Dior also created designs for the theatre and an outfit made for Vivien Leigh by Angels & Bermans, the theatrical costumiers, bears a striking resemblance.

up for us when Camille Paglia remarks, 'A contemporary woman clapping on a hard hat merely enters a conceptual system invented by men.'[43] When she rips down her mother's green velvet curtains to have them remodelled as a sumptuous day dress for visiting the prison-bound Rhett Butler, it is not just an interesting piece of bricolage. Katie Scarlett O'Hara Hamilton is making ready to attack the male bastions of barter and commerce with the trappings of fetish and desire.

At the beginning of the 21st century, Camille Paglia leads a new generation of 'Equity Feminists' who are keen to throw off the acrimony between the sexes which began in the 1950s. While supporting equality before the law and the removal of obstacles to women's advancement in society, she opposes special protections for women. Paglia maintains that the reforming wing of Feminism, to which she belongs, is growing and gathering momentum from a younger generation who are no longer in sympathy with the censorious anti-pleasure wing of mid-20th-century Feminism. It is my belief that the character of Scarlett O'Hara, supported by Rhett Butler in the film *Gone with the Wind,* is the prototype for the post-Feminist woman and that the film set the scene for a return to romantic, feminine, sexually provocative dress emphasizing the differences between men's and women's body shapes.

In *Selznick's Vision*, Alan Vertrees pays tribute to the passion and dedication of the man who he claims created his own and Hollywood's 'magnum opus' in the production of *GWTW.* He describes it as the 'most successful motion picture of the classical Hollywood period',[44] adding his critique to the many documents in praise of the film's production values. He lists its nine Oscars, presented in February 1940 soon after the movie premiered, and sets it in the context of other excellent films released in the same 'annus mirabilis of American filmmaking', including *The Wizard of Oz* and *Wuthering Heights.* Vertrees explains that the film has remained the undisputed biggest hit in the history of cinema. *Entertainment Weekly* in 1994 confirmed it as 'for decades the unassailable Mount Everest of popularity. This Civil War soap opera has still been seen by more people in cinemas (198.5 million) than any other film.' Recent television polls continue to put *GWTW* at the top of the list of films seen by most people, inevitably numbering a high proportion of adult women, from Britain and America, during the 70 years since its release. Evaluating its influence on female fans fifty years later in 1989, Helen Taylor writes, 'It depicted a world of omnipresent women and intermittently stable and dependable men; it showed a society held together – often against heavy odds – by women's energy, labour and ability to "make do and mend". It presented men as objects of mystery and fantasy, creatures who seemed to offer strong shoulders for women to lean on but who all too often vanished into the night, assuring women how capable they were on their own.'[45] Helen Taylor was describing how women felt towards Rhett Butler in the film. Revisiting her findings, at the beginning of the 21st century, I discovered many women still waiting for their own Rhett Butler to arrive bringing a hat from Paris, which only he knew how to wear.[46]

Nostagic designs and women in red

A link between the 1939 box-office hit and the post-war designer came during a decisive moment in planning the V&A's Couture Culture exhibition in 2007. They had acquired a version of Dior's 'Zémire' ensemble a year earlier. It had been a private order from Lady Sekers, wife of the British textile manufacturer, made in an innovative synthetic fabric in red. Mysteriously, it was found stored in a cellar by the Seine in Paris, and a decision was made for it to be cleaned and repaired to become a key piece in the show. One of Dior's most nostalgic designs, it was named after an opera by Grétry, first performed at the royal palace of Fontainebleau in 1771. In thrall to the *Ancien Régime*, Dior first named the creation 'Fontainebleau', but this was crossed out on the chart and replaced by 'Zémire'. From Dior's 'Ligne H' collection, the original model in grey silk satin was shown to Princess Margaret at Blenheim Castle in 1954. It appears in several British and American magazines, in many issues of *L'Officiel de la Couture et de la Mode de Paris* of the times, and in a promotional film. Susan Small, a British company making 'line-for-line' licensed copies, produced ready-to-wear versions that sold in Harrods for 22 guineas. Claire Wilcox, writing about Zémire in her catalogue to accompany The Golden Age of Couture, describes its historical significance, saying it was one of Dior's most consciously historical designs:

> The 'riding' jacket and full skirt have a distinctly eighteenth-century flavour, and are made using traditional construction techniques.[47]

Stressing the longing for the past, inherent in Dior's works, she quotes Edna Woolman Chase, Editor-in-chief of American *Vogue* from 1941 to 1952:

His clothes gave women the feeling of being charmingly costumed; there was a faintly romantic flavour about them.[48]

Again, alluding to Dior's empathy with times gone with the wind, Wilcox suggests:

The attraction and paradox of Dior and many of his contemporaries is that although they established a modern identity for couture between 1947 and 1957, its practice and philosophy were rooted in the past.[49]

A further, rather surprising link with *GWTW* is in the revelation of the connection between the actress, the designer and the 'Zémire' model:

The coup de grâce *is the sign-off when Antonio Banderas, as Clark Gable from* Gone With the Wind, *using the exact camera plot and in the precise pose from the original, is identified as the 'him' everyone wants.*

Christian Dior also created designs for the theatre and an outfit made for Vivien Leigh by Angels & Bermans, the theatrical costumiers, bears a striking resemblance.[50]

A picture of the dress, worn by Vivien Leigh, was sent to me by Eleri Lynn, who wrote to say:

> It was designed by Dior for the 1956 play *Duel of Angels* directed by Jean-Louise Barrault in which Vivien Leigh plays Paola. It, along with the programmes of the play, is in the care of the Theatre Museum, based here at the V&A. It looks just like our Dior 'Zémire' dress in the exhibition, which is why we were initially drawn to it.[51]

There is a woman in red archetype; she is the femme fatale, the fertile goddess of the middle period of women's lives, treacherous and potent. Valerie Steele has devoted a whole book to *the red dress*, in which she explains its symbolism, strongly linked to sexuality; in China and India it is worn by brides because of its association with happiness. She points to the significance of the colour choices for costumes in *GWTW*:

> When Vivien Leigh played Scarlett O'Hara in *Gone with the Wind*, she wore a red dress for several pivotal scenes, most notably when Rhett Butler carried her upstairs to bed.[52]

It is the revealing, crimson, be-feathered number, not unlike the red dress image drawn by David Downton for Golden Age publicity texts, which gave Leigh such agonies of embarrassment. It was this Walter Plunkett creation which caused the despotic Fleming and Selznick to cruelly deride her small breasts. It most epitomizes the scorned woman, and was chosen by Rhett for her to wear to face her critics at Ashley Wilkes's party. Audiences are drawn, in sympathy, to her framed in the doorway of the Wilkes's modest entrance hall. Leigh is filmed in mid shot, to make the most of her sexual display, and then in close-up to show her resolve as she makes ready to face Melanie's disapproving guests. Fashion may have given something back to Vivien Leigh, wearing the Red Poppy dress, with Jean Patou *Joy* perfume for Oscar night, but in the wearing of the red Dior, for a British West End appearance, more of the ghosts of *Gone with the Wind* might well have been laid to rest for Leigh.

During and after the world wars, women in Europe and America had begun to take hold of the reins of destiny in the way Scarlett drove her own buggy and fought her own fights. In each decade of the 20th century, women from both sides of the Atlantic have shared common concerns, influencing each other's progress and policies. The film's prologue, the relationship between Rhett and Scarlett, became the backdrop to Dior's rise to eminence and for Paris to return as a Fashion city. The romantic themes and feminine dresses set up Dior's 'New Look' to seduce American, and European, women back to their homes, aprons cinched round tiny waists, still hoping that tomorrow would be 'another day'. In a tone-setting scene in the film, generous-hearted Melanie says to Scarlett, who is being deliberately provocative and territorial, 'You have so much life.' Then, in a temperamental flourish, our heroine begins a regal procession through the crowds, flirting with everyone's sweethearts as she moves. The camera faithfully follows her, in both middle distance and close-up shots. It moves to her face, then back to our first sight of Rhett Butler. He's standing framed in the centre of the screen at the bottom of the stairs of the Wilkes's grand mansion, in totally chic black-and-white spotted cravat, silver grey trousers and black jacket. As the camera pans up to her looking down on him, she is filmed saying to her companion, 'He looks as if he knows what I look like without my shimmy.' She sees Rhett as a sexual creature from the moment they set eyes on each other. Then the money shot. Swiftly zooming away from her, down the sweeping staircase, is the close-up of Rhett, glass in hand, arms curved insouciantly around the carved balustrade, looking up at her. This cinematic moment, which left millions of fans feeling, like Selznick with Leigh, 'I'll never recover from that first look', was appropriated, not to say successfully hijacked, by Marks and Spencer for its Christmas 2007 television commercial.[53] In the *Christmas Belles* Hollywood pastiche, five girls all want the same thing for Christmas; *him*, thrills, spills and clothes. In *Christmas Belles*, models appear in character: Elizabeth Jagger as Rita Hayworth in *Gilda*, Laura Bailey as Lauren Bacall in *To Have And To Have Not,* Noémie Lenoir as Jane Russell in *Gentlemen Prefer Blondes,* Erin O'Connor as Audrey Hepburn in *Sabrina* and Twiggy Lawson as Bette Davis in *Now, Voyager.* The *coup de grâce* is the sign-off when Antonio Banderas, as Clark Gable from *Gone with the Wind,* using the exact camera plot and in the precise pose from the original, is identified as the '*him*' everyone wants.

Notes

1 The opening words of the film *Gone with the Wind* (1939), dir. David Selznick and Victor Fleming.

2 Helen Taylor, *Scarlett's Women: Gone with the Wind and Its Female Fans* (London: Virago, 1989), p. 95.

3 Ibid., p. 79.

4 Molly Haskell, *From Reverence to Rape: The Treatment of Women in the Movies* (London, New English Library, 1975), p. 125.

5 Ibid.

6 Ibid.

7 Drake Stutesman, 'Storytelling: Marlene Dietrich's face and John Frederics' hats' in *Fashioning Film Stars, Dress, Culture, Identity*, ed. Rachel Moseley (London: British Film Institute, 2005), p. 30.

8 Bronwyn Cosgrave, *Made for Each Other: Fashion and the Academy Awards* (London: Bloomsbury, 2007), p. 38.

9 Ibid., p. 39.

10 Ibid.

11 Ibid., p. 42.

12 Rob Lapsley and Michael Westlake, 'From *Casablanca* to *Pretty Woman*: The Politics of Romance', in *Contemporary Film Theory*, ed. Antony Easthope (New York: Longman, 1993), p. 192.

13 Interviewing *GWTW* fans in 2001, I realized how important the character of Rhett Butler is to the film's influence. Leeds-based Fashion sales manager Margaret Ambler said the things which interested her about Scarlett were her tiny, tiny waist and her clothes, and that 'we would all be swept off our feet if there were more Rhett Butlers around!' A Muslim Civil Servant from Manchester and her London-based barrister sister say of Scarlett, 'She never gave up. She was strong against the odds. The romance helps and the scenery. Everyone could do with a Rhett Butler in their lives.' Asian sisters Rushpal Lali and Jaspal Samra believe it is the 'ultimate romance'. 'Scarlett did not do what was expected. She moved away from the normal. She was inspirational, and as Asians we would not have so many expectations; by seeing Scarlett, we could begin to feel aspirational as women. Sometimes when things are not going so well we will just say to each other let's watch *Gone with the Wind*.' Heather Horry, a Cheshire Inland Revenue officer with three children and a full social life: 'It showed me that by being a woman you could still be independent and have a mind of your own; that you could have both a social and a business life. Scarlett showed how it is possible to make compromises.' Angela Charters, a retired teacher from Liverpool, saw it in her late teens at the cinema with her mother, two aunts and at least two sisters. 'I'm more inspired by Melanie than Scarlett. She was beautiful as well as brave. She had insight and could see good in everyone to such an extent that she was blinded to her husband's infatuation. Scarlett

was a conniving, selfish little bitch, self-considering but fascinating.' Others said, 'Neither Scarlett nor Rhett would conform. Scarlett was a challenge to him. She was so glamorous and then, of course, there is the survival factor. Rhett was mature and experienced. She was cosseted. She became a woman because of the war, surviving against the odds.' 'My temperament is like Scarlett's and I believe that Rhett is the ideal man,' says Rachel Marsden, a beauty therapist from West Yorkshire who has watched the film many times and wanted her children to be named Rhett and Scarlett.

14 Quoted from *'Gone with the Wind* – Rhett Butler' at the Harry Ransom Center, University of Texas, Austin; www.hrc.utexas.edu/exhibitions/web/gwtw/wardrobe/rhett/rhett.html (accessed 12 April 2009).

15 Frances Tempest, e-mail to author, 23 March 2008. She added these observations: 'To a modern eye the colours of the costumes seem very much of their period, featuring, particularly, a repellent salmon pink. Was this early Technicolor? The ballroom scenes feature so many different, and such crude, colours that the only excuse could be the novelty of coloured film. To my eyes the costumes are nothing special, the cheerful Negro workers and servants look as if they have been dressed with little or no thought and throughout the film there is no significant use of detail.'

16 Agnès Rocamora, 'Paris, Capitale de la mode: Representing the fashion city in the media', in *Fashion's World Cities*, ed. Christopher Breward and David Gilbert (Oxford: Berg, 2006), p. 44.

17 David Gilbert, 'From Paris to Shanghai', in *Fashion's World Cities*, ed. Breward and Gilbert, p. 9.

18 Rocamora, 'Paris, Capitale de la mode', p. 46.

19 Christopher Breward, *Fashion* (Oxford; Oxford University Press, 2003), p. 172.

20 *The New Look*, BBC Radio 4, 30 October 2007.

21 Norma Rantisi, 'How New York stole modern fashion', in *Fashion's World Cities*, ed. Breward and Gilbert, p. 117.

22 Ibid.

23 Drake Stutesman, 'Costume trendsetting' in *Film Reference*; www.filmreference.com/encyclopedia/academy-awards-crime-films/costume-TREND-SETTING.html (accessed 12 April 2009).

24 Linda M. Scott, *Fresh Lipstick: Redressing Fashion and Feminism* (London: Palgrave Macmillan, 2005), p. 101.

25 Ibid., p. 102.

26 *GWTW*'s international smash hit status, and its influence on how women wanted to look, could well have been recognized by the French government by inclusion of its producer, David O. Selznick, in the *Légion d'honneur*. Both Christian Dior and Andrew Goodman, director of the New York department

store Bergdorf Goodman, were admitted to the prestigious list, in 1948 and 1949 respectively, for their services to Fashion.

27 Paul Gallico, *Mrs 'Arris Goes to Paris* (New York City: International Polygonics, 1989), p. 60.

28 Drusilla Beyfus, 'The heights of fashion', *Daily Telegraph* online, 14 September 2007, www.telegraph.co.uk/culture/3667939/the-heights-of-fashion.html (accessed 12 April 2009).

29 Valerie Steele, *Fifty Years of Fashion: New Look to Now* (New Haven and London: Yale University Press, 2006), p. 1.

30 Eleri Lynn, 'Preface', *The Golden Age of Couture*, 2008 diary (London: V&A, 2007), writing after the Unravelling Couture conference: 'I would say however, that really, during "the golden age" Paris was the last word in fashion. Front pages of newspapers all over the world were held for the latest Dior look! Dior, Balmain and Fath were the "Big 3" in America – outselling homegrown couturiers. It was really only during the war that America posed a threat to Paris, because nothing was coming out of France! Couture continued, but not on an export level that was competitive.'

31 Nicholas Drake, *The Fifties in Vogue* (London: Heinemann, 1987), pp. 10–11.

32 Ibid., pp. 51–2.

33 Ibid., p. 60.

34 Georgina Howell, *In Vogue: 75 Years of Style* (London: Condé Nast/Random Century, 1991), p. 113.

35 Ibid.

36 Breward, *Fashion*, p. 135.

37 Ibid, p. 136.

38 Valerie Steele in *Paris Fashion*, p. 270, cited in Breward, *Fashion*, p. 177.

39 Breward, *Fashion*, p. 75.

40 Pauline Weston-Thomas, 'Dior's New Look of 1947 and the design called Bar', *Fashion-Era* online, www.fashion-era.com/1950s_glamour.htm#dior's%20new%20look%201947 (accessed 12 April 2009).

41 Didier Ludot, *The Little Black Dress* (New York & Paris: Assouline, 2006).

42 Breward, *Fashion*, p. 138.

43 Camille Paglia, *Sexual Persona, Art and Decadence from Nefertiti to Emily Dickinson* (London: Penguin, 1995), p. 55.

44 Alan Vertrees, *Selznick's Vision* (Austin: Texas University Press, 1998), p. 8.

45 Taylor, *Scarlett's Women*, p. 131.

46 See also Note 13 above.

47 Claire Wilcox, *The Golden Age of Couture: Paris and London 1947–57* (London: V&A Publications, 2007) p. 22.

48 Ibid.

49 Ibid.

50 Ibid.

51 Eleri Lynn, e-mail to author, 10 December 2007

52 Valerie Steele, 'Introduction', *The Red Dress* (New York: Rizzoli International Publications, 2001).

53 The campaign was developed at RKCR/Y&R, London, by Creative director Mark Roalfe, copywriter Pip Bishop and Art director Chris Hodgkiss.

CHAPTER TWO

Audrey Hepburn and breakfast at Givenchy's

As a language, Garbo's singularity was of the order of the concept, that of Audrey Hepburn is of the order of the substance. The Face of Garbo is an idea, that of Hepburn an event.

Roland Barthes, *Mythologies*

Audrey Hepburn had starred in only four major Hollywood films when she caused Roland Barthes such sensation. He was proposing she could represent meaning to audiences beyond those who watched her movies. After her most significant films were released, in the 1950s and 1960s, she became an influence on Fashion followers in Britain and America, encouraging women to use home dressmaking in the class struggle. As 21st-century fans view *Roman Holiday*, *Sabrina*, *Funny Face* and *Breakfast at Tiffany's*, they witness the face that launched a thousand webpages and her popularity persists through digital media. The project she began with European children's charity UNICEF uses her image, protected by her sons, to further the cause. Named at the top of every 'most stylish' list, Audrey Hepburn appears in magazines, on posters, in videos and, occasionally, in the promotion of clothes or jewellery. Clues to this enduring charisma, stirring countless imaginations, are found in the preface to a *Vogue* publication, celebrating the fifties, written by Hepburn herself in 1987:

> I remember the fifties as a time of renewal and of regained security. Postwar austerity was fading and although the heartbreak remained, wounds were healing. There was a rebirth of opportunity, vitality and enthusiasm. The big American musicals came to London; people packed the theatres to see the twice-nightly shows of *High Button Shoes*, *South Pacific* and *Guys and Dolls*. Life was becoming more

carefree and there was a return to laughter and gaiety. The fifties had a special feeling of warmth. Once again one was allowed to be optimistic about the future – the world was functioning again. Above all there was a wonderful quality of hope, born from relief, and gratitude for those greatest of all luxuries – freedom and *peace*.[1]

Her clear vision in assessing the mood of the times, the humanity, sensed here points to a person more multifaceted than merely an interpreter of roles written by others. Her personality was carved from the miseries and hardship, suffered in World War II; yet empathy and optimism became her guiding principles. It may be that Barthes saw, in Hepburn's face, the compassion she was to bring to her political work, and to roles she created, from significant moments in her early life. These childhood experiences led her to spend precious time with her young sons and as the leading 20th-century campaigner for UNICEF, away from the camera and the ateliers of French couture. She was to tell journalists in the 1980s:

> I've known UNICEF a long time, ever since the Second World War when they came to the aid of thousands of children like myself, famished victims of five years of German occupation in Holland. We were reduced to near total poverty as is the developing world today.[2]

Her legend is full of contradictions, of privilege, privations, celebrity, discretion and diplomacy. Born in Brussels on 4 May 1929 into a family of European aristocrats, she starved in Holland during World War II. Although she was seen as a Hollywood product, a Paramount Studio property, she only ever owned homes in Europe. Far from socializing with the movie glitterati, she used her influence to fight for children's rights. At 16 years of age she danced, in secret, to raise money for the Dutch resistance to the Nazis. Remembering the subterfuge and fear of the time, she said, 'the best audience I ever had made not a single sound at the end of my performance'. Her preternatural slimness was put down to the shortage of food during her teenage years. There were limited food supplies. Her family and many others made flour out of tulip bulbs for cakes and biscuits. Her uncle and her mother's cousin were shot, in front of her, for being part of the resistance, and her brother, Ian Von Ufford, died in a German labour camp. She suffered from malnutrition, and developed acute anaemia, respiratory problems and oedema. After she appeared in *Roman Holiday* (1953), *Sabrina* (1954), *War and Peace* (1956) and *Funny Face* (1957), Barthes was to write of her face as 'substance' or 'event'.

She influenced women in the 1950s and 1960s. Through her, they realized they would be judged on how they looked and that it was in their power to alter these perceptions. She was seen as an approachable Fashion idol with an haute couture image, and as an international charity worker determined to redress the suffering of children. Barthes was so convinced by her androgynous magnetism that he argued: 'the face of Audrey Hepburn, for instance, is individualized, not only because of its peculiar thematics: woman as child, woman as kitten but also because of her person, an almost unique specification of the face, which has nothing of the essence left in it, but is constituted by an infinite complexity of morphological functions'.[3]

Roman Holiday deals with notions of celebrity and public image. Through the eyes of the young Princess Ann we see the difficulties and restrictions of being a head of state, always in the public eye.

Barthes' ideas hinted at the influence Hepburn was to exert through her compelling iconography. While his philosophical assertions suggest his unconscious enchantment, it is her screen life that explains its power. Appearing on *The Phil Donahue Show* in 1990, Audrey Hepburn told details of her story; of how she believed her survival and the possibilities freedom brought were her life's greatest gift. She explained that it was not so much bravery or stoicism which made her work at being ready, to play a part, or be on time for every appointment – 'the curtain goes up even if you're not there' – but the strict disciplines of dance training. She said that good manners, insisted on by her mother, were learned as a way of being kind to other people. The scene in *Breakfast at Tiffany's* when Holly Golightly rampages around her flat as she learns that her brother has been killed was shown to demonstrate her dramatic acting ability. She turned the compliment round, saying, 'Talk about therapy in movies, I've never broken a light in my life.' If she had the time to write her memoirs, it might contain emotions and feelings, but she would avoid an actual autobiography because there were so many other people involved.

By 1990 she was seriously involved with her work for UNICEF, which she knew through the Red Cross when it had taken part in the liberation of Holland. Her success in cinema meant she could devote time and money to this cause. The delight in her film work was still evident 30 years on, as she told the television audience, 'I wanted to be a dancer but had to earn a living doing little bits in movies for extra bucks.' Sympathy for the suffering of others seems to have been uppermost in her mind for most of her life. At the time of the interview, she was involved with the New World Symphony Orchestra, in a series of fund-raising concerts in New York, Philadelphia, Chicago and Houston. As UNICEF's goodwill ambassador, she narrated texts she had chosen 'from the *Diary of Anne Frank*'. Talking of meeting children from Ethiopia, travelling in a tiny aeroplane and being given weeds from the desert by them, she said:

> It was the most beautiful bunch of flowers I ever had. They knew I'd come from UNICEF. They don't know about Paramount but do know about UNICEF.[4]

Taking the sentimentality out of charity work, celebrating the depth and breadth of its influence, she explained her feelings:

> I knew about this side of Africa, about Bangladesh. The way to deal
> with it is by doing something. Maybe I would have a good cry every
> so often. I know what's being done to help the 500 voluntary agen-
> cies with their marvellous work. It's about saying, 'how about a cup
> of tea?' and going there and making it.[5]

She recalled the movies she had made as a 'constant source of pleasure
and the best cure for coming out of the war'. Also, she enjoyed remembering her first months in theatre, appearing twice nightly: 'All the
friendships and the music were totally therapeutic and a happy
experience.'

Money for the resistance

Audrey Hepburn's credentials for becoming a Hollywood star were
much stronger than might be expected from the surprise expressed, by
American commentators, over the success of *Roman Holiday* in 1953.
The movie industry's publicity machine was possibly taken off guard
as a European stole the limelight during a time when there were many
home-grown talents around – Grace Kelly, Marilyn Monroe. American
film writer Molly Haskell, quoted on an Audrey fan site, describes the
phenomenon:

> She appeared as fragile as a cut flower, but for someone who looked
> as if she might blow away with a strong breeze, Audrey Hepburn
> proved astonishingly durable as a star. She lit up the screen in 1953,
> as the hooky-playing princess in *Roman Holiday*, and from then on
> set her own pace and style with a look that decidedly ran counter
> to then-prevailing standards of female beauty. She was patrician,
> exotic, boyishly slender at a time when the accent was on big-
> breasted bombshells and girl-next-door types – and even the latter
> had hourglass figures. Yet her blend of bohemianism and haute
> couture, of rebel and royalist, took fire and the best directors in
> Hollywood fell over each other in their eagerness to work with her.[6]

Hepburn had danced to raise money for the resistance in Holland
during WWII, and studied drama and worked as a photographer's
model, when she moved to London in 1948. She had already made a
few films and appeared in the 1951 Broadway play *Gigi* when she was
given the lead in *Roman Holiday*. Her co-star, Gregory Peck, had the
foresight to ask for her name to be featured with his, above the title.

So when she won an Academy Award, a Golden Globe and a BAFTA, for her performance, Paramount would be seen as having recognized her potential. Molly Haskell writes of the seemingly magical rise to stardom for Hepburn:

> But then, there was always something miraculous about this creature who, while playing a princess, was enacting a fairy tale of her own, the one in which a young unknown is plucked from obscurity and becomes a star overnight. Well, not complete obscurity. The daughter of a Dutch baroness and an English banker who deserted mother and daughter when Audrey was six; Hepburn grew up in Nazi-occupied Holland and went to London on a dance scholarship. She was working as a model and bit-part actress when, shooting a British film on the Riviera, she met Colette. The writer was dazzled and handpicked her for the lead in the Broadway version of *Gigi*. This performance got her the part in *Roman Holiday* opposite Gregory Peck – and an Oscar to boot![7]

Roman Holiday deals with notions of celebrity and public image. Through the eyes of the young Princess Ann we see the difficulties and restrictions of being a head of state, always in the public eye. In the opening scenes Hepburn's character is compared to the British royals of the time; to the British Queen's younger sister, Princess Margaret, who was something of a dissenter, preferring unpredictable commonplace experiences rather than the strictures of public service.[8] The film's opening scenes include montaged, actual footage of state visits in Europe and a voiceover tells of how these diplomatic sorties would improve trade relations in Paris. Seeing Hepburn, as Princess Ann, relieve the pain of wearing formal court shoes by slipping her foot out, undercover of her full-skirted dress, during meetings with diplomats, we are allowed into her personal world. These moments in *Roman Holiday* are when her audiences began to feel an intimate connection with the actress, as Rachel Moseley observes:

> We will be privy to 'the private and secret longings of a princess, her innermost thoughts as revealed to your Rome correspondent in a personal, exclusive interview' complete with 'love angle and pictures', as Joe Bradley later describes his 'scoop' – which, aside from the princess and her companions, only the viewer shares.[9]

The formal, repetitive, schedule drives the fictional princess crazy. So she escapes the grand house and, wearing her most simple clothes, appears on the streets of Rome. We know there is a different world waiting, one of rural Italian food suppliers at markets and international poker-playing journalists. The tipsy, exhausted princess is found asleep on a low stone wall by one of them, an American, Joe Bradley, played by the urbane Gregory Peck. Back in his attic rooms, she begins to find out about simple domestic detail in the informality of a bachelor's pied-à-terre. Looking at the design of a white shirt, she tells him, 'I've never been alone with a man before.' For the audience there is dramatic irony, realizing that an heir to a throne is wearing borrowed pyjamas. He only realizes who she is when he hears the news about her disappearance, next day. In a scene between Joe Bradley and his editor, they discuss angles and trends. 'Youth must lead the way,' he is told. In 1953, this

The sight of Peck and Hepburn on an Italian Vespa scooter made it an object of desire for style-conscious youth, as important as the Gaggia espresso machines when Britain briefly took on Modernism.

75

was a topical theme in the context of access to a young princess. Her observations, on world conditions, would be worth a fee to the journalist of $250, but her 'views on clothes worth a lot more, perhaps a thousand'. From that cinematic moment on, Audrey Hepburn would represent the dynamic interaction between Fashion and class structures. It was to be both her on- and off-screen character; a role in which she would demonstrate how position in society dictates how Fashion is consumed. Looks count in the transmission of meaning in a movie but the script, written by undisputed left-winger Donald Trumbo, gave us an early inkling of Audrey Hepburn as a class and dress cipher.

Audiences saw her as a political signifier whose style could be copied. *Roman Holiday* was written by Trumbo, but fronted by Ian McLellan Hunter while Trumbo was under surveillance by the House Un-American Activities Committee.[10] Some of his thoughts are voiced through Joe Bradley (Gregory Peck). He longs for hard news reporting, with a 'one-way ticket back to New York to a real newsroom'. He is beginning to tire of the world of *la dolce vita,* where he spends time gambling and scratching around for money. While he is being set up to exploit his contact with the princess, she is free to wander around Rome. Hepburn seems to be in control of her own on-screen makeover, choosing to visit an on-street hairdresser. Her long dark curls are shortened. She is given her trademark fringe, copied by thousands of young women across America and Europe in the 1950s. It was not a sign used to create the myth of Roman-ness, like Marlon Brando's haircut as Mark Antony in *Julius Caesar,* identified by Barthes. Her transformation frees her to be frivolous. It is the beginning of a democratizing iconography for her followers. 'You model, cool, just what I wanted,' says the shopkeeper as Princess Ann swaps her offending pumps for flat sandals – symbols of pilgrimages or childhood. 'Your friends, I don't think they will recognize you,' she is told with clever irony. Pamela Church Gibson believes this was when Hepburn became doubly important to how women see themselves. They could see the possibilities for becoming liberated, youthful adventurers and being able to take on a new way of dressing for their own generation.

> Her appeal to women was twofold, as an engaging and childlike temporary fugitive from routines and rules and as an elegant clothes-horse who also possessed a more casual, affordable, off-duty, or pre-

transformation, uniform of simple tops, narrow trousers and flat shoes. She was also remarkable for popularizing the slim, boyish figure – which would endure on and off screen – in an era of big-breasted stars.[11]

The princess's fresh image is reflected in a shop window at the Spanish Steps, now Rome's focal Fashion district and home to Bulgari, Cartier and Louis Vuitton. Academics regard Hepburn's new egalitarian image, at this moment, as not sexual, attracting a female rather than male gaze. Pamela Church Gibson, looking back to the scene, sees it representing a reverse Cinderella fantasy, as the aristocrat takes on the persona of a free citizen. She recognizes how it was a significant marker in encouraging women to buy into the way they looked: 'It most

When she returns from Paris she has learned how to live, 'how to be in the world and of the world'. The disparities between the rich businessmen broth-ers and the chauffeur's enigmatic daughter mean they had hardly looked at her before she was dressed in haute couture.

certainly acted as invitation to imitation and to new modes of fashion-related consumption.'[12]

Character-controlled

During this first on-screen, character-controlled transformation the princess is seen having the distinctive gamine hair cut which was copied by young women everywhere. She rolls up her sleeves, belts her waist and, putting on flat sandals, starts the youthful style which would be universally appropriated. The look she seemed to invent was created for her in the atelier of Rome's oldest and most famous designers, the Italian Fashion house Fontana.[13] While on her flight of freedom Princess Ann (Hepburn) is photographed, paparazzi style, by Joe Bradley's photographer colleague, Irving Radovitch[14] (Eddie Albert), in league with him to sell a major scoop. Her status is frequently emphasized during the course of the narrative. She never carries money, does not know its worth. He's scratching around, as a gambler, understanding its value only too well. Rachel Moseley, whose mother introduced her to the star when she was a girl, researched these indicators of class, evident in Hepburn's early films. It began a search to find out exactly what it was like: *Growing up with Audrey Hepburn.* By the time the book was published, in 2002, she had interviewed three generations of Audrey fans – those who admired her in the 1950s and 1960s, and others from the 1990s. Saying that *Roman Holiday* is one of the filmic discourses which constructs Hepburn against 'frilly' femininity, Moseley expands her discussion of Hepburn's importance to her early fans:

> In *Roman Holiday* Hepburn's character escapes from the fairy-tale femininity within which the film places her from the start, transforming herself into a pared-down, modernised and more casual version.[15]

At the end of the progressive fairytale, when Princess Ann knows she has to return to the dutiful life as head of state, director William Wilder has the princess come face to face with a 20th-century world, from which she would usually be excluded. Musicians and extras play modern jazz and dance bebop on a large river-cruising motorboat. As the film ends with Hepburn, more regal than before greeting her paramour, among other members of the Press corps, at a briefing, we are left admiring the love-struck couple's reserve and their professional dedica-

After her move from little girl, in Edith Head's printed pinafore, to the sophisticate wearing 'yards and yards in the skirt' of her soignée, sculptured, black-and-white strapless Givenchy, Sabrina becomes the objective of every man in sight.

tion. If William Wilder's *Roman Holiday* captured the 1950s era of innocence and possibility, then it was these cinema audiences who became enduringly hooked on the city and the actress who fired their imaginations.

> *Roman Holiday* gave some their first sight of this fashion arena; it crystallized their growing awareness of the virtues of Italian style and its particular importance for young people. Rome had become a popular holiday destination for those who could afford the possibilities offered by the wider availability of air travel ... Film, therefore, can be seen to function as the poor person's 'air travel, transporting audiences not only to places they could not afford to visit, but also serving as a showcase for styles and fashions they might not otherwise see.[16]

Writing on cinema and consumption in *Fashion's World Cities*, Pamela Church Gibson proposes that the sight of Peck and Hepburn on an Italian Vespa scooter made it an object of desire for style-conscious youth, as important as Gaggia espresso machines when Britain briefly took on Modernism. She also thinks the actress's on-screen transformation from formal, Dior-corseted royal to lightly clothed casual tourist was not only important to the narrative but crucial to Audrey's becoming a popular role model. Church Gibson makes the observation that in the 1990s rags-to-riches movie *Pretty Woman*, the heroine does not have the same degree of autonomy:

> But where Julia Roberts, even in 1990, needs guidance from her rich lover, and a helpful hotel manager, Hepburn is usually able to control her own costume changes, to know what she wants and what will suit her.[17]

In 1992 Hepburn paid tribute to her co-star, Gregory Peck, who had insisted on her having equal billing with him. They were an alluring pair with his clean-cut yet rangy looks and her ingenuousness. An added bonus were their heights: his 6 ft 2 ins to her 5 ft 7 ins. It allowed the couple to be seen in genuine rather than constructed poses, in contrast to scenes with actors who, because of their miniature, photogenic features, are often filmed to make tiny men seem as tall as their partners. She said he had promoted a 'totally unknown hoofer' and that he was really 'the beautiful guide, the gentle hero' he appeared on screen. The chemistry between these two entrancing characters contributed to the film's potency as a style marker. Celebrating the prized craftsmanship inherent in the Italian Fashion industry, Church Gibson suggests that the film was responsible for furthering its influence:

> But *Roman Holiday* not only launched Hepburn's career and innumerable imitations of her haircut and make-up – it made of Rome an acknowledged capital of women's fashion as well as the locale for romance and source of the more stylish man's inspiration.[18]

After *Roman Holiday*, Audrey Hepburn was seen as *the* movie actress to be cast in parts dealing with transformation through Fashion. She was not perceived as a Hollywood starlet plugged into the general fifties dynamic. She carried her own romantic mystique, a more elaborate

European mythology, with her. Writing the self-help tribute *What Would Audrey Do?* more than 50 years later, Pamela Keogh defines her staying power:

> Audrey is still showing us how it's done. As a style icon, her influence is unrivalled. In 2006, *New Woman* magazine voted her the Most Beautiful Woman of All Time. On Seventh Avenue, in Hollywood, in the halls of *Vogue, People* magazine, or *InStyle*; to describe something (or someone) as 'very Audrey' is shorthand for the absolute height of chic.[19]

Paramount costume designer Edith Head's extravagant *Diorlywood* creations were worn by Hepburn, as the princess, in *Roman Holiday*. She was responsible for the clothes for the film overall, with the Fontana sisters' designs chosen for scenes in the city as Hepburn took on her signature, ordinary, looks. Edith Head, a lifelong friend of Audrey Hepburn, was given full credit for the costumes in *Sabrina*. However, this leading actress was not simply dressed by a French couturier on-screen, but visited Paris to commission the clothes, both in character and off-screen. Bronwyn Cosgrave's insider information, for her Hollywood Oscar story *Made for Each Other*, reveals scenes of heartbreak for the doyenne of costume design, Head. It was reported that Hepburn thought she needed authentic French haute couture to support the narrative in which her character lived, for a while, in Paris. So after persuading director Wilder they should look to Europe:

> Hepburn was thrilled to learn that to curb the expense of paying custom duties, she would embark on a solo Paris shopping mission and personally select couture for *Sabrina* at the Paris *maison* Hubert de Givenchy, operated from a Gothic mansion on rue Alfred Vigny.[20]

It was recorded in Edith Head's memoirs that her heart was broken, and the gossip surrounding the decisions ranged from accusations that it was the behaviour of a temperamental 'rank-pulling' star to Wilder's defence that it had been the script which inspired Audrey Hepburn to turn to Paris. A lifelong relationship began between the couturier Hubert de Givenchy and the actress. In film credits, Edith Head appears as Costume Supervisor. Her designs for high-society characters, surrounding chauffeur's daughter Sabrina in her tomboy to trophy, object-of-desire triumph, gave Head scope to interpret Fashion for dances, board meetings, and family gatherings for several important roles and a large supporting cast. Hepburn, who won an Oscar for *Roman Holiday*, was nominated again for *Sabrina*, one of six nominations the film received. It won only one, for costume design. Although Edith Head was given the award, it was Givenchy's designs which gave Hepburn's transformation the chic, the je ne sais quoi, to enchant European and Francophile American audiences. He was not credited, and Head accepted the award without including any reference to additional pieces. It was said that Hepburn was devastated and called Givenchy to express regret. Her promise that it would never happen again was kept, according to the designer.

The look became the symbol of youthful non-conformity when she danced a defiant modern jazz sequence in a moody, underground Paris bar in Funny Face. *Clothing company Gap was given permission to use this sequence to promote its skinny pants in 2006.*

In the opening moments of the film it is clear that we are dealing with a class drama. The family Sabrina and her chauffeur father, Thomas Fairchild (John Williams), attend is seriously rich. He is content with the social order. Set on the North Shore of Long Island, *Sabrina* was filmed on the estate of Paramount chairman Barney Balaban to achieve the sense of affluence the Cinderella comedy required. Hepburn's aristocratic European voice poses interesting levels of irony as she meets the dowager Maude Larabee, played by Chicago vaudevillian Nella Walker, and asks, 'Have I changed, have I really changed?' Even with the finishing school élan and her Parisian designer makeover, her father advises caution about a relationship with his employers. As a chauffeur, he believes the limousine window barrier, between back and front seats, should not be breached. Disparaging 1950s growing egalitarianism, he observes, 'Democracy can be a wickedly unfair thing. Nobody poor was ever called democratic for marrying someone rich.'[21]

American wealth is celebrated throughout the movie, and an underlying theme surrounds the work ethic leading to these riches. Larabee company office sets, with their sleek and shiny, spotlit cocktail cabinets and Alexander Calder mobile, are examples of the high Modernism which Hollywood supported and commissioned. Linus Larabee (Humphrey Bogart) promotes the project, explaining how the future of industry will depend on the plastics they are testing. Hepburn's character Sabrina represents 'good' in the fairy-tale tradition, with the magical potential for being able to change hearts and minds. She is innocent, unspoiled, beautiful and able to use love to fight against the evils of greed and materialism. Director Billy Wilder's biographer, Charlotte Chandler, notes that he chose to play up Hepburn's 'Cinderella quality'

> evident in her first appearance in the film, when a full moon sits over her shoulder. This fairy tale theme is also echoed in the film's opening narration. Though Hepburn narrates, she is not in character as Sabrina, and this sets the scene for the idyllic story. The class shift and Sabrina's infatuation with older men are also fairy tale-type elements[22]

For this fairy tale to become a modern-day myth for cinema audiences, it was important they should see Sabrina as an archetypal legendary virgin. Writer Ernest Lehman persuaded Wilder to avoid including a sex scene between Sabrina and Linus Larrabee. He thought it would harm Hepburn's image, and both writer and director agreed that Hepburn's ingenuousness was key to making the role believable. Sabrina is mysterious. She tells her father, when he is warning her to be realistic about her position in society, 'No, father, the moon's reaching for me.' When she returns from Paris she has learned how to live, 'how to be in the world and of the world'. The disparities between the rich business-men brothers and the chauffeur's enigmatic daughter mean they had hardly looked at her before she was dressed in haute couture. Church Gibson, in *Fashion's World Cities,* reminds us of the influence exerted by French Fashion designers:

> Although the film is set mainly on Long Island, it is her Parisian wardrobe that enables her to bewitch both brothers – and to make the women of Manhattan high society look frumpy. She showed American – and other – audiences that Paris had an undeniable right to its position.[23]

Fashion's alchemy

After her move from little girl, in Edith Head's printed pinafore, to the sophisticate wearing 'yards and yards in the skirt' of her soignée, sculp-tured, black-and-white strapless Givenchy, Sabrina becomes the objec-tive of every man in sight. She explains to David Larabee she has always been around, 'just over the garage'. She is described by her friends, the Larabee retainers, as the prettiest girl, in the prettiest dress, the best dancer; the belle of the ball, they say, with 'such poise as though she belonged up there'. Her father's fears about disturbing the social system – 'I don't like it' – are confirmed, as imperious Mrs Larabee, hearing of Sabrina's cordon bleu skills, condescends to her: 'You must come over and cook something special for us.' David, the brother she is in love with, is being set up to combine marriage with a plastics merger. When Linus sees Sabrina on a tennis umpire's seat, in Givenchy, they agree the change in her is 'as if a window has been thrown open'. He learns she does not want money; she wants love. Hepburn's charming version of 'Yes We Have No Bananas' helps the dour Linus unwind a little, on a boat trip, deputizing for his champagne-glass-injured brother. He tells her, 'No man walks alone, from choice.' She observes, 'Paris isn't just for changing trains', a line setting the scene for her next international sortie in *Funny Face*. *Roman Holiday* and *Sabrina* put Audrey Hepburn at the centre of women's 'makeover' fantasy projections. She had been changed from princess to chauffeur's daughter to company director's lover through the alchemy of Fashion. Hollywood decided Audrey Hepburn was ready to star in a film about the industry, and it was ready to have the controversy between itself and Academia aired. Hepburn became a signifier, in the broad narrative of Fashion, by playing roles which became part of its legend. She starred in Fashion films, where a look, or trend, is taken up by audiences, and in films about Fashion. A look that did take off was the basic black skinny pants and long-sleeved top of the Rive Gauche intellectual, or beatnik, worn by Hepburn in *Sabrina*:

> She also reminds us again that she can control her own shape-shifting, dressing down on screen, in bohemian black turtleneck and trousers, for a confrontation with the elder brother.[24]

In it, she cooked for Linus, in the Larabee's trés Modern office apartments. Removing the towel from around her sleek, dark form and asserting her new found bourgeois confidence, she says, 'Sorry I can't stay to do the dishes.' The look became the symbol of youthful non-conformity when she danced a defiant, modern jazz sequence in a moody, underground Paris bar in *Funny Face*. Clothing company Gap was given permission to use this sequence to promote its skinny pants in 2006. Some of Hepburn's fans were disturbed by the appropriation of the image, but for Gap, with its ethical approaches to marketing, it proved a fine partner. A release, which takes note of the UNICEF campaign Gap supported,[25] was put out from their San Francisco headquarters in September of that year:

> This week, the skinny black pant is back at Gap with the introduction of a new, groundbreaking campaign featuring original film footage of timeless style icon Audrey Hepburn. The campaign, entitled 'Keep it Simple', is centered on innovative television spots incorporating a memorable scene of Audrey Hepburn dancing in the classic film *Funny Face*.[26]

Inhabiting the materialistic, driven world of the glossy Fashion magazine, full of catwalk couture, *Funny Face* inspired no contemporary Fashion trends other than the black skinny basics introduced in *Sabrina*. There is no doubting the influence of Paris. Hubert de Givenchy is named in the opening credits. If Hollywood gave Fashion back to Paris through *Gone with the Wind*, it continued its patronage with *Sabrina* and *Funny Face*. As an amusing dance movie, *Funny Face* improved Hepburn's stock as a matchless talent and revived Fred Astaire's standing as the world's most accomplished dance partner. Cellar bar scenes are a parody of Art house cinema and yet, overall, the movie is neither slick Hollywood nor deeply important European. As a satire on the Fashion industry, pre-dating BBC TV's *Absolutely Fabulous* and the 20th

She is making her own artistic decisions: 'Never mind what I'm going to do.' Descending the steps, refusing to take any more instructions – 'I can't stop, take the picture, take the picture' – Hepburn is empowered and empowering.

Century Fox hit *The Devil Wears Prada*, it fails as a romantic or musical comedy. Unlike its descendants, *Funny Face* features the work of only one French couturier and he, Givenchy, is fictionalized in the character of Paul Duval (Robert Flemyng). Audrey Hepburn appears in 11 Givenchy ensembles in her role as bookseller turned model. Fred Astaire's Dick Avery was written in tribute to the highly acclaimed Fashion photographer Richard Avedon, who supervised the photography for the film. Hepburn's book shop assistant is characterized as an uptight black-stocking, talking in riddles about every kind of '-ism'. Pushed outside while editors and photographers use the gloomy bookish interior, she is pictured looking into the bookshop window. This *mise en scène* forms part of the continuing Hepburn narrative which began during her stroll around the shops in Rome and culminated in Tiffany's window in New York. A reluctant model, persuaded by photographer Dick Avery, Jo Stockton travels to Paris having had her makeover begun in New York. Hollywood allows America this style status before encouraging audiences to fall in love with Paris. Jo Stockton wants to hook up with the philosopher Emile Flostre, a charlatan whose beliefs are a scriptwriter's ridiculous version of Existentialism. He loses out because of his lechery or possibly his lack of Gershwin musical numbers. So Hepburn's image remains unsullied by notions of casual sex, but her role, as free-spirited intellectual, is undermined by the wacky parody of Existentialism she is required to espouse, and her contact with the poseurs who surround her. However, by focusing on Fashion photography, having Richard Avedon's stills as articulation, the film places Audrey Hepburn at the centre of Fashion's new philosophies. The importance of *Funny Face* to Hepburn's involvement with Fashion comes from director Stanley Donen's conscious referencing of Richard Avedon:

> The images are, however, carefully prepared and composed, as their use in Donen's film makes clear. The photographs are integrated into the film as freeze-frames that punctuate sequences depicting fashion shoots involving Hepburn and Astaire.[27]

Acclaimed American photographer Avedon acted as visual consultant to the film, and his technique of high shutter speed and shallow-focus images, to catch his subjects as if in flight, was used in the Paris couture scenes. Douglas Smith, lecturer in French at University College Dublin, encapsulates the marvels of the film's photography:

> One of the most strikingly composed images captures Hepburn in the Louvre, running across the bottom of the grand staircase that leads up to the winged victory of Samothrace, her draped arms outspread in imitation of the Greek statue.[28]

Freedom and autonomy

It is the photographs of her face which progress the Hepburn myth for and beyond Fashion. Details become mere outline, eyes, nose and mouth, in the red-lit darkroom at the offices of fictional magazine *Glamour,* as Astaire, as Avery referencing Avedon, experiments with cutting and fixing the likeness. This is also the moment when he persuades Hepburn to take part in the Paris Fashion shoot, so she can meet her cult philosopher. Commenting on Roland Barthes' ability to take ideological meaning from photographs, in his paper 'Humanism in Post-war French Photography and Philosophy', Smith writes:

> Hepburn's image is one of change, of youth maturing, switching hairstyles, and clothes, from one image to the next. Hepburn is the existentialist ideal of beauty, open to endless self-transformation; she embodies the star as event.[29]

Funny Face inspired Smith's approach. He sees that Hepburn's uncompromising character takes on a challenge. She is set up to reconcile the values of Education and Art with those of Photography and Fashion:

> the film stages a conflict between the competing claims of photography and philosophy, a contest that photography apparently wins, since it is the photographer and not the philosopher who 'gets the girl'. But the woman in question is a philosopher too, and it is ultimately the empathy between the photographer and his philosopher model that secures the happy ending.[30]

Smith argues that the manipulation of the bookseller, away from her practice of librarianship and study to become a much-photographed

Fashion model, is an example of the imposition of an outside agency on the freedom of an individual. Taking up Barthes' suggestion that Hepburn's face is capable of expressing an infinite variety of emotions, Smith identifies expressions of 'freedom and autonomy'. He is persuaded that in Avedon's stills of Hepburn in movement, 'we catch a glimpse of the contradictory funny face of post-war humanism'. In the role of Dick Avery, Astaire directs Hepburn in an extraordinary feat of homage to Avedon in the *mise en scène* between stills. In the first of the series of the 'Fashion shoot' she is named 'bird of paradise', appearing in Givenchy, with diamonds in her hair. Modelling a pale pink 1950s waisted jacket, she is directed to be 'happy'; then sad like Anna Karenina, told 'you may not know that kiss again'; 'kooky' while fishing; then, as Isolde, asked to be 'furious with Tristan'. In the spectacular setting of the Louvre, Hepburn's character takes back her original free-thinking control. She reverses the process begun in the offices of *Glamour* when bookseller Jo Stockton is hijacked to become a Fashion cipher. After days of being Avery's puppet, Stockton knows how to stage the moment of double articulation; when a pose brings extra meaning to the clothes. She can predict what her mentor might demand. Avery tells his model, 'You've outgrown me.' Then Hepburn's voice is heard at the top of the gallery's imposing staircase. She is making her own artistic decisions: 'Never mind what I'm going to do.' Descending the steps, refusing to take any more instructions – 'I can't stop, take the picture, take the picture' – Hepburn is empowered and empowering. Signified as victorious, her alter ego is enabled to occupy the intellectual high ground she had envisioned, for herself, before visiting Paris.

Inspired by the film's stimulating scenario, Susan Sellers, too, deals with post-war France's discussions of Philosophy and Photography. Writing in *Harper's Bazaar*, in 1995, she reflects on the heady mix of progress and stasis occupying philosophers, and their abstract ideas of how the real might be expressed through Photography. She sees that Hollywood is also involved with the intellectual distractions occupying Smith:

> Stanley Donen's Paris-set musical *Funny Face* (1956) articulates these concerns in the dilemma faced by its librarian-turned-fashion-model protagonist, who is torn between the competing claims of photography and philosophy.[31]

She believes that *Funny Face* plays a part in the construction of modern woman, arguing that the Hollywood film musical is often used to show how 'European cinema has defined itself in relation to a Hollywood product'. Including *Gentlemen Prefer Blondes* (1953) with *Funny Face* in her critique, she explains:

> Both these musicals place their female heroines in Paris as American tourists. The cultural transactions involved in watching a Hollywood product in France are thus illustrated on, as well as beyond, the cinema screen. This allows us to consider the ways in which Hollywood constructs a specific European screen identity and how this identity offers differing pleasures to the musicals' stars and audiences.[32]

Narrative links

In 1957 Hepburn was being described, in publicity material, as a 'relatively unknown Belgian actress who made an indelible impression on women, who emulated her looks and style throughout Europe and America'. So when invited to play Holly Golightly in *Breakfast at Tiffany's,* she was not expected to leave her European identity at Ellis Island. Dressed, inevitably, in Givenchy, she speaks an Anglo-American patois, peppered with idiosyncratic bon mots. In her back-story, Holly has been encouraged to speak French to lose an 'Okie' twang. Her agent, O.J. Berman (Martin Balsam), who devised the strategy, calls her a 'real phoney' because she believed in her own re-invention. Hepburn devotees have no reason to suspend their disbelief in the character's authenticity, nor dispute the validity of her construct, as an alternative self-directed heroine. Placed at the top of many fans' lists of most resonant images, the opening of *Breakfast at Tiffany's* is for me a high point in women's liberation. Audrey Hepburn frees modern woman to be more herself than she has ever been before, as she steps out from a yellow cab between New York skyscrapers in the early hours of the day. Gazing into Tiffany's window – 'nothing really bad could happen to you there' – holding her portable coffee, taking a bite from a donut, wearing tiara and pearls, we are convinced that anything is possible at any time. Before the hippy weirdness of third-wave Feminism in the seventies, and the limp inadequacies of millen-nial post-Feminism, there was, in *Breakfast at Tiffany's,* a vision of sophisticated escapist heaven where men and women all behaved like grown-ups. In an opening scene, Patricia Neal, as Mrs Failenson, 'decorator' and sponsor of out-of-work writer Paul 'Fred' Varjak, talks of returning from Rome, making a narrative link from Hepburn's first significant movie.

Breakfast at Tiffany's is importantly Modern. It uses cinema's most advanced camera techniques and film stock, and deals with notions of mental health, freedom, independence and autonomy. Holly Golightly speaks of her angst, calling symptoms the 'mean reds', of men being exploiters, 'Quelle rat!' She buys a typewriter ribbon for the 'kept' author, which signals her as an enabler. 'I'm his agent,' she jokes. 'He's already got a decorator.' It takes on one of the central tenets of Modernism in the main characters' utopian desires to create a better world. Holly Golightly has already escaped the oppression of small-town, of second-wife, domesticity, and Paul Varjak returns to writing 'sensitively felt promising prose'. The tone of the film is so Modern that it verges on the post-Modern. Holly has re-invented herself, and Varjak is writing the story as it's happening. She won't return to the old safe traditional life, and he gives up being financially supported by an older woman. In a DVD extra showing original trails for the film, we are told, 'It's everything you've ever wanted to do and Audrey Hepburn's the one you've wanted to do it with.'[33]

Truman Capote, the novelist whose book was adapted for the screen by George Axelrod, wanted Marilyn Monroe to play Holly Golightly. Pamela Church Gibson imagines what Monroe's Hollywood glamour might have brought to the part, but considers what a loss that particular casting would have meant to Fashion:

> Certainly, the cinematic 'fashion moment' created by the opening shots of the film, the juxtaposition of Hepburn's quirky elegance with the streets of Manhattan at daybreak, would not have entered the collective consciousness in the same way, not provided such a gift for the cinematic image banks, so frequently ransacked by fashion editors, stylists and photographers.[34]

In Rachel Moseley's studies of Hepburn as a role model for fifties, sixties and nineties women, she recognizes the meanings Barthes saw in Hepburn's face:

The passivity suggested in this emphasis on appearance is not simple. Her face is an *event.* This potential contradiction (simultaneous activity and passivity) in Hepburn's persona is frequently expressed through a discourse which figures her as at once creator and created, artist and model, active and passive.[35]

Hepburn's life in Fashion began sometime before fans poached her style from *Roman Holiday* and her zany panache from *Breakfast at Tiffany's.* British society photographer Norman Parkinson took pictures of her for *Vogue* in 1952, after novelist Colette had persuaded her to become Gigi on Broadway. In *Roman Holiday,* Hepburn was

Audrey Hepburn frees modern woman to be more herself than she has ever been before, as she steps out from a yellow cab between New York skyscrapers in the early hours of the day. Gazing into Tiffany's window – 'nothing really bad could happen to you there' – holding her portable coffee, taking a bite from a donut, wearing tiara and pearls, we are convinced that anything is possible at any time.

fortunate to have the talents of Wilder and Head, with their skills in cinema, to make an influential Fashion film. They used certain camera angles, scripting, music, lighting, acting and clothes to create Hollywood glitz and European Art house authenticity. Christopher Breward, writing *Fashion* for Oxford University Press (2003), includes two of Audrey Hepburn's films in his 'Influential fashion films' list of 12 American and European movies: *Roman Holiday* (USA, 1953) introduced Audrey Hepburn's distinctive look, while *Breakfast at Tiffany's* (USA, 1961) was the last of Audrey Hepburn's screen collaborations with Givenchy.[36]

Dismissing *My Fair Lady* (UK 1964) as an 'overblown interpretation of historical dress', and as part of a series of '50s/60s Hollywood block-busters' with some 'tenuous links with contemporary trends', Breward describes it as 'essentially designed with spectacle in mind', recognizing how Fashion needs more than mere referenced details for inspiration.[37]

Vogue's relationship with Audrey Hepburn began in the 1950s, when her every change of appearance and role was recorded throughout the decade. In 1954 she married Mel Ferrer after they appeared together, that year, in the Broadway production of *Ondine,* for which she won a Tony as best actress. By September 1955 British *Vogue* saw Hepburn as a fascinating star whose personal life was worth investigating. A spread over two pages, with pictures of the actors at their home in Italy, captures the spirit of their enchantment:

> Two grave, unusual actors with children's eyes, they married after co-starring in Giradoux' *Ondine* on Broadway last year. Her looks – close, drenched hair, an orphan-boy alertness, limbs which fall into the ballet positions – have created a new ideal of beauty. He, too, moves like a dancer; fences – as in *Scaramouche* – like a master; has an off-beat charm seen in essence in *Lili.* They are now in Rome (here, at their villa), filming the Ponti de Laurentiis *War and Peace.*[38]

Looking back to these years, for *Vogue* in 1987, Nicholas Drake described Hepburn as 'like a portrait by Modigliani where the various distortions are not only interesting in themselves but make a completely satisfying composite'. *Vogue* recorded that during the filming of *Sabrina* (1954) Hepburn had enlisted a 'rising young Parisian couturier,

Hubert de Givenchy to design her wardrobe'. It was the beginning of a lasting friendship and working relationship. In her role in *Funny Face* (1957) she was involved in modelling countless Givenchy creations – as beatnik bookworm transformed into the world's most glamorous mannequin by a fashion editor with 'pizzazz'. The editor, played by Kay Thompson, was inspired by celebrated *Vogue* editor Diana Vreeland. From Vreeland's obituary notice, written by Bernadine Morris for the *New York Times* in 1989, we are reminded:

> 'She was and remains the only genius fashion editor,' Richard Avedon, the photographer, said yesterday. Their professional relationship at *Harper's Bazaar* and *Vogue* was the inspiration for the movie *Funny Face* starring Fred Astaire and Audrey Hepburn.[39]

Hubert de Givenchy was thrilled by his relationship with Hollywood, through Hepburn, and said, 'After *Sabrina,* Audrey requested my clothes for all her films with a contemporary setting, which is how I came to design the outfits she wore in *Funny Face, Love in the Afternoon, Breakfast at Tiffany's, Charade, Paris when it Sizzles* and *How to Steal a Million.*[40]

It was suggested that her influence was so powerful, their friendship so constant, that there was a symbiotic relationship between the French designer and the Belgian actress. As well as the clothes for the films, he also made her dresses for her second wedding and her sons' christenings, and their christening gowns. The Givenchy clothes Audrey Hepburn wore symbolize the designer at the height of his powers. In his use of silk prints and embroidered fabrics, he drew on the expertise of skilled French textile workers. In his flawlessly detailed separates, high-style coats and elegant ball gowns, he represented the matchless art of Parisian haute couture. We might ask the question, 'Did Audrey create Givenchy or was it the other way round?' American designer Ralph Lauren, knowing the value of serendipity, was to say that Audrey Hepburn could pick what was right for her from his own collections and added:

> You could take Audrey into Sears, Roebuck or Givenchy or an army surplus store – it didn't matter, she'd put something on and you'd say, 'It's her!' Very few people can do that.[41]

He also thought the balance in the relationship with the French couturier was tipped in favour of the actress:

> I truly feel Audrey gave Givenchy a look. As time went on, they collaborated, but I think she picked what was Audrey out of Givenchy.[42]

Audrey Hepburn is almost certainly seen as a brand by Mark Tungate. In his book *Fashion Brands*, he writes of how Italy sells its Fashion. He explains how an advertising campaign for Tod's loafers used sophisticated trend setters – Cary Grant, Jackie and John Kennedy, and Hepburn – to sell the shoes:

> Not saying these people wore the shoes but 'linking the brand with a certain insouciant style'.[43]

In commenting on Hollywood and its importance to spreading Fashion's message, Tungate connects the Italian elegance of Armani clothes, featured in *American Gigolo* (1980), starring Richard Gere, and also recalls:

> Designers had been dressing stars for years. Hubert de Givenchy was famous for outfitting Audrey Hepburn.[44]

He attributes some of Burberry's life to the Hepburn phenomenon, thinking that her appearance in *Breakfast at Tiffany*'s, in the signature trench, may have helped as the 'brand rumbled along through the 1960s and 70s'. Missing no allusion to her branding potential, Tungate comments on the longevity of her important movies:

> The film *Roman Holiday* (1953), starring Gregory Peck and Audrey Hepburn, still looks like a fashion plate.[45]

Rachel Moseley knew of Audrey Hepburn through her mother, who had grown up with her, as a screen idol, in the sixties. Later, when her career as a film writer led her to investigate Audrey's star qualities in more depth, she was motivated by the response of women, over decades, to turn her studies into a full-length book. Moseley says Hepburn's screen career was associated with 'rites of passage and transformation stories – the sorts of myths and legends which influence young women'. She explores Hepburn's 'enduring fascination' in this context, and writes of how the image appeared in 'endless features' on how to achieve the Audrey look. Fans Moseley questioned might see a Hepburn character as 'a girl from a not very rich family who wanted to be someone',

Some of Burberry's life came from the Hepburn phenomenon, from her appearance in Breakfast at Tiffany's *in the signature trench which helped as the 'brand rumbled along through the 1960s and 70s'.*

and so many identified with her. She tells of how Hepburn is still a force to be reckoned with and is 'cited as the favourite star of young British [women] celebrities such as Darcey Bussell, Jayne Middlemiss and Martine McCutcheon. She celebrates how Hepburn gave women the opportunity to play more than one role, in more than one outfit, able to be themselves as students, fashion models, cooks, teachers, librarians, city dwellers, tourists or philosophers, whether buying or making their own looks:

> For some, then there was clearly more labour – physical and emo-
> tional – involved in producing an acceptably feminine self in this
> period than for others who were able to embrace more openly the
> 'freer' femininities of the 1960s. Hepburn's image was flexible
> enough to offer and enable both.[46]

Taking us behind Paramount's sets in her monograph *Made for Each Other*, Bronwyn Cosgrave tells of how 'Hepburn steeped herself in fashion, reading European magazines', and reveals that 'she appeared in a French comedy because the producer allowed her to keep the Christian Dior gown she'd worn for a walk-on role'. Edith Head, Paramount's chief designer, speaking from a costume point of view and leaving some of the mystique behind, said that Audrey's fittings lasted hours rather than minutes.

Undergraduates see Audrey Hepburn as an inspiration to designers, someone who remains an influential figure because of her unconventional looks. They realize how important Hepburn is to the Fashion industry because of her many Internet appearances. Writing for a blog site, 24-year-old Wang Wei reports on an earlier interview:

> 'My look is attainable,' she [Hepburn] told Barbara Walters in 1989. 'Women can look like Audrey Hepburn by flipping out their hair, buying the large glasses and the little sleeveless dresses.' In truth, though, it was not at all easy to capture the essence of Audrey. Just ask the millions of women who tried. For designer Michael Kors, 'women wear things that they just take for granted, but without Audrey Hepburn they probably wouldn't be wearing them'.

Young women commend her 'imperfections' and are interested in the opinions of their mid sixties grandmothers who talk of the styles Hepburn wore in her films. They think the key to her longevity is tied in with notions of class and classiness. Wang confirms Hepburn's unchallenged allure and quotes director Billy Wilder:

> After the release of *Roman Holiday*, her Hollywood debut, the fashion world never would be the same. Director Billy Wilder once said: 'After so many drive-in waitresses becoming movie stars, there has been this real drought, when along comes class; somebody who actually went to school, can spell, maybe even plays the piano. She may be a wispy, thin little thing, but when you see that girl, you know you're really in the presence of something. In that league there's only ever been Garbo, and the other Hepburn, and maybe Bergman. It's a rare quality, but boy, do you know when you've found it.'[48]

Knowing the most popular image is Audrey in *Breakfast at Tiffany's* in the black Givenchy dress and pearls, today's Fashion followers recall other looks and scenes; headscarves, climbing through a man's window at night, her party, her cat! They feel she made a similar impact to Jackie 'O', but that her influence may diminish to be superseded by figures like Michelle Obama. For students from Asian or Caribbean backgrounds, Audrey Hepburn seems less of an influence than other Hollywood stars like Sophia Lauren and Vivienne Leigh. Some think there may be the risk of overexposure, seeing her sometimes as a cliché. She is recognized because her face appears on products, 'everywhere from placemats to posters', even if students have not seen her films. Cathy Horyn, in the *New York Times* in 2008, uses the significant moment from Capote's book *Breakfast at Tiffany's* to begin a review of contemporary chick lit:

> Truman Capote said of *Breakfast at Tiffany's*, his classic novella of a New York glamour girl, that he was trying to prune his writing style, achieve a more subdued prose. Of course, Holly Golightly became the lodestar to designers as well as to millions of young women who have been enthralled by her single-minded spirit and by the image evoked by Audrey Hepburn in the opening shot of the film, as the cab races up Fifth Avenue and deposits her in front of Tiffany's.[49]

British students tip *Breakfast at Tiffany's* to be the film which outlasts all her others. Some have been introduced to Audrey at very young ages by their grandmothers. As a Fashion statement, the large white shirt and eye mask combo from *Breakfast at Tiffany's* is mentioned. They picked up on the Gap ad; they know what an extensive website presence Hepburn has; they are fascinated by her elusive quality, describing it as 'difficult to pin down'. They know of her as a fifties/sixties signifier and believe she will continue as a cult figure. Horyn confirms their expectations, explaining how Holly Golightly was part of the extravagant bluff, the clever ambiguity, the Barthian recuperation, practised so effortlessly by Audrey Hepburn:

> But fashion wasn't important to Holly. Despite the Paris wardrobe in the movie version, she made it clear she thought the whole thing was something of a wonderful joke, a bore. Take it or leave it. That was her appeal. As she said, explaining why she didn't stick around

Hollywood and become an actress, 'My complexes aren't inferior enough.'[50]

The resonant *mise en scènes* – the Tiffany's window, Gregory Peck's 'missing' hand joke in *Roman Holiday* – are memorable moments for today's fans. They believe Fashion writers will continue to use her as a referent for stylishness. Jennifer Dunlop (Fashion, Media and Promotion BA, Huddersfield University 2008/9), said she remembered the cigarette holder and white Grecian dress, the amazing costume jewellery and big hats and classic Burberry trench from *Breakfast at Tiffany's*, adding, 'Her style was so timeless you could wear any of her clothes today and not look out of place. She didn't follow trends, so she will always be in style.' Many young women have seen up to six of Hepburn's films. Her image has been identified on any number of products, coasters, clocks, room dividers, notebooks, postcards, screen-prints. Making an interesting connection between an ill-fated aristocrat with something of a reverse Cinderalla story and Hepburn, Lauren Maxwell (FMP) points out: 'Marie Antoinette has held the interest of generations of young women for over 200 years, so I don't see why there would be an end to the interest in Audrey Hepburn', believing the attraction is because 'she has something women will always aspire to have'. Jessica Ainsworth (FMP) defends her heroine's well-protected image as Hepburn was featured as one of the celebrities Coleen Rooney mimicked, saying, 'I thought it was awful, because Audrey Hepburn was so admired and Coleen Rooney isn't.' Hepburn is part of sixth form Film Studies, as well as a favourite of mothers and grandmothers. Students write of her image's value to the vintage clothes market, and in the encouragement of Pop art. They describe Hepburn's films as legendary. Post-Feminist Fashion students, more interested in how Hepburn dresses than in influential narratives, wonder whether Givenchy has carte blanche to use her image for its promotion. Orlagh Mullholland believes Hepburn's 'beauty and elegance transcends decades, epitomizing, the strong independent woman draped in grace and composure'. She is seen as part of Fashion's continuing narrative with a face, retaining innocence, and a style models continue to imitate.[51]

Her interest in clothes, theatre, her sense of nostalgia and her relationship with the French designer Hubert de Givenchy created the legend which Audrey Hepburn and her films have become. Givenchy

Textile specialist Katherine Higgins, talking to Antiques Road Show *viewers on BBC1 in November 2007, told how Laura Ashley's scarf-making business took off as a result of Audrey Hepburn's wearing a scarf in a certain way in* Funny Face *(1957).*

said of her, 'She was capable of enhancing all my creations. And often ideas would come to me when I had her on my mind. She always knew what she wanted and what she was aiming for. It was like that from the very start.' These views, attempting to assess what Audrey Hepburn gave to Fashion, are part of the story of her appeal. As well as Hepburn being the subject for discussion among designers and journalists, academics are attracted by her charisma. Rachel Moseley's researches around Hepburn led her to discover that she was a star who had a special relationship with her audiences. Placing Hepburn in a separate category from other screen muses, she says, 'It is debatable that all feminine images are produced for a male gaze and Audrey Hepburn ... is one such instance.'[52] Michael Specter, reviewing John Galliano's career in the *New Yorker* in September 2003, suggested that his designs were more suited to the uses of a PR campaign than for haute couture. He was missing the point about how Fashion promotes itself, but allowing the opportunity to assess Hepburn's reputation into the 21st century. Describing the horror caused by Galliano's appointment to head up Givenchy, he wrote:

> When Arnault actually gave Galliano Givenchy's job, late in 1998, many people were shocked (including the sixty-eight-year-old Givenchy himself, who learned about the appointment when he read it in a news release issued by his own press office). Galliano became the first British designer to take over a major French fashion house in nearly a century and a half – since Charles Frederick Worth was appointed by Napoleon III to dress the Empress Eugenie. It would have been difficult, under any circumstances, for the staid French fashion establishment to accept the appointment of a foreigner to run a firm whose refined image was represented most famously by Audrey Hepburn.[53]

Pamela Church Gibson, in the mapping of Fashion's cities in which women consume and are consumed, speculates on the film star's claims to Fashion influence and sees Hepburn's image as a 'principal fashion referent':

> Hepburn's androgynous image, so appealing to women, and her dual role as Fashion icon and anti-Fashion champion have retained their appeal precisely because of their subversive potential.[54]

As a thrilling Fashion symbol and international diplomat, she continues to inspire new generations of film fans and Fashion lovers. Whether seen as kitten, child or woman, there is no doubting what Audrey Hepburn gave to her audiences. She had the supreme confidence of knowing that, no matter how desperate life might once have been, there was always the chance to transform the world through politics and peacekeeping. It was this that enchanted us. Barthes spent most of his life hiding his homosexuality from *Maman* and the world, yet the 22-year-old actress stirred his unconscious. He sees her as someone who could provoke an événement, which in French carries the added meaning of sexual climax, beyond the sense of an event in English. It could have been her youth which roused the 44-year-old French cultural critic to suggest that she had the power to instigate a coming, a happening, an issuing out; but I suggest that it was Hepburn's philosophical and political mythology which inspired his excitement.

Notes

1   Foreword, Nicholas Drake, *The Fifties in Vogue* (London: Heinemann, 1987), p. 6.

2   Quoted by Megan Lane, 'Audrey Hepburn: Why the fuss?', BBC News website, 7 April 2006, http://news.bbc.co.uk/1/hi/magazine/4884428.stm (accessed 3 May 2009).

3   Roland Barthes, *Mythologies* Tr.Jonathan Cape, 1972, Vintage, London, 2000

4   Quoted from *The Phil Donahue Show*, 1990, http://www.youtube.com/results?search_type=&search_query=Hepburn+Phil+Donahue+Show&aq=f (accessed 3 May 2009).

5   Ibid.

6   Molly Haskell, 'An ode to the most elegant of actresses', *Audrey1* website, http://www.audrey1.org/archives/74/absolutely-audrey (accessed 3 May 2009).

7   Ibid.

8   In 1980 Princess Margaret visited a Haberdashers' school in Cheshire. During a tour of the Science rooms she told me, as a journalist, how her children would rush up and down carpeted areas to create static electricity before coming over to give her a slightly electrifying kiss. This liking for simple everyday experience was felt as an emotional need by the fictional princess in *Roman Holiday.* In a reverse Cinderella narrative, audiences are able to empathise with the heroine's longings even though her life is far removed from theirs.

9   Rachel Moseley, *Growing Up with Audrey Hepburn* (Manchester: Manchester University Press, 2002), p. 35.

10 Trumbo, along with nine other writers and directors, was called before the House Un-American Activities Committee as an unfriendly witness to testify on the presence of Communist influence in Hollywood, in 1947. Trumbo refused to give information. After conviction for contempt of Congress he was blacklisted, and in 1950 spent 11 months in prison in the federal penitentiary in Ashland, Kentucky. In 1993 he was awarded the Academy Award posthumously for writing *Roman Holiday* (1953). The screen credit and award were previously given to Ian McLellan Hunter, who had been Trumbo's front.

11 Pamela Church Gibson, 'New stars, new fashions and the female audience: Cinema, consumption and cities 1953–1966', *Fashion's World Cities*, ed. Christopher Breward and David Gilbert (Oxford: Berg, 2006), p. 92.

12 Ibid.

13 The Sorelle Fontana atelier overlooks the Piazza di Spagna in Rome. The couturier's designs are still worn by Hollywood stars and international royalty. The Fontana sisters didn't just achieve their dream of opening an

atelier; they came to own one of the most famous in the world, synonymous with glamour and elegance.

14 The character Irving Radovitch in *Roman Holiday* is often acknowledged as the original paparazzo, although the expression was created only after Fellini's *La Dolce Vita* (1960), with the photographer named Paparazzo played by Walter Santesso.

15 Moseley, *Growing Up*, p. 107.

16 Church Gibson, 'New stars', p. 93.

17 Ibid., p. 94.

18 Ibid.

19 Pamela Keogh, 'Introduction', *What Would Audrey Do?* www.pamelakeogh.com/pdf/wwadIntroduction.pdf (accessed May 3rd, 2009).

20 Bronwyn Cosgrave, *Made for Each Other: Fashion and the Academy Awards* (London: Bloomsbury, 2007), p. 80.

21 Quotation from the film *Sabrina*, dir. Billy Wilder, 1953.

22 Charlotte Chandler, 'Sabrina', *Nobody's Perfect: Billy Wilder, a Personal Biography* (New York: Simon & Schuster, 2002), pp. 171–6, http://tags.library.upenn.edu/tag/film+1950s (accessed 3 May 2009).

23 Church Gibson, 'New stars', p. 96.

24 Ibid.

25 Quoting the press release issued by Gap, September 2006: 'In celebration of the launch of the "Keep It Simple" ad campaign, Gap is making a generous contribution to the Audrey Hepburn Children's Fund. The Audrey Hepburn Children's Fund is a non-profit organization created to continue Ms. Hepburn's international appeals on behalf of children around the world', http://www.gapinc.com/wps/portal/gapinc/media

26 Ibid.

27 Douglas Smith, 'Funny Face: Humanism in Post-War French Photography and Philosophy', *French Cultural Studies*, 16:1 (2005), pp. 41–53.

28 Ibid.

29 Ibid.

30 Ibid.

31 Ibid.

32 Susan Sellers, 'How Long Has This Been Going On? *Harper's Bazaar, Funny Face* and the Construction of the Modernist Woman', *Visible Language*, 29 (Winter 1995), p. 119.

33 From voiceover for trail, *Breakfast at Tiffany's*, dir. Blake Edwards, 1961, bonus feature, *The Audrey Hepburn Collection*, 5 DVD set, Paramount Pictures, 2006.

34 Church Gibson, 'New stars', p. 102.

35 Moseley, *Growing Up*, p. 35.

36 Christopher Breward, *Fashion* (Oxford: Oxford University Press, 2003), p. 136.

37 Ibid., p. 130.

38 From British *Vogue*, September 1955.

39 Bernadine Morris, 'Diana Vreeland, editor, dies; voice of fashion for decades', obituary, *New York Times*, 23 August 1989, http://www.nytimes. com/1989/08/23/obituaries

40 Hubert de Givenchy, 'Audrey Hepburn', *Audrey Hepburn* MySpace blog, 9 December 2006, http://blogs.myspace.com/index.cfm?fuseaction=blog.view &friendld=100388398&blogld=203322385 (accessed 3 May 2009).

41 Ralph Lauren, 'Citations d'Audrey Hepburn', Audrey Hepburn website, http://audrey.hepburn.free.fr/divers/citations.htm (accessed 3 May 2009).

42 Ibid.

43 Mark Tungate, *Fashion Brands* (London: Kogan Page, 2005), p. 32.

44 Ibid., p. 119.

45 Ibid., p. 169.

46 Moseley, *Growing Up*, p 83.

48 Ibid.

49 Cathy Horyn, 'And the plot thinned ...', *New York Times*, 24 July 2008 (accessed 3 May 2009).

50 Ibid.

51 Vox pop conducted with Fashion students by the author, February 2009.

52 Rachel Moseley, 'Respectability sewn up: Dressmaking and film star style in the fifties and sixties', *European Journal of Cultural Studies*, 4:4, p. 475.

53 Michael Specter, 'The fantasist: How John Galliano reimagined fashion', *New Yorker,* September 2003. http://www.michaelspecter.com/ny/2003/ 2003_09_22_galliano.html (accessed 3 May 2009).

54 Church Gibson, 'New stars', p. 106.

CHAPTER THREE
Vivienne Westwood and Anglomania at the Met

It is the appropriation by society of a form, or a use, through rules of manufacture, that creates a garment, not the variations in its utilitarian or decorative quantum. If a woman places a flower in her hair this remains a fact of pure and simple adornment, so long as the use (such as a bridegroom's crown) or the positioning (such as a flower over the ear in Gypsy dress) have not been dictated by a social group; as soon as this happens it becomes a part of dress.

Roland Barthes, *The Fashion System*

Witty women designers Elsa Schiaparelli and Vivienne Westwood have their emblematic Fashion worn by the rich and adventurous and their brilliance reflected by inspired museum curators. Schiaparelli's career was star-studded and full of controversy. Declared bankrupt in 1954, many believed it was the end of her story. But when she donated 71 items from her personal wardrobe to the Philadelphia Museum of Art, Pennsylvania, in 1969, it began an association confirming her ascendancy. Schiaparelli now appears in Surrealist and solo shows across the globe. Westwood's retrospective, the first held for a practising designer, began at the Victoria and Albert Museum in London in 2004. After touring to Australia, Shanghai, Taiwan, Tokyo, Düsseldorf, Bangkok, Thailand, San Francisco and Milan, the exhibition was meant to end in the UK, in Sheffield, four years later. Then, at the request of the Westwood organization in 2008, it continued on to Hong Kong and Beijing.

Links between Schiaparelli and Westwood are being drawn, and those who observe their lives see intriguing connections. As a post-Modernist drawing on Art's narratives and experimenting with textiles,

Westwood is not compared to her contemporaries as, for example, Schiaparelli to Chanel. Designing when Modernism was at its height, they were often defined by their disparity. Schiaparelli, who saw Fashion as Art, and Chanel, who regarded it as Dressmaking, were seen as rivals in the 1920s and 1930s. Chanel was brought up in an orphanage, entered the demimonde of millinery and couture, and became the mistress of influential people. Schiaparelli, from a family of scholars and scientists, born in a Roman palazzo, rebellious and questioning in her conservative, upper class Italian household, pushed the bounds of acceptable behaviour; the vivid pink, which became her signature colour 'Shocking',[1] was remembered from seeing begonias from her pram. Some of her most famous designs reference the moons and stars, studied by her uncle, Giovanni Schiaparelli, the eminent 19th-century astronomer. Comparisons were made between the two women until their deaths, yet Coco Chanel had very little in common with Elsa Schiaparelli, whose timeless inventions made her peerless. Coco was an orphan who shook off her poverty-stricken beginnings, fraternizing with the haute bourgeoisie, designing elegant, wearable, costumes for their wives. Elsa, in her early twenties, travelled to England to care for the children of her sister's friend. She met and married Count William de Wendt de Kerlor, a member of a philosophical society. The couple lived on Elsa's substantial dowry on the French Riviera before arriving in New York in 1916, where their daughter Yvonne, nicknamed Gogo, was born. A few months later Elsa divorced William, and supported herself working as a translator and scriptwriter. It was during this period that Schiaparelli learned the art of self-marketing, practised by American businesswomen who seemed more pushy than their European sisters. Returning to Paris, leaving her sickly daughter in a Swiss boarding school, she was soon enjoying friendships with Cocteau, Picasso, Picabia, Stravinsky and other artists she had met in New York, including Man Ray and Marcel Duchamp. After joining fellow socialite Blanche Hays, from West Village, New York, she moved to Paris in 1921, where Poiret 'took her under his wing':

> Her fashion career began almost by accident. Independently wealthy, she was free to socialise but lacked a vocation. After dabbling in sculpture, she started to design clothing, but with little success. Then, in 1927, came the sweater that gave Schiaparelli her big

break. According to legend, it was her Armenian concierge who knitted it. Another version says Schiap tracked the woman down after a friend had tipped her off. Concierge or not, she asked the Armenian woman to knit the garment from one of her sketches. After three attempts, she was delighted with the result – a simple black sweater with a white trompe-l'oeil bow at the neck.[2]

Schiaparelli worked as a freelance for small Fashion houses, and the breakthrough came in 1927 when *Vogue* described the sweater of hers as 'an artistic masterpiece'. In her biography from 1954, she wrote, 'All the women wanted one immediately.' The sweater appeared in the *Ladies' Home Journal*, without a mention of the designer. Indeed copyright, a major concern for the French Fashion industry between and

Schiaparelli worked as a freelance for small Fashion houses, and the breakthrough came in 1927 when Vogue described the sweater of hers as 'an artistic masterpiece'. In her biography from 1954 she wrote, 'All the women wanted one immediately.'

after two world wars, was an aggravation for Schiaparelli for much of her professional life. In 1927, it seemed that Macy's in NY thought its customers were not ready for her avant-garde Fashions. However, a French Art Deco exhibition held in 1928 at Lord and Taylor, the US upscale speciality department store, changed hearts and minds, and Schiaparelli's designs were soon being sported by fashionable middle-class Americans. Her business dealings, as well as her designs, were ahead of the times. In 1927, her empire expanded when she became an equal partner with Charles Kahn, in association with Galleries Lafayette, and although sweater design copies continued to create hostility between Paris and American stores, by 1930 French couture was able to bring in some restrictions. During the showing of Schiaparelli's retrospective in Paris in 2004, Pamela Golbin, Musée de la Mode et du Textile curator, told the journalist Alix Sharkey:

> Again and again Schiaparelli blazed new trails: she was the first conceptual designer, the first to do thematic collections, the first to produce fashion shows as spectacle and entertainment rather than glamorous business appointments. She was the first couturier to use man-made fabrics and to replace buttons with zippers, and the first designer of any kind to issue press releases. But more than anything else, she was the first to understand the power of marketing.[3]

In 1933 Schiaparelli opened her own London salon and began featuring British woollen fabrics in her collections: tweeds and hand-knits, loving Scotland with its tartans, bonnets and tams. This sourcing of British textiles was a practice taken up by clever, creative descendants Jean Muir and Vivienne Westwood. A legal dispute over the desertion of her cutter, Albert Cezard, to the couturiers Norman Hartnell was distressing to the business, but she continued to view Britain as her second home, with her small, smart, expensive mews house in London. Her career prospered through her alliance with the British film and theatre industry, and between 1933 and 1939 she designed costumes for 30 films and plays. Her London salon closed down just weeks before Britain entered into WWII. The London Press suggested it was the result of the damage done by copyists, rather than the threat of the serious international crisis about to unfold. By 1935, the businesswoman in Schiaparelli was flourishing. She and her talented, American public relations supremo, Hortense Macdonald, took a stand at the first French trade fair in Moscow. As sole representatives of French couture, they lined their booth with press clippings printed on silk; the floor was covered in exclusive Colcombet's black 'tree-bark', crêpe with a fan-shaped display of international Fashion magazines. Writing for a student pack that accompanied the 2003/4 Philadelphia exhibition, Dilys Blum captures the excitement of the Art Deco era:

> Since 1935, Schiaparelli had been presenting thematic collections at her salon, theatrically staged with dramatic lighting, backdrops and music. A fashion editor who regularly attended these events recalls that the front rows were filled with royalty, politicians, artists, film stars who pushed towards the models 'as if it were rush hour'.[4]

The Soviet trip and the marriage of one of Schiaparelli's sales assistants, Bettina Jones, to a former Communist Party member led to the right-wing newspaper *Je suis partout* adding to its 'anti-semitic rantings' by rumouring that the Schiaparelli salon was closing in London, in favour of opening one in Moscow. Positive comments about the Moscow trip were only carried in the 'Red' press in France and Britain, while America remained neutral. *Vogue*, in an uncharacteristically political move, printed a cartoon by Miguel Covarrubias, 'The Impossible Interview', showing a meeting between Elsa Schiaparelli and Stalin, which implied that Stalin was so much of a Soviet, military, dictator that he could have nothing to share with the international artist and socialite. The incomparable Schiaparelli, expressing her philosophy in her autobiography, seems to have believed that Fashion has its own ineffable alchemy, beyond affairs of state:

> Fashion is born by small facts, trends, or even politics; never by trying to make little pleats and furbelows, by trinkets, by clothes easy to copy, or by the shortening or the lengthening of a skirt.[5]

She took a pragmatic view of party politics, designing for both royalists and republicans so that women could meet the uncertain political temper of the times. Alix Sharkey, reviewing the major retrospective of her work at the Musée de la Mode et du Textile in Paris in 2004, sets it, in the thirties, in the context of its contemporary Art:

> The zenith of her career was the period from 1935 until the outbreak of the Second World War. In 1936 she introduced her Egyptian look with pagoda sleeves, and made gowns with zippers in a contrasting colour. She also produced her desk suit, a twinset inspired by Dali, with false and real pockets, all made to look like desk drawers. During the 1937 to 1938 season her Surrealistic designs had the fashion world gasping. She turned again to trompe-l'oeil, with a jacket bearing a woman's profile, drawn by Jean Cocteau. She had Dali paint the famous lobster dress. She did a dress covered in musical notes, and another using a Dali-designed fabric that appeared to be ripped. Dali loved collaborating with Schiap, as he did on a black velvet purse shaped like a telephone, with an embroidered gold dial. It was during this period, too, that Schiaparelli set the standard for fashion shows as spectacular entertainment, with a series of themed collections including Music, Circus, Butterflies, Commedia del Arte, Astrology and Cash & Carry. Each show was more flamboyant and extravagant than the last.[6]

Bankruptcy

In an abbreviated history of Schiaparelli's life at the end of Dilys Blum's catalogue for the 2003/4 exhibition, there is a neat allusion to the fractious relationship between France and the States. Blum records that in February 1928 the French limited their sales of Coca-Cola. Summarizing Schiaparelli's astounding life, Blum notes that she bought a house in Tunisia in 1950, where, it is said, she began focusing closely on Modernity. Givenchy left Schiaparelli's house in 1951, and began his own company in 1952. In the same year, Schiaparelli herself started the first designer eye-glass company in the USA, and in 1953 licensed designs for a number of different lines with American makers. She introduced the perfume 'Success Fou', and a separates line with Pat Sandler. *Shocking Life,* her biography, was published in 1954 and in December Schiaparelli's couture salon, the Place Vendôme Maison, filed for bankruptcy. Chanel returned to couture, also in 1954, and went on to found her international label. Alix Sharkey, writing in his review, describes the zeitgeist:

Schiap misunderstood the profound changes that had taken place during her absence. Refusing to curb her imagination and flamboyance, she found her designs no longer captured the public mood. Meanwhile, a new generation of male designers – led by Christian Dior – was poised to take over. Eventually realising her moment had passed, Schiap retired as a designer and closed her couture house in 1954, before publishing her autobiography.[7]

Elsa Schiaparelli died, in her sleep, in her Paris home in November 1973, having begun a second life as a celebrated artist, as a result of the donation of her costumes to the Museum of Art in Philadelphia in 1969. Since the day textile curator Elsie McGarvey accepted the gift, Elsa Schiaparelli's work has been cherished and shown in major exhibitions worldwide. Dilys Blum was at university at the time of Schiaparelli's stunning donation to Philadelphia, not dreaming of making museums a career. Nevertheless, in attending a 'Dec Arts' seminar she may have been taking an unconscious interest in its world, she tells me. Writing a brief history of Fashion for the student pack for the Shocking exhibition in 2003/4, she summarizes Schiaparelli's allure:

It was Schiaparelli's bold, whimsical approach to fashion which allowed her to differentiate herself from other designers in the 1920s and 30s. Chanel once described her as that 'Italian artist who makes clothes', but it was her artful approach that made her distinctive. She built upon fashion trends that had been developing since the late 1800s, branding them with her own unique sensibility. Although many of the designs are over sixty years old, her revolutionary approach continues to influence the fashion world of today.[8]

Anne d'Harnoncourt, the revered Philadelphia Museum of Art director who died unexpectedly in June 2008, was internationally renowned for her work with the museum. Writing the foreword to Dilys Blum's *Shocking! The Art and Fashion of Elsa Schiaparelli*, she explains the rationale behind 'the spectacular gift of seventy-one of her own designs', which, together with 88 models and 5,800 original sketches given to the Musée de la Mode et du Textile in Paris in 1973, became an 'unprecedented overview of Schiaparelli's extraordinary career and an exciting sense of just how far she was able to push the boundaries of fashion into the realm of art'. Anne d'Harnoncourt, typically generous in her praise of colleagues, included this tribute to the work of the curator in her introduction:

> Dilys Blum, the museum's inspired and indefatigable Curator of Costume and Textiles has devoted the better part of five years to research into Schiaparelli's life and art, and the intricate interweaving of images and text in this publication bears witness to her profound understanding of Schiaparelli's achievement.[9]

Lack of pomposity

An earlier showing of Schiaparelli's collection was as part of Best Dressed: 250 Years of Style, which ran at the Philadelphia Museum in 1997/8. It drew on more than 200 costumes and accessories from the Museum's holdings of Western and non-Western dress. Exhibition texts place Schiaparelli's work as part of the world of international celebrity:

> A selection of important late nineteenth-century gowns designed by great Parisian couturiers, including Charles Frederick Worth; works by renowned twentieth-century fashion designers, such as Elsa Schiaparelli who gave the Museum a significant collection of her work; and one of the most popular items in the Museum's collection, the wedding dress worn by Princess Grace of Monaco, the former Grace Kelly of Philadelphia.[10]

Dilys Blum, who had been with the museum since 1987, began work on *Shocking!* after *Best Dressed* in 1997. She was encouraged by Anne d'Harnoncourt 'who had always wanted to do something with the collection'. Making connections between Westwood and Schiaparelli for me in 2008, she sees both designers taking on the considerations of Art:

> There was no discussion as to whether fashion was art. We had been collecting textiles and costume since our founding in 1876 and it was a given. I love Westwood. I saw her show in London and then, later, in Milan. She reminds me of Schiap in another time. Like Schiap her collections tell stories, and offer an ironic commentary on the times. Schiap seems more subtle, but that is, probably, hindsight.[11]

During the 1937 to 1938 season her Surrealistic designs had the fashion world gasping. She turned again to trompe-l'oeil, with a jacket bearing a woman's profile, drawn by Jean Cocteau. She did a dress covered in musical notes, and another using a Dali-designed fabric that appeared to be ripped. Schiaparelli's Lobster dress, illustrated above, was printed from a sketch drawn by the master silk designer, Sache.

There is a refreshing lack of pomposity about much of America's attitude to education, class and protocol, which Dilys Blum accepts as 'a given', and yet she is, no doubt, aware of the difference between European and US sensitivities, made especially evident when the Americans take on the French. What pleasure the Italian aristocrat's scintillating gift will have given America's museum elite, as they exported their collection to the European spiritual home of Fashion. Dilys Blum told me how Pamela Golbin curated Shocking for Paris in 2004:

I organized the original exhibition, which was shown here in Philadelphia. Pamela then added other material, from her collection, and reworked the exhibition for a French audience, which was understandably more clued into French history, the haute couture, etc. We had more audiovisual material here including film clips as well as paintings by Dali, Man Ray, etc. that related to the collections. The two exhibition presentations differed considerably, in part, because of the differences between the museums, i.e. Art versus Fashion, and audiences.[12]

Blum's urbane overview, taking in American ownership of decades of Old World Art, is a reflection of America's attitude to Cultural history in general. The Metropolitan Museum of Art, in New York, values Art as treasured legacy, and by owning collections of works from across the known universe demonstrates America's prowess at 19th- and 20th-century empire building. Texts from the Philadelphia Museum's website indicate how Schiaparelli was considered the undisputed trendsetter of her era.

Writing in *The New Yorker* in 1932, Janet Flanner observed that 'a frock from Schiaparelli ranks like a modern canvas,' and the Paris fashion designer herself defined dressmaking as an art rather than a profession. The Philadelphia Museum of Art celebrates the extraordinary Elsa Schiaparelli, acknowledged by her contemporaries as the style arbiter of the 1930s, in the first major retrospective exhibition and catalogue, to examine the ways in which her creations mirrored the social, political, and cultural climate of her times.[13]

Michael Bracewell, in the *Independent on Sunday*, in August 2004, saw mainly Art when he visited the Musée de la Mode at du Textile in the Louvre on the last day of the Schiaparelli exhibition in Paris. He refers to her spectacular use of heavenly signs, which she studied through her uncle's telescope – both artist and scientist:

Glittering in crepuscular light, garments and jewellery of such strangeness and ceremonial elegance appear as an exhibit of supernatural artefacts. A white tulle veil embroidered with a slithering cascade of silver-blue serpentine tendrils; a midnight blue jacket encrusted with gold and silver astrological signs; a suit studded with mirrored panels; sheath-like evening gowns – one lavender, its bodice an impossibly elaborate tracery of pearls; a circular neck-lace of transparent cellulose acetate, ornamented with luminous insects ...[14]

He has no qualms about using the language of Art to discuss Fashion; applying its tropes to emphasize Fashion's claims to Art's status and expressing the idea that creative impulses, rendered material, are no respecters of field or discipline:

> Not since Vivienne Westwood and Malcolm McLaren's earliest punk clothing and accessories, made for Sex and Seditionaries in 1976, has modern fashion known an edge and elegance, or a fusion of concept and aesthetic, to compare with Schiaparelli's merger of technical brilliance and artistic vision.[15]

Inventive wildness

As she began her exciting association with the world of Vivienne Westwood, Claire Wilcox, Curator of Fashion and Textiles at the V&A, had to confront the Fashion/Art debate head on, at the hands of the international controversialist Suzy Menkes, reviewing Radical Fashion at the museum in 2001. Eleven renowned fashion designers – Azzedine Alaia, Hussein Chalayan, Comme des Garçons, Helmut Lang, Jean Paul Gaultier, Maison Martin Margiela, Alexander McQueen, Issey Miyake, Junya Watanabe, Yohji Yamamoto and Westwood – were invited to take part in a mixed media show. It involved individual shoots with celebrated photographers for the accompanying book, *Radical Fashion*, edited by Wilcox, and site-specific electronic music for each designer's installation. Menkes, in the *International Herald Tribune,* 23 October 2001, challenged the rationale behind the V&A's exhibition. Suggesting it would be impossible for visitors to make any spontaneous, radical, statements of their own because the exhibition was full of every inven-tive wildness, already, she implied that the eccentricity inherent in the collections spilled onto the opening night party:

> where Vivienne Westwood's marigold curls matched her display of dresses, Azzedine Alaia showed off his hourglass creations and Alexander McQueen brought his Mom to witness his installation of fashion scenes from a madhouse.[16]

Judging the show 'visually compelling', she especially enjoyed popular programmes – a three-hour odyssey of Helmut Lang's catwalk movies and 'Westwood's voluptuous nymphs or Jean Paul Gaultier's witty couture' brought to life. However, Menkes hits us with the question, 'But is the exhibition radical – in any of the various meanings of the word?'

> 'It's not that the designers have claimed to be radical – it's our summing up,' says Claire Wilcox, the show's curator, who selected the 11 designers, from Alaia to Martin Margiela to Junya Watanabe. 'There is an ambiguity to the word "radical",' she says. 'It has associations with politics and with the street. It means literally "from the root", but it is taken here as meaning "uncompromising".'[17]

Claiming the 'curator has compromised her pivotal role by encouraging the designers to make their own selections and to choose how to display them', Menkes asks if 'avant-garde fashion has become instant museum pieces', are 'designers considered more as artists than as frock makers?' Defending their bold decisions, Wilcox told the columnist:

> What I find exhilarating is that the designers do constantly surpass one's expectations, and they do it in a material culture. Art is conceptual, but fashion is based on material qualities, it is worn on the body; yet it can be empowering and life changing.[18]

During the run of Radical Fashion, Westwood, who was liaising with Wilcox in preparation for the full retrospective in 2004, said:

> But as soon as you begin with a word like 'radical' to describe fashion, you are faced with a paradox. To do anything original, you have to build it on tradition.[19]

While working with the V&A on her exhibition, between 2001 and 2004, Westwood's collections echoed themes from her 1980s output:

> asexual 'ethnic' cutting, using predominantly rectangular and triangular gussets and some semi-circles and curved seams, in an exploration of the natural dynamic of the fabric.[20]

It was at earlier stages in her career that Westwood's own affiliation with the museum had begun. Valerie Mendes, curator in the textiles

She may not have known how much this obsession would become the backbeat to the rest of her own professional life. She describes his encouragement, as they created the bleached, razored, prototype Punk hair said to have influenced David Bowie, saying, 'He took me by the hand and made me more stylish.'

and dress department, who helped influence later changes in how exhibitions were constructed, said during 'Collecting for the Future' in 1990 that she hoped items would not 'survive in isolation, or else people in the future are going to be very puzzled'. She was demonstrably far-sighted in acquiring the V&A's first outfit from Vivienne Westwood's World's End shop in 1981.

Categorized as a woman who grew up with a fierce intellectual curiosity, there is some doubt whether Westwood would ever have found this lust satisfied without her chance meeting with Malcolm McLaren.[21] He was in a permanent state of revolution against his bourgeois background. This fascinated Westwood, whose gentle artisan roots were not objectionable to her. Of his rebellion, she was to remark, 'Malcolm's a one-off.' It was their passion for clothes that united them. When they met, *hippyness* was at its height, but they did not identify with its looks or its ethos. Roland Barthes, sceptical about this colourful grubby sect, in 'A Case of Cultural Criticism', from 1969, also spotted the underlying hypocrisy embedded in its philosophy. He saw the taking on of the dress, and behaviour, of simple poor peasantry as a way of the 'haves' seeming to identify with the 'have-nots', in a masquerade of solidarity, costumed as replicas of their lumpen forebears:

> This poverty turns the hippy's choice into a copy, a caricature of economic alienation, and this copy of poverty, though sported only lightly, becomes in fact distinctly irresponsible. For most traits invented by the hippy in opposition to his home civilisation (a civilisation of the rich) are the very ones which distinguish poverty, no longer as a sign, but much more severely as a clear indication, or an effect, on people's lives: under-nourishment, collective living, bare feet, dirtiness, ragged clothing, are all forces which, in this context, are not there to be used in the symbolic fight against the world of riches but are the very forces against which we should be fighting.[22]

It seems to me that in rejecting 'essential hippyness' Westwood and McLaren had allied themselves with Barthes' position. Curiously, this would have chimed with McLaren's concerns at the time; with French politics and philosophies, from 1968. From a Situationist inclination, McLaren and Westwood's politicization of clothing set the scene for Punk, anarchy and iconoclasm, and also for its commodification. Nevertheless, none of their collections were restricted to a single vision, nor were they designed to signify their support for either Peace or War. Jon Savage, in an interview for *The Face* in January 1981, cited by Wilcox (2008), writes:

> McLaren's anti-authoritarianism was a guiding principle but he effortlessly combined this with a love of Fashion, saying, 'It's the thing that makes my heart beat.' Westwood affirmed: 'Malcolm has always been totally fascinated by clothes. They're the most important thing in his life, really.'[23]

She may not have known how much this obsession would become the backbeat to the rest of her own professional life. She describes his encouragement as they created the bleached, razored, prototype Punk hair said to have influenced David Bowie, saying, 'He took me by the hand and made me more stylish.' In the exhibition catalogue, described by Westwood as 'my book', Wilcox's considered prose exactly contextualizes Westwood and McLaren's rapport with Punk:

> In this incarnation the shop supplied the sartorial identity for the Punk movement.[24]

Westwood's success may well depend not just on her inventive research into expressions of status but also on the hard work symbolized by her perfectionism:

> Other shops, however, used Westwood's ideas but without the attention to quality and detail of design that was characteristic of all the Sex and Seditionaries clothes.[25]

Nor did other Fashion outlets have a history of rebellion to inspire their legends or logos. When McLaren and Westwood opened shops – Sex in 1974 and Seditionaries in 1976 – they were at the helm of the Punk movement. Rebecca Arnold, commenting on their moves into the retail sector, believes that they marked turning-points in the way we shop for Fashion:

> It brought art school strategies of subversion into the previously calm world of retail, turning consumption into an anarchic act, loaded with menace and threat.[26]

By the early 1980s Westwood was beginning to see herself as a designer, after she and Mclaren had decided she should concentrate on Fashion and he on Music. She began to research ideas and techniques at the National Art Gallery and at the V&A, and recalls:

> I started work on the Pirate collection utilizing a shirt pattern that had been used for 500 years.[27]

Still listening to her Pygmalion, she decided to follow McLaren's advice and use the pattern exactly as it was, without any adaptation. Claire Wilcox believes, at this stage, Westwood realized that for her to create clothes, which had seemed sexually attractive in the past, she would have to reconstruct the clothing faithfully. Jon Savage was to write in *The Face*:

> The clothes are superb: inverting style codes in a way that's both subtle and shocking ... A jacket uses a traditional sports jacket cloth, yet is cut mediaevally, with the sleeves slashed to reveal a dazzling flash of orange patterned satin.[28]

It was the Pirate collection that, by being seen in Fashion magazines, attracted buyers. Wilcox explains how the Media began to take an interest in the alternative, non-Fashion-trained Westwood, who had begun her career assisting an anarchist, making clothing with semiotic rather than commercial intent:

> Although Punk had received a great deal of Media coverage and certain stylists, such as *Vogue*'s Grace Coddington, were following her closely, the Fashion world had up until then regarded Westwood as a subversive shop-owner rather than a serious designer.[29]

Punk

When anarchists, the avant-garde or the radically political move on to start other movements, seeming to renege on earlier positions, they are accused of hypocrisy or cowardice. The British bourgeoisie, for example, is particularly defensive about those who move on from an unconventional youth to make money, and are judgemental about how it is made. Westwood's success, commercially, is seen as a disavowal of original principles even though activists are often engaged in encouraging new generations to think for themselves. In 'Turning Rebellion into Money' from the website *Eat French Bread,* in 2007, blogger Ag commented on how Westwood, and McLaren, went on to turn their Fashion inventions into a lively retail business while still involved with Punk. Summarizing the end of the 20th century as a time when people began to operate autonomously, communicating with other individuals without the need for support from 'dominant' systems, she records:

> Today an industry of highly paid 'cool hunters' roam the globe looking for new fringe activities and styles to commodify. The new

generations have seen that any clear definitive style is too easily reduced to cartoon copies and appropriated by the mainstream, so they pastiche dead styles, and ideas, to create something that refuses meaning and categorisation.[30]

With Westwood, and McLaren, seen as political innovators as well as trend-setters, there seems to be general confusion about how they could have developed. They did not see themselves as architects of happenings but as influences on how their peers expressed themselves through their clothes. The Situationists in 1960s France may have made it plausible to use Art for political demonstrations but this did not rule out moving on to create meanings in other ways:

> Entrepreneurial activity is not always counter-revolutionary. McLaren and Westwood are sometimes said to have undermined the purity of the collective creative impulse of punk by opening their King's Road boutique and making the style available for purchase over the counter. But without the likes of them the distinctive style and what it stood for would not have been unified and remembered.[31]

Elizabeth Wilson, the British doyenne of Fashion academics, writing 'Urbane Fashion' for *Fashion's World Cities*, reiterates the idea that it was because of the work of Westwood and McLaren – their association with Punk, together with his music management and promotional skills – that, for the first time, pop music and Fashion were marketed simultaneously to become somehow indivisible.

Gentle parody

Claire Wilcox interviewed Valerie Mendes, the curator who acquired the first Westwood for the V&A, to discuss Westwood's second collection, Savage, from 1982:

> From the museum's point of view we wanted to include her work very much; she is at the forefront of ideas, her impact on the cut of clothes has been considerable and while her ideas can be extreme her clothes are wearable.[32]

Buffalo followed Savage, and then Punkature, and by 1983 Westwood was on the Paris Fashion circuit. In 1984 VW designed Hypnos at the house of her new business partner, Carlo d'Amario, in the Italian Alps. He now manages the company Vivienne Westwood Limited. He remained in Italy, handling production partnerships, in 1986, when she returned to England and re-opened 430 King's Road. Influenced by fabrics and artefacts from Scotland and the regions, Westwood began designing with materials which would lead to her being given a Queen's Award for Exports. The Scottish Isles and the vision of a little girl in a Harris tweed jacket, on a London tube – 'Everyone around her was being noisy and rowdy, but she looked quite serene' – set the tone for her work for the next 10 years. Claire Wilcox explains:

> Shown at Olympia in Spring 1987 to the accompaniment of classical music and traditional brass bands, Harris Tweed was Westwood's first show for two-and-a-half years. Although the move towards a more traditional, fitted look had started in the summer, in the Mini-Crini collection, she could now further explore the potential of British fabrics and styles in Harris Tweed ... She paid homage to the tailoring traditions of Savile Row and the jacket she designed then, named the Savile jacket, still features in her collections today.[33]

Charting Westwood's progress in the Media, Wilcox accepts that her clothes were a gentle parody of establishment styles and that the Fashion Press had begun to respond to the Westwood enchantment:

> One hunting-pink Barathea Harris Tweed suit with black velvet trim and brass buttons was memorably photographed by Snowdon for British *Vogue* (which by now was becoming seriously interested in Westwood) amongst the Horse Guards at Buckingham Palace.[34]

By 1999 Westwood was so steeped in Art, and so involved with her investigations into how specific materials could respond to ways of draping and cutting, that Wilcox wrote of her collection from this year:

> La Belle Hélène (S/S1999) was inspired by Rubens' portrait of his second wife Hélène Fourment (*Hélène Fourment with a carriage*, c. 1639). The movement, tension and elasticity of materials in the painting were explored in stretch wool and cotton and silk suiting that moulded the body. Evening fabrics consisted of lace mounted on wool or organza and garments made of plaited ribbon, while prints inspired by Matisse formed blocks of hand-painted colour, to resemble a canvas, especially in a painterly ultramarine. The clothes were accessorized with ballerina shoes and flat sandals, as Westwood's

sense of the body returned to an appreciation of its lithe animation.[35]

After she had shown in Paris and had studied the dress of the French aristocracy in paintings, Westwood was quoted in the book accompanying the V&A's The Cutting Edge: 50 years of British Fashion 1947–1997 exhibition:

> On the English side we have tailoring and an easy charm, on the French side that solidity of design and proportion that comes from never being satisfied, because something can always be done to make it better, more refined – hence an elaboration that always stops short of vulgarity – and then that 'je ne sais quoi', the touch that pulls it all together.[36]

Her passionate curiosity is assuaged by her continuing research into the past; producing collections 'using clothes as a cultural carapace, each laden with historical references, imbuing the wearer with a self-awareness, a pleasure in being observed and "read"'. Commenting on Always on Camera, 1992–3, Wilcox explains that Westwood's love of painting was further communicated through her clothes, and that she seems unconcerned about having her designs appropriated:

> Instead of simply reproducing an image on fabric, Westwood began to create clothes inspired by portraits that emulated the very quality of the artist's brushwork. As usual, she was open about her influences, confident that no one else could achieve what she could – for even if the clothes were copied, the original ideas, which gave them such resonance, would be absent.[37]

Given the opportunity to speak for herself in a video made for the exhibition, Vivienne Westwood explains that the 'biggest compliment' she seeks is for her clothes to be seen, not as hers, but as belonging to and being worn by 'beautiful women'. It sounds self-deprecating and modest but, if truth were told, it means she hopes her clothes have a transformational quality; that they carry symbols, which provoke intellectual consideration. When journalists first began writing about Westwood they described her clothes as 'unwearable'. She believes a Press who had been viewing pictures taken from extreme angles during catwalk shows made this judgement. Westwood maintains that most

It was the Pirate collection that, by being seen in Fashion magazines, attracted buyers. Wilcox explains how the Media began to take an interest in the alternative, non-Fashion-trained Westwood, who had begun her career assisting an anarchist, making clothing with semiotic rather than commercial intent.

clothing has no rapport with the body and is made of shoddy materials that she would not be happy to wear. In response to this exasperation, she intends her designs to be a 'criticism of mediocrity in dress'. She plays with erotic exposure, attempting to change the way we see the body through altering the silhouette. She proposes that through traditional tailoring something quite startling can be constructed. Using very high heels to lengthen legs immediately and round the bottom, the waist and top half of the body, 'the thorax', is made to look tiny. Then, with a décolletage created using corseting techniques from 200 years ago and beautiful tight tailoring, the silhouette resembles 'an ant on stilts'. She explains that the head comes out looking more important, and that the shoes form a pedestal to give particular power and expression to the most erotic part of the person, the face. Her collections start from tailoring, essentially part of man's dress. Her inspiration comes, in an especially English way, from when ladies adopted men's Fashions:

> In the West there is a complementary exchange between English tailoring and French couture; with lots of trouble taken, attention to detail and everything fits perfectly. Essentially this is the point in Fashion where glamour and romance meet, when there is some-thing people have never seen before, but is like a perfume, which carries connections of something people knew already.[38]

Westwood describes her method as 'synthesising things from the past'. As she works with today's fabrics, she realizes there is the pos-sibility of using them in ways not explored before, arguing that 'Fashion is the manipulation of materials'. Inspired by Balenciaga and Dior, whose looks were part of her youth, she remembers how, in the 1950s, proportions were changed. She notes that then the hip was pushed forward, the back curved and the nose was going up. She reinvented this image, using a cage and putting fan pleats over it, suggesting that the silhouette can be distorted in other ways. Recognizing that in her career she has dealt with traditional and archetypal beauty in both clothes and in models, she states her philosophy:

> Having had the privilege, for 20 years, of working in Fashion I have never diffused or dispersed my vision – always keeping to the heart of it. It is a criticism against everything else. I am comfortable in assuming this arrogant position because I am so appalled by the banality of everything else. If I do achieve an influence it will be something very, very worth while spending my life doing.[39]

Idiosyncratic vision and commercial arenas

Britain's most admired Fashion journalist, Hilary Alexander, whose *Telegraph* pieces include fascinating esoterica, probably finds Westwood and her work near to her own heart. She writes on Paris Fashion week in Spring 2008, and celebrates Westwood's skill in taking her idiosyn-cratic vision into the commercial arena:

> 'Amazonia,' declared Dame Vivienne Westwood, before the start of her show last night in Paris, coming over all Fitzcarraldo in a hand-painted, jungle creatures-shirt and Brazilian military cap. The show combined 17th-century perceptions of the waist with a fantasy of people living in a forest or jungle, thrown on their inner resources

and the environment for their survival – AND, of course, their clothes. Strange, multi-coloured insects, birds, snakes, suns, moons and foliage were splashed in broad brush-strokes on oversized anoraks, gaucho-shirts, long, wrap-around skirts, trousers, loose jackets, kilts, blanket-capes and long wizard-like robes. The models' face-paint – whiskers, tattoos, green eyes, smudged lips – was also inspired by the children's naïve paintings … eclectic signatures of a Westwood Gold Label collection: wide-shouldered velvet trouser suits; printed 'work' dresses hitched up over leggings and flat shoes with toes shaped like the blunt end of a hammer-head shark; jackets with Montagu-and-Capulet slashed sleeves; faux fur capes; and drop-waist dresses in lemon and beige silk and metallic taffetas, accessorized with corsets, wide belts with seed-pod and 'head' buckles and polished wood pendants.[40]

Dilys Blum has remarked that the Philadelphia Museum of Art is not concerned with whether Fashion is Art, or not Art, and the journalists who saw Westwood's work as unwearable were not commissioned to look for intellectual narratives on Fashion's catwalks. They may have missed a trick, but the haute bourgeoisie, who make the exhibitions, do not overlook the theoretical content in Westwood's clothes. Andrew Bolton, ex-V&A, who joined the Metropolitan Museum of Art in New York in 2006, curated the exhibition Anglomania: Tradition and Transgression in British Fashion. He placed Westwood's work in the context of Englishness. Using an ironic, theatrical and historical gaze, he drew on the work of late 20th- and early 21st-century British designers. Gaby Wood chose to contrast two spectacular Fashion bashes as the starting point for her review of Anglomania. Her report for the *Observer* in April 2006 is reminiscent of Chapter 14 in *The Devil Wears Prada,* when Andrea Sachs is dumbfounded by the glory of a gallery party:

> If *Vanity Fair* thinks its Oscar party is glamorous, that's nothing compared to the pride *Vogue* takes in organising the annual Costume Institute Ball, an event recently described by *New York* magazine as 'the most excessive, obsessive, competitive, stage-managed, micro-managed, luxurious, fabulous party of the social season'. And that was putting it mildly.[41]

The 'Costume Institute Ball judiciously combines the rich, the famous and the impossibly fabulous in a single military operation', Wood enlightens; and in contrast to the Chanel show the year before, she was expecting 'some very bad behaviour at the Anglomania opening'. As well as true Brit sponsorship by Burberry, a landing party of UK guests, the Duke of Devonshire, designers Westwood, McQueen, Galliano and Chalayan launched Anglomania. Writing of whether she should expect to be welcomed with 'opening arms' or a 'burgeoning backlash', Wood lists influential British people in American Fashion: *Vogue* editor Anna Wintour, Glenda Bailey at *Harpers Bazaar* and Andrew Bolton, curating this, his first New York exhibition after leaving London. He found that (Anglo)mania was about more than just Fashion:

> When I started thinking about the exhibition I became much more aware of a new passion for things English. British bands such as the Arctic Monkeys and Franz Ferdinand were getting more airplay on the radio. You'd get on the subway and see people reading Zadie Smith or Alan Hollinghurst. There seems to be more of an interest in British culture in general. And on the catwalk you see references to it – in Rei Kawakubo's and Junya Watanabe's recent collections, for example – either to British street style or to icons of Britishness, like the Union Jack flag. It made me think it was the right moment for the exhibition.[42]

Saying that the premise of the show was a 'two-way street', with influences flowing in both directions between London and New York, Wood sees the exhibition looking back over 30 years to when the clothes in Vivienne Westwood and Malcolm McLaren's shop Seditionaries were in a dialogue with England's history – 'reinventing itself according to the way it is seen from the outside'. Wood quotes ex-pat Andrew Bolton focusing on what makes the show work abroad:

> aspects of English culture that have driven Anglomania abroad and which designers like Vivienne Westwood and John Galliano both parody and celebrate in their work.[43]

She observes that 'national effects are never as simple as they seem', and that a figure like Westwood, by accepting OBEs and damehoods, is collaborating with an established part of British society which she and her fellow anarchists, from 30 years ago, might well have expected to be replaced at the beginning of the 21st century by other hierarchies. Andrew Bolton took the opportunity to explain how anachronistic and eclectic were the choices made by Fashion designers, arguing that the mixed period rooms at the Met were highly appropriate contexts for their displays:

> Westwood and McQueen have looked at periods where they would use architectonic structures to heighten femininity, but their references are rarely literal, so they might combine a 1740s panier with a 1890s bustle. They advance the silhouette of fashion by combining past ones.[44]

Bolton also seems to suggest that even those who appear to be cutting-edge are sometimes, rather, influenced by the past:

> Hussein Chalayan, who's always classified as a futurist, also has a sense of history. If you look at that great coffee-table skirt, it has the silhouette of an 1840s crinoline.[45]

If English eccentricity is regarded as just for fun by the non-English, then Wood suggests that Anglomania is not a show which could have been put together by the V&A in the way it was done at the Met in New York. She asserts:

> It is, altogether, Englishness for export, and would have been far too wrapped up in more complicated notions of class had it been staged in London.[46]

Andrew Bolton was, it could be said, running with the hare and hunting with the hounds, having so recently departed the 'sceptre'd isle'. Perhaps not exactly seeing himself as still wearing a Westwood 'hunting-pink' jacket, he steered Wood away from an overly trans-Atlantic perspective:

> Stereotypes can be as dangerous as hell, but they are so potent. And you can't avoid thinking about stereotypes, when it comes to Englishness, because it's a romantic construct in the first place – unlike the idea of Britishness, which is much more political.[47]

Writing in *The Englishness of English Dress,* in the chapter 'Vivienne Westwood's Anglomania', Rebecca Arnold sees Westwood as a designer whose work springs from a thoughtfulness associated with the academic process. She remarks on Westwood's 'fascination with French art and fashion as a source for her meticulously researched collections'. She

Buffalo followed Savage, and then Punkature, and by 1983 Westwood was on the Paris Fashion circuit. In 1984 VW designed Hypnos at the house of her new business partner, Carlo d'Amario, in the Italian Alps. He remained in Italy, handling production partnerships, in 1986, when she returned to England and re-opened 430 King's Road.

explains how Cut, Slash & Pull S/S 1991 was a fusion, using 18th-century corset designs embossed with a detail from a Boucher painting, which she integrated with 20th-century photographic techniques and plastic faux boning supported by stretch fabric to create a new highly decorated erotic Fashion. The synthesis is achieved in the following process:

> French influences are absorbed and integrated into her strategy for a future culture built on the past. She projects her love of history and frustration with the late twentieth century onto clothes that are fantasies of aristocratic distinction, historical models that, like her 1991 'Dangerous Liaisons' jacket, whose etiolated cut, rich silk ground and painted floral borders cross boundaries of gender and national identity.[48]

Between Radical Chic and her own retrospective, Westwood collections echoed her themes from the 1980s in an exploration of the dynamics of the fabric, with robust androgynous forms and obvious geometry from rectangular and triangular gussets to semi-circular and curved seams. In *Fashion, Desire and Anxiety*, Rebecca Arnold examines Westwood's political themes and shows how in her Fashion they replicate society's current concerns. She is aware of how Westwood responds to the mood of the moment:

> In Britain during the recession of the early 1980s Westwood dressed her models in the bulk of wadding petticoats, dyed dull browns and olive greens worn with silky bras over the top of hooded T-shirts, paying homage to the way women in the Third World flaunted such trophies of Western dressing.[49]

Fabulous publicity

Westwood told listening admirers at the opening of her retrospective in Sheffield in May 2008 that the underwear as outerwear had been McLaren's idea. She was filmed for an episode of the television documentary *British Style Genius*. Watching the recorded launch, I briefly glimpsed Claire Wilcox, who no doubt was pleased to be picking up this fresh information on provenance of artefacts. She was probably less delighted with the diva's next comments. *British Style Genius* series editor Michael Poole threw light, and the medium's considerable resources, on the question of the extraordinary power of the construct of 'Englishness'. The programme maintained that the influence of this 'nation of shopkeepers' and tailors is exerted over the rest of the world. The five-part documentary, first broadcast on BBC2 in Britain in 2008, aimed to see 'what makes British style distinctive and influential'. Anthropologist Ted Polhemus, interviewed for 'Fashion Rebels', the second in the *Genius* series, said the British were renowned for 'wild Fashion' and Colin McDowell, Fashion Fringe founder, felt that 'rebelliousness is ingrained in Brits'. Hat designer Stephen Jones immediately insisted that Fashion would not be the way it is unless Vivienne Westwood 'had been around', and Anna Wintour of *Vogue* US clinched the concept, being filmed saying, 'I think the English designer is afraid of nothing.' Forgetting the implications of being avant-garde or outrageous for Fashion's sake alone, Hilary Alexander, the journalists'

Fashion writer, made the Media point that, of course, designing like this 'could generate fabulous publicity'. In this 'Rebels' episode, Dame Vivienne was seen opening 'her' show in Sheffield, the city close to her birthplace in Derbyshire. Far from its being an innocent, nostalgic, trip to the provinces, Westwood focused on being as mutinous as possible. Ignoring the cherished values of museum curators – dismissing any duty of care for the costumes – she said:

> I don't care if people steal a pair of the shoes, or whatever. It doesn't matter. Don't worry about it. If people touch it and light makes it fade a bit. It doesn't matter.[50]

It was at this point in the film, in a piece of editorializing probably designed to excuse her cavalier attitude to the exhibition displays, that directors included remarks which revealed Vivienne Westwood's global success. Why should she be concerned about the loss of a few historic pieces when her current empire was at the height of its commercial success? We learned her company's turnover was £110 million in 2007, with 60 boutiques opening worldwide, and catwalk shows taking place twice a year in Paris, Milan and London.

Positioning mannequins

Louise Pullen, the Ruskin Access Curator at the Millennium Galleries in Sheffield, helped to set up the 2008 Westwood exhibition working alongside the designer's team. She noticed how they spent time positioning the mannequins and determining the look of the garments once they had been condition-checked. She explained how curators feel, working with those from the commercial world outside the museum:

> It can be a little daunting to see objects, which a curator would treat with great care manoeuvred and draped into shapes that may cause damage to them – BUT this of course is necessary to display them in just about any way, shape or form. One more extreme example perhaps is the 'Winterhalter' ball gowns, which sweep over the edge of the plinth; these are likely to get some damage during the show. This draping was a stipulation of the VW team, yet it is also understandable from a curatorial viewpoint: they wanted to present their creations as they were meant to be seen on the catwalk so visitors could see the dresses in the best light, and so the drapery could be appreciated.[51]

Shown at Olympia in Spring 1987 to the accompaniment of classical music and traditional brass bands, Harris Tweed was Westwood's first show for two-and-a-half years. Although the move towards a more traditional, fitted look had started in the summer, in the Mini-Crini collection, she could now further explore the potential of British fabrics and styles in Harris Tweed ...

The collaboration between the V&A and Dame Vivienne's people appears to have been a clash of two cultures – a discourse between interpreters and the interpreted. The pragmatism inherent in taking on a curatorial role is central to how work is shown; yet Louise Pullen's perfectly professional responses to my investigations are revealing:

> Returning to the gloves issue, according to best museum practice, these should usually be worn unless there is something about the object, or the bulk of the gloves that might damage the object. By the time we worked with the VW stylists they did usually wear gloves, but the V&A team I worked with, had I think, been un-nerved by the lack of gloves in previous set-ups, especially as they do own some of the garments. Yet, again it does seem understand-

able; the VW team work with the clothes, day in and day out, at a practical level and if they are not used to wearing gloves, would not think to wear them.[52]

As the exhibition continued round the globe, V&A, curators realized that the Westwood collection, which had been fitted to mannequins for more than four years, was beginning to show the strain, particularly on the tight bodices. It was a concern, even though without this process the garments would not have been out, being seen by thousands of visitors with otherwise no access to this Fashion celebration. Here is the dilemma at the nub of gallery life – the question of whether curators are the guardians of objects or archives. Louise Pullen recognizes the differences between them:

> Curators see museum objects as the possessions of the city and its citizens. Most of the garments in the show belong directly to the VW archive; ultimately, they can do what they like with the clothes. They might see them as a resource to use as they need or want, without the same thought for their longevity.[53]

As a student of costume, Louise Pullen regards Vivienne Westwood's output as a tribute to historic textile crafts and making, admiring her use of treasured British traditional fabrics, tartans, prints:

> Her versatility and creativity is inspiring. Her starting point in anarchic fashions and inclusion now of everything from day-wear to elegant garments for country or evening wear shows a definite development through her career; her clear inspiration from, but obvious adaptation of historical elements of dress and decorative arts is fascinating.[54]

Alisa Richardson, Exhibitions Designer at the Sheffield Galleries, remembers that the Westwood team had been concerned about how much space was available, for the Pirates section. She tells of how they were delighted, later, with the effect museum staff had achieved, believing it recreated an atmosphere reminiscent of the World's End shop, allowing visitors closer viewing of the garments.

> We have been asked to provide the next venue – Hong Kong – with many of the specs and dimensions of our gallery designs so that they can emulate/recreate them.[55]

Thrown into the murky waters of Fashion politics during her clashes with the *New York Herald Tribune*'s Paris-based Suzy Menkes, Claire Wilcox is cautious about being drawn into debate about Fashion or Art now, and suggests she would rather let others form their own opinions and arguments for and against. Asked whether her role had been compromised by the Westwood team's input, she supposed her training and experience are what she relies on to give her the professional distance she needs: 'I pride myself on remaining as objective as I can, by contextualizing living designers' work.'[56]

Westwood's roots in anarchy and dressmaking make her seem, simply, determined to have women valued because of how they look. I wondered what Claire Wilcox felt about any political compromises Westwood may have had to make: if her substantial success means she and her colleagues, including McLaren, will have worked towards

Anglomania was launched by a landing party of UK guests, the Duke of Devonshire, designers Westwood, McQueen, Galliano, and Chalayan, with true Brit sponsorship by Burberry.

achieving fame and financial rewards for their efforts, whether we should consider Westwood as an important artist/designer or as a publicity manipulator who uses controversy to build a Fashion empire. Her reply, 'Probably both', leads me to make up my own mind. Although this book is about the promotion of Fashion, this chapter is about the collision of Art and Commerce in the service of Fashion. Westwood's association with the anarchist McLaren confuses critics, and her training, which was not in a fashionable Art school, has given the Fashion establishment an opportunity to see her as an outsider. Her approach to creativity is certainly that of an intellectual, even though, as late as 1997, serious journalists were seeing her as a figure of fun:

> At any given time Westwood has a least two, maybe three sentences, on the go concurrently, uttered in hushed Derbyshire tones that career and collide until they either explode into meaning, often minutes and even hours later, or at times peter out entirely leaving anyone who's interested to fill in the gaps. She sounds like a character in an Alan Bennett play, which only adds to the impression of naivety.[57]

In this Susannah Frankel *Visionaries* interview (1997), the journalist moves on to give her remarks context and positioning Westwood as an eminent designer rather than an amusing caricature:

> For the autumn/winter '97 season, Vivienne Westwood, the undisputed grande dame of British fashion, returns, in all her glory, to open London Fashion week after an absence of six years.[58]

Vivienne Westwood has not stopped being a rebel since the 1970s, nor has she stopped being an intellectual since, in 1961, her Art dissertation was awarded a distinction at St Gabriel's College in Camberwell. Then, fellow students remember her as pleasant, outstanding, pretty and a loner, and as someone who 'didn't come to group photographs'. Now students of Fashion and Art have the privilege of hindsight and the opportunity to make judgements about Westwood retrospectively. Louise Pullen made the significant point that when Westwood and McLaren began their careers in clothes they were selling in the centre of an important capital city. There was the chance of encounters with members of the aristocracy, which led McLaren to say of Diana Spencer's visit to their shop: 'The clothes fell into the wrong hands!' Looking back over 30 years, to when people like Westwood and McLaren were making minute ripples in the British class pond, Louise Pullen reflects on those waves:

> She wanted to make people confident or heroic through these clothes; to change social status, not in the received sense of the word, but still to give off a strong social message. These clothes are now rare, not only because they were fragile but because they were worn (in both senses of the word). Yet these clothes were still for those who had money. Whilst they were not couture, they still came from a King's Road boutique.[59]

Political alignments

In an attempt to pin down Westwood's elusive enchantment Louise Pullen mentions how, even in collections based on street influences drawn from hip hop or graffiti, they were bought by people who could afford to buy into the Westwood label. She believes that when VW moved on to the Harris Tweed period using Savile Row tailoring techniques to make fake crowns or imitations of ermine capes, worn by members of the peerage, it may have been 'out of a sense of fun rather than rebelliousness'. However, these are the clothes which raise questions about Westwood's political alignments, and Pullen identifies the Fashion problems which continue to occupy Westwood:

> Today's VW suits and evening dresses seem more about giving someone stature rather than status – it is the cost of them which adds any element of status. They are made to make any wearer feel good, but yet come with a price tag. The Red label is more affordable, thus opening it to a wider market, but VW herself states that to dress really well you need full couture; still the preserve of the rich. I think in the end, it is one of those circular riddles.[60]

When Vivienne Westwood moved the production of her Red label to the powerhouse of technology that was the clothing industry in Italy in 1993, her business changed 'beyond all recognition'. This may have been the moment when manufacturing and distribution problems for the company became academic. Susannah Frankel wrote of its expansion to become a business with a turnover of £20 million in 1997. Visitor figures to the Westwood retrospective since 2004 are a marketing coup which leads me to speculate on its influence, raising the Westwood annual turnover up to £110 million in 2007. Before Sheffield, between 2004 and 2008, over three quarters of a million people saw the exhibition internationally. The highest visitor numbers after the V&A (170,834) were in San Francisco and Taipei, at just under 150,000, followed by Tokyo, where the number was near to 95,000. Anna Fletcher, V&A exhibitions co-ordinator who provided these figures, comments:

> She epitomises Britishness, with her use of tartans and traditional styles and materials, and audiences abroad seem to really enjoy anything British. In addition, I think some people world-wide, are quite interested in the social history of London, in the 1970s, and the punk movement, in which Westwood played a part, and others are interested in the craftsmanship of her couture and the historical references in Westwood's work.[61]

A set of revealing, regional, data showing the impact on an economy of such a popular exhibition were supplied by Eric Hildrew, Sheffield Museums Market Research & Campaigns officer. These figures are an indication of how crucial Art establishment endorsement can be to wealth creation. During the Sheffield 2008 showing, 42 per cent of visitors said they were in the city specifically to see Vivienne Westwood: The Exhibition. Postcode analysis indicated that fans had travelled from major northern cities, Bradford, Leeds, Manchester, York and Nottingham. Up to 16,800 visits to Sheffield resulted from the exhibition, with over £1,000,000 being contributed to the local economy. Of the people who came to Sheffield specifically to see the exhibition, 12 per cent stayed overnight, resulting in 2,016 stays or an economic impact of £274,000. Day visitors to the city created a total gain of £420,000, with residents adding another £406,000. Said to be three times as lucrative as recent sporting events, it built new audiences, with 30 per cent of viewers attending the Millennium Gallery for the first time; retail spend was up by 35 per cent and café spend by 25 per cent. Forty three per cent of visitors to the Vivienne Westwood exhibition were from social classifications A and B, compared with 23 per cent ABs within the Sheffield City Council administrative boundary. The exhibition attracted a target demographic of 18-to-35-year-olds, representing 36 per cent of all visitors, which surprised the organisers. They had identified their core audience as '35–55 year old females, interested in their appearance, style, and clothes-shopping; well-educated ABs who were left wing once upon a time'. Hildrew explained: 'So we got

Westwood explains how Cut, Slash & Pull S/S 1991 was a fusion, using 18th-century corset designs embossed with a detail from a Boucher painting, which she integrated with 20th-century photographic techniques and plastic faux boning supported by stretch fabric, to create a new highly decorated erotic Fashion.

the AB bit right, but we were out on the age – it turned out younger women were really into Westwood too.' They noticed during the run that there were 'a lot of very well dressed late teenage girls, who had obviously put on their finest, specifically to come and see the show!'. Assessing how Westwood could be seen in the museum context, Hildrew made the following contribution:

> What I think we under-estimated was the interest in VW as a kind of heroine of fashion and self-expression … All of this seems very zeitgeist for exhibitions in general – visitors are increasingly looking for personal relevance and interaction – they don't just want to stare at the crown jewels passively – that top down approach doesn't wash anymore.[62]

Communications Professor Angela McRobbie identifies Westwood's significant power, influence and marketing talent, seeing them as a clever strategy developed from her ability to invent her own persona, with a mixture of faux naivety and practised pedantry.

> This exonerates her from the charge of taking liberties with history. She can delight in the production details of the dresses of Marie Antoinette, for example, without any broader references to their symbolic significance as signs of unacceptable wealth and luxury in the context of the French revolution.[63]

She also recognizes how Westwood uses a light touch when she finds it necessary to discuss her own skills in Arts and Crafts, making them seem part of a more political theoretical position:

> It is quite admissible for Westwood to say, as she did in her recent [sic] television series, 'my work is anchored in English tailoring'. Or that creativity comes through technique, or that fashion is 'the manipulation of materials, as it is with painting'.[64]

Schiaparelli's work was celebrated at the Philadelphia Museum of Art in 2003, in Paris in 2004, and during the Surrealist exhibition at the V&A in London in 2006. It was at this stage, in the revival of interest in her, that the rights to the name were negotiated in a move to ensure ownership, ahead of a label re-launch by Diego della Valle, president of the Milan luxury accessories house Tod's SpA. The V&A Vivienne Westwood retrospective set off from the Pennine hills, in winter 2008, once again on its overseas journeys to set bells ringing on cash tills around the Pacific Rim. Admired and celebrated by fellow Fashion designers, Dame Vivienne achieves more fulfilment, during frequent feats of self-actualization, than the women she parodies, either Baroness Thatcher or the British Queen Elizabeth II. There are no peers to critique them, nor catwalk shows to delight in their wit and skills. Whatever Westwood and McLaren set out to do, politically, in the 1970s, they could not have imagined how their project would grow to become a dynamic 21st-century commercial success, or that an academically inspired exhibition celebrating their vision would travel round the world continually on view for more than five years.

Notes

1   'The single exclamatory word most associated with Schiaparelli is "Shocking!" This was the name given to her best known perfume, launched in 1937 (in a bottle designed by the Surrealist, Leonor Fini) and to the colour "Shocking Pink", which became Schiaparelli's equivalent to the vivid blue which defines the art of Yves Klein.' Michael Bracewell, *Independent on Sunday*, 29 August 2004.

2   Alix Sharkey 'Didn't know one end of a tape measure from the …' *The Independent*, 13 March 2004. (Note: Alix Sharkey is one of Britain's best-known freelance journalists, writing regularly for the *Guardian*, *Observer*, *Sunday Telegraph* and others. From 1992 to 1995 he wrote a regular weekly column for *The Independent*. A former editor of fashion magazine *i-D*, news editor at MTV Europe and BBC TV presenter, he is currently Contributing editor to British *GQ*.)

3   Ibid.

4   Dilys E. Blum, *Shocking! The Art & Fashion of Elsa Schiaparelli*, Philadelphia, 2003, www.philamuseum.org/micro_sites/exhibitions/schiaparelli/kids/schiap-pack.pdf (accessed 19 April 2009).

5   Dilys E. Blum, *Shocking! The Art & Fashion of Elsa Schiaparelli* (Philadelphia: Philadelphia Museum of Art, 2003), p. 72.

6   Sharkey, *The Independent*.

7   Ibid.

8   Blum, *Shocking!*, www.philamuseum.org/micro_sites/exhibitions/schiaparelli/kids/schiap-pack.pdf (accessed 19 April 2009).

9   Blum, *Shocking!* (Philadelphia: Philadelphia Museum of Art, 2003), Foreword.

10 From 'Best dressed: 250 years of style', 21 October 1997–4 January 1998, Philadelphia Museum of Art, www.philamuseum.org/exhibitions/1998/3.html (accessed 19 April 2009).

11 Dilys Blum, e-mail to author, 2 September 2008.

12 Blum, e-mail to author, 27 August 2008.

13 From *Shocking! The Art & Fashion of Elsa Schiaparelli*, 28 September 2003–4 January 2004, Philadelphia Museum of Art, www.philamuseum.org/exhibitions/2004/64.html (accessed 19 April 2009).

14 Michael Bracewell, 'Dream lover', *Independent on Sunday*, 29 August 2004.

15 Ibid.

16 Suzy Menkes, *International Herald Tribune*, 23 October 2001.

17 Ibid.

18 Ibid.

19 Ibid.

20 Claire Wilcox, *Vivienne Westwood* (London: V&A, 2008), p. 30.

21 McLaren and Westwood's initial meeting has not been firmly established. There is speculation that he spotted her from a London bus but there is no authenticated account.

22 Roland Barthes, *The Language of Fashion*, trans. Andy Stafford, ed. Andy Stafford and Michael Carter (Oxford: Berg, 2006), p. 112.
23 Interviewed by Jon Savage in *The Face*, January 1981, cited in Wilcox, 2008, p. 16.
24 Wilcox, *Vivienne Westwood*, 2008, p. 13.
25 Ibid, p. 14.
26 Rebecca Arnold, *Fashion Desire and Anxiety: Image and Morality in the 20th Century* (New Brunswick, NJ: Rutgers University Press, 2001), p. 47.
27 Wilcox, *Vivienne Westwood*, p. 15.
28 Ibid. p. 16.
29 Ibid.
30 Ag, 'Turning Rebellion into Money', *Eat French Bread* blog site, May 2007.
31 Ibid.
32 Wilcox, *Vivienne Westwood*, p. 17.
33 Ibid., p. 20.
34 Ibid., p. 21.
35 Ibid., p. 30.
36 Quoted in catalogue for The Cutting Edge: 50 Years of British Fashion 1947–1997 by Amy de la Haye, V&A exhibition, 6 March–27 July 1997.
37 Wilcox, *Vivienne Westwood*, p. 25.
38 Westwood quoted from video accompanying exhibition, viewed at Sheffield Millennium Gallery, July 2008.
39 Ibid.
40 Hilary Alexander, 'Paris Fashion Week', *Daily Telegraph*, 26 February 2008.
41 Gaby Wood, 'The Brit Apple', *The Observer*, 9 April 2006.
42 Ibid.
43 Ibid.
44 Ibid.
45 Ibid.
46 Ibid.
47 Ibid.
48 Rebecca Arnold, 'Vivienne Westwood's Anglomania', in *The Englishness of English Dress*, ed. Christopher Breward, Becky Conekin and Caroline Cox (Oxford: Berg, 2002), p. 171.
49 Arnold, *Fashion Desire and Anxiety*, p. 24.
50 Quoted in 'Fashion Rebels', second part of UK TV series *British Style Genius*, BBC2, Autumn 2008.
51 Louise Pullen, e-mail to author, 11 September 2008.
52 Ibid.
53 Ibid.
54 Ibid.
55 Alisa Richardson, e-mail to author, 22 September 2008.
56 Claire Wilcox, e-mail to author, 26 August 2008.

57 Susannah Frankel, 'Vivienne Westwood', in *Visionaries: Interviews with Fashion Designers* (London: V&A Publications, 2005), p. 96.

58 Ibid.

59 Louise Pullen, e-mail to author, 11 September 2008.

60 Ibid.

61 Anna Fletcher, e-mail to author, 3 September 2008.

62 Eric Hildrew, e-mail to author, 20 September 2008.

63 Angela McRobbie, *British Fashion Design: Rag Trade or Image Industry?* (London: Routledge, 1998), p. 110.

64 Ibid.

CHAPTER FOUR
Mary Quant and the JCPenney blockbuster

When I read in a fashion magazine that the accessory makes spring-time, that this women's suit (of which I have a photograph in front of me) has a young and slinky look, or that blue is in fashion this year, I cannot but see a semantic structure in these suggestions: in every case, and whatever the metaphorical detours taken by the wording, I see imposed upon me a link of equivalence between a concept (spring, youth, fashion this year) and a form (the accessory, this suit, the colour blue), between a signified and a signifier.

Roland Barthes, *The Fashion System*

Mary Quant fascinates people as people fascinate Mary Quant. Fashion feeds from her fervour, her love of fun and clothes. The industry admires her because she understands its strategies. Yet it was the British Post Office which signalled her greatness, putting a little black dress on one of a series of stamps, celebrating 50 years of Modern design in 2009. No one was more surprised than Mary Quant when she found herself in the company of celebrated 20th-century Modernists. Successful at the promotion of Fashion, like Westwood coming from Art and not Couture, she is seen as innovator rather than designer. She refuses to take credit for the miniskirt, knowing it was, partly, from the street and that everyone, including André Courréges, was hacking away at hemlines in the sixties. It is the impulse towards Modernism which gave her the power to transform lives through Fashion; its optimism informs her biography and continues to inspire her thinking. Recent journalism reveals her importance as a guide for those who follow. When the designer Luella Bartley was interviewed and photographed with Quant for *Vogue*'s 90th anniversary,[1] she held that the Fashion industry could learn much from *Quant by Quant*, her idol's own record of events. Before Bartley launched her own international Fashion label, she had read the autobiography five times. First published in 1966, when Quant was just 30 years of age, it chronicles her early life, her Fashion projects and inventions, and is one of very few biographies to have 'profit margins' and 'stock difficulties' listed in its index. Commending youthful resourcefulness and zeal, it opens with the introduction of Alexander Plunket Greene, who later became Quant's husband. He was attending Goldsmiths' College, London, at the time when she was studying Art illustration there in 1952. Even in those early days, as a student, she recognized the powerful pull of personality:

> I had to wait three months before he noticed me and during that time I just watched from the outskirts of a posse of disciples who surrounded him constantly, hanging on his words, rushing about to fetch and carry for him and generally imitating his style.[2]

Greene was acting as front man for their worldwide Fashion enterprise when I interviewed them 29 years later, in 1981. This partnership was crucial to their success but it was Mary Quant's understanding of Modernism, from earlier influences, which gave it its edge. Both her parents were awarded Firsts by Cardiff University. They spent World War II educating children who had been evacuated from around Britain, moving from one part of the country to another with their own children, Mary and her younger brother, Tony. Her parents' vocational lives were the cornerstones of Quant's early years, so when she observed Plunket Greene's cavalier attitude towards academia it appeared in stark contrast to her own. He seemed to use college pretty much for its socializing potential:

> And it was only when I went to Goldsmiths' that, for the first time in my life, I realized that there are people who give their lives to the pursuit of pleasure and indulgence of every kind in preference to work.[3]

Modernism

She was set up to become a professional woman by her background and powerfully exact interpellation. Her parents made no difference between

When the designer Luella Bartley was interviewed and photographed with Quant, for Vogue's *90th anniversary, she was quoted, at the shoot by David Bailey, as saying that the Fashion industry could learn much from her idol's record of events.*

their expressed hopes for Mary and those for her brother. In interviews in 2009 she was still reminding journalists of her egalitarian origins, pointing out that both her mother and father were teachers. In the biography she wrote:

> It was made absolutely clear to both of us, from the start that we would have to earn our own livings. My parents never even considered the possibility that marriage might be a way out for girls. I was made terribly aware that it was entirely my own responsibility to make a success of my life.[4]

Loathing the 'ornate' clothes she was obliged to wear, handed on from a cousin, she made every effort, even as a child, to alter them. In tune with Modernism before Goldsmiths', she noticed interesting styles from dance clothes worn by other children, and stored these inspirational ideas away for future use. She did not imagine, in her wildest dreams, that she could be professionally involved with Fashion:

> But all the time I was growing up it did not occur to me that I could earn a living from something that was so much fun.[5]

She writes of questioning accepted ideas, wondering why adults in the forties and fifties always wore gloves. Her scientific mind made her ask why high heels were put on for dancing, and why women were anxious about having matching shoes and handbags. Before she was 10 years of age she was motivated, consciously or unconsciously, by prevailing trends. Although Modernism was not envisioned as a specific style, it is a term embracing many Design ideas and Art movements, all of which reject ornamentation and support abstraction. Modernists believe in a 'less is more' philosophy, encouraging clean simple forms and use of new technologies to bring the advantages of Modernity to society as a whole. Students educated from the 1930s to the 1960s in Europe and America were involved with the movement. It had begun in cosmopolitan centres in Germany and Holland, as well as in the cities of Moscow, Paris and New York. Quant's inclination towards this key 20th-century ideology is apparent. Her hatred of what she describes as 'over-accessorization' came from observation, and so she developed a philosophy which would later alter the way women were to look:

> Eventually I decided that such rules were totally irrelevant to modern-day living. Rules are invented for lazy people who don't want to think for themselves.[6]

Mary Quant and her brother were inventive and were always managing 'to stir up a certain amount of havoc' while living in various towns and villages. This need to make something happen was accompanied by an interest in how to make money. While staying in lodgings related to a boarding school she briefly attended, she noticed how the owners smartly used children's food rations to sell as extras to grateful adult paying guests. Instead of grousing about some possible exploitation, she recalled:

> It struck me as an extremely bright idea and, so far as I could find
> out, it seemed to work well. This was my first introduction to Big
> Business![7]

The Quants' entrepreneurial activities, giving sailing lessons to visiting families and taking them on all-day picnics round the Pembrokeshire coast, were extended to running an agency to clean the boats and return holiday makers to their trains. When the weather was unsuitable, there was sewing. The indications that one day Mary Quant would become an enterprising businesswoman are here and the scene was set. There was a growing affluence in post-war Britain. Young people no longer needed to contribute part-time pay to the family budget. They could spend disposable income on fun and Fashion.

By the time Alexander Plunket Greene and their partner, Archie McNair, were about to open Bazaar in 1957, Quant's life had begun to sound like several episodes of *Grand Designs* and *Mary Queen of Shops* combined. They had to negotiate the pitfalls of planning permission, underpin buildings with gallons of expensive concrete, withstand accusations of wrecking heritage buildings and diplomatically woo local business dragons, whose sinister hidden agendas were in conflict with their own. The launch of their restaurant, Fantasy, some time before the Fashion boutique Bazaar, was so successful that they decided to give a party for the shop's opening. This was when Quant wished she had known about Fashion PR's first diktat: know who writes about your project for which audience, talk to them and invite them to your events.

> Our whole approach was so unprofessional that it is not surprising
> none of them turned up. Some of them sent junior assistants.[8]

A lone journalist from *Harper's Bazaar* wrote about 'a pair of mad house-pyjamas'. Frequently quoted since, with the wrong punctuation, Quant followers are led to believe that late Fifties designers were expected to come up with something for lunatics to wear. At the time, the popular Press did not focus on Fashion, but might mention the antics of aristocrats in society columns:

> Alexander Plunket Greene, kinsman of the Duke of Bedford, opens
> shop in Chelsea[9]

Neither the Fashion industry nor the Fashion Press could have predicted that within seven years the Quant/Plunket Greene venture would grow to

> go well over the million mark and the clothes I was to design would be in 150 shops in Britain, 320 stores throughout America and also on sale in France, Italy Switzerland, Kenya, South Africa, Australia, Canada and, in fact, in just about every country in the western world.[10]

When an enterprising American manufacturer bought the pyjamas, with the avowed intention of copying them for his home market, Mary had to console herself with thinking that having a design used for mass production could be seen as a compliment. She was concerned about how easy it was to copy a design and make money out of it without protection for the originator. It did inspire her to concentrate on design and so enroll on an evening course in cutting. However, they did not research into manufacturing and wholesaling and continued to pay full retail price for fabrics from Harrods. She began to see that there wasn't much profit being made, especially as customers, who were also friends, dropped in for cocktails permanently on offer at any time of the day or night. They discovered they had spent £3,000 on entertaining in their first year. On one occasion, having sold everything in the shop, Mary dashed back to her flat, being used as manufacturing base, to pick up the one remaining finished dress, only to have it taken from her in the street outside the shop. The fanatic rushed inside and paid for it without trying it on. Then they knew they would have to put the business on a more formal footing. Soon after, they found themselves in the middle of what is variously described as 'Youthquake', or the 'Swinging', or 'Revolutionary', sixties. Quant charted its progress in her writing:

> We were in at the beginning of a tremendous renaissance in fashion. It was not happening because of us. It was simply that, as things turned out, we were part of it.[11]

She witnessed the sociological changes afoot at the time, changes being brought about by post-war Modernist thinking. She recognized how the world's Press would follow trends and map behaviours in major cities.

There was hardly a day when Chelsea was not mentioned or featured in one way or another in the newspapers. Chelsea suddenly became Britain's San Francisco, Greenwich Village and the Left Bank. The press publicized its cellars, its beat joints, its girls and their clothes. Chelsea ceased to be a small part of London; it became international; its name interpreted a way of living and a way of dressing far more than a geographical area.[12]

Here she pre-dates the intellectual motivation behind *Fashion's World Cities*, in which the powerful relationship between metropolitan modernity and Fashion culture is mapped. In taking the lead from her customers, rather than controlling the way women should look in her designs, she was in tune with Barthes' questioning of the author's divine

Mary Quant was so impressed with the youthful people around her, whether doctors' daughters or dockers' daughters, that she researched fabrics to make their lives easier and more eventful.

authority. She offered a 'multi-dimensional space, where Art could be interpreted' in the centre of the cosmos which was post-war regenerated London,

> The Chelsea girl, the original leather-booted, black-stockinged girl who came out of the King's Road looking like some contemporary counterpart of a gay musketeer, began to be copied by the rest of London and watched with interest by others all over the country. Soon the 'look' was to be copied internationally. This girl's challenging clothes were accepted as a challenge. It was she who established the fact that this latter half of the twentieth century belongs to Youth.[13]

Quant looked for a rationale behind the well-springs of this revolution and concluded that no one designer is ever responsible:

> All a designer can do is to anticipate a mood before people realise that they are bored with what they have already got. It is simply a question of who gets bored first. Fortunately I am apt to get bored pretty quickly. Perhaps this is the essence of designing.[14]

Quant is not just an observer of consumer behaviour, passions and histories. She is a reviewer and critic commenting on the relationship between wearers, their clothes and the practices which create them:

> Once only the rich, the Establishment, set the fashion. Now it is the inexpensive little dress seen on the girls in the High Street. These girls may have their faults. Often they may be too opinionated and extravagant. But the important thing is that they are alive ... looking, listening, ready to try anything new.[15]

She recognizes the importance of dress to happiness, and values the psychological advantage of feeling part of Fashion. She sees clothes design as a decorative Art, being most speedily communicated, and of most importance, because of its intimate connection to the body. She writes of the 'delicate art of putting oneself across ... socially, professionally and commercially'. In responding to the 'girls in the High street' she was setting the agenda, taking it away from the rich and the Fashion establishment. She knew their need for experimentation had to be met, whether 'dukes' daughters, doctors' daughters or dockers' daughters'. They wanted to try out the new. She delights in their questioning spirits and in their lack of pretension. Admiring them 'tremendously', she rejoices in this Modern 'classless' rebellion:

> They will not accept truisms or propaganda. They are superbly international. The same clothes are worn in Britain, Europe and America.[16]

Chosen by Quant in her campaign to change the way clothes were designed and worn, these 'dolly birds' were dynamic allies as postwar 1950s London was not exactly a hotbed of modernizing ardour. Design thinking at the time saw an incompatibility between Fashion, and femininity, as Modernists denigrated decoration. Until Hepburn and Quant, it was impossible for women to see that being frivolous and fun-loving did not depend on the number of frills worn but on the amount of freedom and control clothes gave to the wearer. Before Quant, the newly rich planning a party in Britain would have their dressmakers run up a glittery Alma Cogan or Shirley Bassey copy. There would be the risk of rivals describing them as looking like a 'tube of Bacofoil'. If HBO's *Mad Men* costume research is reliable, there was little but department store versions of Dior's New Look for professional Americans either. Realizing that both Europe and America were beginning to question Paris's supremacy, Royal College of Art designer Sylvia Ayton said, 'They were looking at us and we were looking at them.' For a V&A interview, she explains:

> Until the 1960s, London's clothing industry operated in the shadow of the great Parisian couturiers. Paris, with its focus on made-to-measure garments for a fabulously wealthy, elite, group of women, was the hub of international fashion. But suddenly, with the growth of the youth market, London began to set the pace.[17]

Professor Valerie Steele, of the Fashion Institute of Technology, New York, looking beyond the strictures of a fading hegemonic haute couture, assesses the London scene of the mid sixties and distinguishes the 'mods' as the most significant of the prevailing trends:

> The term was an abbreviation of 'modern' and unlike the aggressively flamboyant teddy boys and rockers, the mods developed an

understated style of streamlined modernity that marked the first really important phase in youth fashion.[18]

Identifying herself with the characteristics of Modernity, Quant differentiates it as a movement encouraging change, embracing technologies which would make life more enjoyable for men and women:

> It is the Mods ... the direct opposite of the Rockers (who seem to be anti-everything) ... who gave the dress trade the impetus to break through the fast-moving, breathtaking, up-rooting revolution in which we have played a part since the opening of Bazaar.[19]

At the critical moment when Bazaar first opened, the Plunket Greene/ Quant project was taken under the wing of Archie McNair. Whether Luella Bartley was ever to need this sort of advice in the future or not, Mary Quant covers the nuts and bolts of running a rag trade venture for everyone, as she explains how they were happy to be joined by an accountant:

> Costing is a talent in its own right. It is like the most nerve-wracking gamble in the world when you start to cost a dress. You have to find out first whether you get the right quantity of material at the right price. Then you have to work out just how much all the things that go into the finished dress are going to cost. In theory it should be easy enough but dresses have to be made in different sizes and obviously large ones take more cloth than small.[20]

She also adds, as a guide to practitioners, that if you are working on the basis that the worst will happen, it will, because the price will be too high in the first place. Coming to how customers can be attracted to look at new collections, she touches on the tricky matter of tempting journalists to take an interest:

> If, in fact we estimate that we will sell 750 of a particular dress, and we are wrong, and only a hundred are sold, either because it is not a good dress, or, for some reason, it does not catch the eye of the buyers or of the fashion Press, we are in frightful trouble.[21]

Archie McNair did much to make the operation more professional, but it was the design of the clothes that led to manufacturers becoming interested. Maybe they sensed Quant had access to ingenious market research – people-watching in Chelsea. If anyone was responsible for encouraging the rise of post-war youth culture, it was Mary Quant. Her insights made it possible for retailers to see customers as arbiters of taste:

> The young will not be dictated to. You can be publicized on national network television, be written up by the most famous of the fashion columnists and the garment won't sell if the young don't like it. I admire them tremendously.[22]

She began to commission manufacturing out to the experts, using the best in each market. As a model for Modernity, she set out to learn what was technically feasible, deliberately making use of mass-production techniques, working closely with top technicians. In another feat of professionalism, they found themselves working with the man who specialized in overseas Fashion trips. David Wynne Morgan, who had been at school with Plunket Greene, was still working in Fashion in 2007, when I met him. His first words on Quant, in December 2006, were, 'She's a genius.'[23] For some of the 40 years between his Bazaar liaison and then, he was chairman of Hill and Knowlton, *Mad Men* archetype in New York. During the heady days of the 1960s, he took Quant, her clothes and models to be part of a Fashion show at the Palace Hotel, St Moritz. Quant wrote:

> The grandees of the British Fashion world like Victor Stiebel, Mattli, John Cavanagh and Worth were all sending a part of their latest collections. David wanted to include a few items from Bazaar.[24]

Wynne Morgan told me that Noel Coward, celebrity composer-playwright, staying at the hotel and camping it up after the show, had said, 'I've never been so proud to be British.'[25] Quant, analysing Wynne Morgan's PR strategy in the sixties, thought the styles from British designers were 'beginning to show signs of growing too grand for words'. She recalls the hazards of showing abroad, of satisfying Customs' protocol and of keeping up with extraordinary models in elaborate wigs. Splendid ball gowns, in a splendid ballroom, would upstage her pleated flannel above-the-knee frocks, so she decided:

> The only possible way was to break the tempo of the whole evening, with one great burst of jazz and let the girls come in at terrific speed in the zany, crazy way in which my clothes should be shown.[26]

Recording that the audience was anticipating dignified evening dresses, not models clowning around in lace trouser suits with fur hats:

> the thing was that they were expecting to see nothing but the grand clothes of the haute couture. They had already seen and possessed plenty of them. They had several minks of their own in their wardrobes. I am sure they felt there was nothing new in fashion for them to see.[27]

Models wearing Quant's white stockings and flannel dresses, or tunics over red sweaters with matching red legs, pranced down the runway to 'hot jazz', and although Bronwen Pugh threw off her coat revealing that she had forgotten to put on a dress, the show was a success:

> The grandees and the millionaires wanted these clothes. They had everything else; all the minks and ball gowns they could use; the silk shirts and the silk trousers; the stretch pants and leopard tops. But they hadn't any fun clothes. This was something quite new to them and I had no idea to what extent this look was to grip people's imaginations and how popular it was to become.[28]

This potential worldwide venture was helped along by Quant's association with the hairdresser Vidal Sassoon, whose business brilliance was measured by Wally Olins in *Corporate Identity* (1989). Sassoon did not rely on zeitgeist or the inventions of customers to develop his project. He decided to express identity through Design, using it as a commercial strategy to add value, carrying out 'a minor revolution using Design in various ways'. Olins describes how Sassoon created a new niche market position aimed at increasingly affluent younger people:

> Sassoon saw a commercial opportunity in the hairdressing world of the 1960s and he exploited it with great flair and energy. Of course, he used all the classic identity tools: products – the styling of hair and hair-care products that went with maintaining the appropriate appearance; environments – the layout and interior design of his salon; information – publicity, advertising and PR, at which he was remarkably successful; and behaviour – the relaxed informal atmosphere created by his own staff inside his salons.[29]

Plunket Greene and Quant were members of an exclusive band of modernizing characters whose ventures were to transform London into an international shopping heaven. Olins marks out Vidal Sassoon, saying:

> In a sense we can consider Sassoon an earlier version of all those fashionable retailers who found and subsequently developed niches in the marketplace: Benetton, Esprit, Next and the rest, all owe something to Sassoon.[30]

At one time the Plunket Greenes thought of forming a joint company with Terence Conran and his second wife, the author Shirley Conran.[31] Founder of Habitat, Conran had designed Mary Quant's Knightsbridge shop; he invited her to create the uniforms for his salespeople, and had

When David Bailey dropped in to socialize in Bazaar, she was inspired by his love of the models and his imaginative photography. She had a Bazaar window dressed to look like a Bailey photographic shoot.

Sassoon cut their hair and Terence Donovan take photographs at the opening.

Inventive, adventurous spirits like Quant were happy to draw on the talents and skills of colleagues and agents, but as an artist she would continually come up with individual inventions for clothes and publicity. When David Bailey dropped in to socialize in Bazaar, she was inspired by his love of the models and his imaginative photography. She had a Bazaar window dressed to look like a Bailey photographic shoot. By 1963 the clothes were such a success that Quant's second branch was opened and the Ginger Group, a lower-priced line appealing to a wider clientele, was launched. She was at the heart of the Modernist momentum yet it would take the hindsight of the British Post Office to identify that this was what made Quant a worldwide influence. She was much too close to see that she was interpreting an international movement. At the time of the second Bazaar opening, she wrote:

> Fashion is the product of a thousand and one different things. It is a whole host of elusive ideas, influences, cross-currents and economic factors, captured into a shape and dominated by two things ... impact on others, fun for oneself. It is unpredictable, indefinable. It is successful only when a woman gets a kick out of what she is wearing; when she feels marvelous and looks marvelous.[32]

Synthetics

Making the pertinent point that short skirts had automatically excluded older or larger women from being fashionable in the 1960s, Bonnie English in *Catwalk to the Sidewalk* sees how Quant's clothes appealed to an emerging demographic: the working girl. Manufactured from easy-care, crease-resistant washable synthetics, they were designed for people on the move. Knowing there were eight million women going out to work in Britain, Quant thought, no matter what form of transport they were using, they would not want to worry about what to wear: 'Dressing to go with the job and fit in with the sort of life a woman leads has always been a problem.' Researching into these ideas, she looked at what Dr Ernest Dichter at the Motivational Research Institute in New York had discovered. She learned:

> Fashion is a tool of competition, in the sexual sense, but it is also a tool to compete in life outside the home. People like you better, without knowing why, because people always react well to a person they like the look of. It is an integral part of taking a job.[33]

She concluded that 'the modern girl is much more feminine than we imagine her to be' and in compiling a set of criteria to understand women's style she used the notion of 'square' to guide her investigations. Her deductions are key to keeping up for everyone, and certainly prefigure advice on offer today in television programmes such as *What Not to Wear* and *Ten Years Younger*:

> A 'square' – who is by no means always an intellectual – also is one who cannot be bothered to keep up with the changing trends of fashion. She is a little low on nerve. She is utterly resigned to never being right in fashion at the right moment; she would rather like to be but she is always finding out that just as she had got to like some feckless innovation, it is suddenly older than time.[34]

The sixties revolution, which saw London represent the UK at the centre of the Fashion universe, was written about by Peter Laurie in *Vogue* US in 1964: 'Probably no other [city] in the world offers us the opportunities that are here. Wherever enthusiasm, energy, iconoclasm or any kind of creative ability are needed, you'll find people in their mid-twenties or younger.' Quant was the spirit of the age, and how! When she decided to find mass producers for her clothes, it opened up the opportunity for everywoman to wear thrilling modern designs, the sort of avant-garde pieces which had only been available to the fashion-conscious, well-heeled, upper middle classes until then. She delighted in the success of her venture and revelled in her ability to be ahead of the rest:

> The description one journalist gave of the show at Courrèges this year might well have been a word picture of our first showing at Knightsbridge Bazaar. It was described as 'a display of far-out fashions that swing down the runways to the way-in beat of progressive jazz'.[35]

She tried to stick to her intention to democratize access to Fashion by keeping clothes within the budget of working girls, and saw it as a goal to beat couturiers on price:

> The nerve wracking thing for me was that although Pierre Cardin and Norman Hartnell were showing expensive clothes, none of my things cost more than twelve guineas ... and most of them were around the twelve pounds mark! I had to keep reminding myself that this was the whole point of what we were doing.[36]

Ernestine Carter, curator, writer and editor, who believed that Fashion is as intellectually relevant as Architecture, saw Mary Quant being in the right place, with the right talent, at the right time. She included her with Chanel and Dior, who had given women status, introducing designs through couture collections. Quant responded to her customers' desires, drawing on ideas from children's clothes, encouraging freedom of movement and activity. By the time Dick Hebdige was writing *Subculture: The Meaning of Style* in 1979, he had concluded that the Quant phenomenon was part of the discourse on fashion consumption and fine Art. Christopher Breward, whose scholarship has moved Carter's proposition along, while acknowledging Quant's impact seems distrustful of 20th-century promotional strategies:

> Mary Quant epitomized the energy of London's young fashion scene from the founding of her boutique in 1957 to the end of the 1960s. Her style was characterised by its simple child-like shapes and bold, flat colours which were complemented by a deliberately naïve but highly successful succession of 'publicity stunts' engineered to promote a thriving international business.[37]

The irony suggested here depends on Quant's own version of events which, Breward thinks, was written with a certain disingenuousness. Indeed, it is difficult to appreciate from the biography that there were dedicated promotional agencies in place, helping to sell British Fashion abroad. Young designers had set up the Association of Fashion Designers, and the established trade was supported by the government-sponsored Clothing Export Council from the 1950s. Quant's account implies that the promotion of their project was really a matter of having journalists stumble across them by accident:

Clare [*Vogue* reporter Lady Clare Randlesham] walked in … Perhaps 'walked' is the wrong word. Clare doesn't walk! Then she turned to me. 'What do you mean opening a shop like this and not telling me about it? How could you do such a thing! Have any of the fashion girls seen these clothes?'[38]

Randlesham, who was sharper at picking up Fashion intelligence than other journalists at the time, became their supporter. Her confidence impressed Quant. She guided them and invited 'all the right people' to their first Press party. Quant still thought they were far too unimportant to really be noticed by Fashion pundits who still seemed to be sending assistants. An innovative show with pheasants, bought

This potential worldwide venture was helped along by Quant's association with the hairdresser Vidal Sassoon. He did not rely on zeitgeist or the inventions of customers to develop his project. He decided to express identity through Design, using it as a commercial strategy to add value, carrying out 'a minor revolution using Design in various ways'.

from Harrods, as props, thawing out and bleeding over the journalists who had turned up, is described by Quant:

> … girls came whizzing down the stairs, an outsize glass of champagne in one hand, and floated round as if they had been to the wildest party or looking dreamily intellectual with a copy of Karl Marx or Engels in the other hand.[39]

Deciding to make sure the Quant phenomenon was being thoroughly reported, Randlesham 'let everyone know about it', organizing Iris Ashley to give them a full page in the *Daily Mail*:

> Alexander says that it was Clare Rendlesham who inspired us; Iris Ashley who made us known to the masses; and Ernestine Carter who gave us the accolade of respectability.[40]

Felicity Green, who joined the Mirror Group in the early 1960s, engineered important changes to Fashion journalism in this democratizing process. She was first Associate editor of the *Sunday Mirror*. Then, as Associate of the *Daily Mirror*, she began to promote the influence of women throughout the paper. Her efforts have been recognized by the Fashion industry and by the Press. In the early 1990s she became a senior lecturer, teaching Fashion Journalism at St Martin's School of Art, and in 2005 she was elected to the *Press Gazette* Hall of Fame. Interviewed for the V&A in 2004, she described the politics of Fleet Street in the 1960s:

> At that time we were selling five million copies a day and we had an overlap with the *Times* at one end and people who couldn't read at the other, so our readership was fairly broad. I felt I wanted to relate clothes to people: where you might wear them, how you might wear them, clothes making a statement about you. In other words I think what I brought to the paper was something new in the way of presentation, in that I made fashion into features, I made it relate to your life, to your money, to your attitudes, to your prejudices, to your pleasures. People want to imagine themselves in the clothes, they want to see clothes in their mind's eye, they want to relate them to themselves. I felt we had to talk to readers and we had to make fashion come alive and I reckon we did it.[41]

Exhilaration to her readers

She refused to be silenced in the face of reactionary ignorance. In tune with the times, drawing on her relationship with the movers and shakers of the era, she defied her bosses and reformed the way Fashion was reported:

> When I had Mary [Quant's] first mini skirts in the paper our chairman, Cecil King, did not approve at all of what I was doing. He said, 'How long are you going to continue to put those ridiculous clothes in my newspaper … how long do you propose to go on with this?' And I said, 'well, as long as they are news. And what will you do with me if I do continue to put them in the paper?' … and he said, 'I will arrange for you to be fired' and walked on by. That was about the only guidance I ever got. But what I wanted to put in the paper were trends and news to inform and entertain … our readers couldn't afford Hardy Amies or Norman Hartnell.[42]

Green remarks on the need, then, for Fashion to become more Media savvy. In a changing economic climate when consumers were waiting to be directed towards the most entertaining way to spend their money, she wanted to inform them. She knew how difficult it was to make features out of Fashion journalism without the help of other creative professionals. In Chelsea's King's Road and Kensington High Street a revolution might have happened, but it was not reflected in newspapers' ability to bring this exhilaration to their readers:

> There was a schism right through this world of fashion, there was resentment from one side, from the older generation thinking it was all perfectly dreadful … and on the other side it was – 'We're doing our own thing and how brilliantly.' You were wearing cheap clothes, you were proud to be wearing cheap clothes, cheap clothes were fun. It had been a serious business before then and only a serious business. [Designers] were always willing, and rather excited to co-operate with the fashion journalists but there was no PR working for them so contact was a problem. The other thing I remember about that time was model girls who arrived when you set up a shoot, they arrived with a big bag with their curling tongs, their make-up, their hairdryers, and various accessories, their own shoes,

handbags etc. There were no hairdressers, no make-up artists, there were no stylists, it was you and the model and you worked it out between you.[43]

Alexander Plunket Greene and Quant handled breaking into the American market with a growing professionalism. They set out to do their own market research in New York, ahead of appointments, but they had been briefed to contact a 'merchandizing expert' called Tobe with a column in the *New York Herald Tribune*, syndicated throughout the States. She did not like their collection and greeted it with a common American expletive. Undaunted, they visited the head-quarters of *Women's Wear Daily*, 'the most powerful fashion newspaper in the world and the Bible of the American fashion industry'. *WWD* loved their clothes, raving about 'what they called the new international look'.

> English chic is fiercely NOW … by the young for the young … coky [*sic*], not kooky. Where did the English chic come from? It has always been there but it's on an added fashion wavelength now. Where is English chic going? How high is the moon?[44]

Valuing take-up by the Trade Press, knowing it acts as catalyst for other journalists and is the seal of approval by Industry informers, Quant writes of how leading Fashion writers followed suit:

> Sally Kirkland of *Life* magazine read what *Women's Wear Daily* had said and she phoned to say she would like to see our clothes. Rosemary McMurtry of *Seventeen* magazine was so enthused that she suggested a special promotion; Eugenia Sheppard of the *New York Herald Tribune* sent an assistant to see us and we were written up on her pages. We lived in a whirl of excitement.[45]

There seems to have been a more formalized approach to Quant's onslaught on America than the haphazard marketing strategies which marked their original attempts to alert British Fashion Press and buyers. Edward Rayne lunched with them at their hotel on the same day as the *Life* journalist's visit. Rayne was chairman of the Incorporated Society of London Fashion Designers (ISLFD), and his success at persuading American press and buyers to view British collections was celebrated in *Vogue*. He had a special relationship with America and H&M Rayne was the first British firm to introduce machinery from the US to make the sole of the shoe more flexible. He arranged for the Plunket Greenes to meet Geraldine Stutz, the vice-president of up-market store Bendell. Stutz was the first retailer in America to carry the ready-to-wear collections of European designers Jean Muir and Sonia Rykiel, too. Mary Quant was thrilled with the interest taken in them by the American Press and Fashion trade. She soaked up all there was to learn about the business from these transatlantic marketing maestros:

> The greatest thing that ever happened to me, professionally, was that first trip to the States. It changed my whole thinking. I had never met women so professional in their approach to business who could work at the pitch they do.[46]

Visiting the crucible of Modernity, Quant was impressed by America's facility with technology, tuned in as she was to its ethics and aspirations. Praising their accurate sizing system as revolutionary, she records:

> They seem to know how to mass produce for every possible female shape. I found that if a woman knew her size she could just walk into any shop and buy off the peg without trying on. The most she might have to do would be to turn up the hem or shorten the sleeves.[47]

Quant knew what made commercial sense and wondered why the youngest newcomer to a clothes company would be given the crucial job of grading sizes, saying that such a novice would add an inch indiscriminately over a whole garment:

> Proportioning is desperately important to mass production. It is in fact, the very crux of modern design ... When you grade up a dress, you can't simply add an inch or two to the hem and an inch or two on all the seams ... It takes real originality and designing sense to do it. There is something almost sculptural about it ... it is a job for the expert, not the beginner, however gifted that beginner may appear to be.[48]

America loved the London Look. In 1957 Quant signed a contract with JCPenney to create clothes and underwear for the wholesale market.

In a reverse arrangement, she was convinced by the informal 'preppy' style of American coordinates that separates were versatile and ideal for the young:

> Co-ordinates are a godsend to the woman with sizing troubles. Not all bust sizes are in the exact proportion to hip measurement that manufacturers have decided to regard as normal. Not everyone is made to the exact pattern of a size 12 or 14 or 16. Anyone with such a problem can buy the top she wants in the size she is looking for, then pick from a multitude of skirts on the separates rails that go with the blouse.[49]

She also sets out to right the marketing wrongs of distribution and stockists. Noticing how tricky it was to find co-ordination between promotion and point of sale, she describes the need for retailers to make sure their publicity is synchronized with delivery and distribution:

> I found I could look through a copy of *Seventeen* or *Mademoiselle* or *Glamour* and see the most exciting-looking clothes, but when I wanted to buy one of these, it was awfully difficult to find one in the shops.[50]

Quant came back from her first trip to America determined to spread its enthusiasm for selling Fashion back to Britain and reach more of the British market. In 1958 she launched the Ginger Group, a mass-produced version of the look, with US manufacturer Steinberg's. Noting the differences between selling Fashion in Britain and in the States, Quant believed that in the late fifties and early sixties shoppers would be less likely to be disappointed by the timing of publicity and supply chain management in Britain. She also recognized that London had led the way in changing the focus of Fashion towards the young:

> As a country, we were aware of the great potential of this change long before the Americans or the French. We were one step ahead from the start; we are still one step ahead and we have simply got to stay that way.[51]

Penney's London-based agents were responsible for recognizing Quant's potential. Paul Young, a junior in the control buying office, had seen her stories in *WWD* and in *Life* and was determined to find

out more about them. They overheard him on their office phone explaining how he wanted to promote Quant. He had seen various designers
in Paris, Italy, Spain, Denmark, Sweden and Ireland, but concluded:

> There is nothing to touch Mary Quant. I absolutely believe that our
> whole project should be launched on this girl. Forget about the
> original idea of a European promotion.[52]

Concerned about how selling through the major chain store JCPenney
in the US would affect her image as a freewheeling individual cutting-
edge designer – 'We had no idea what the reaction would be' – she let
her principles guide her:

> Our decision was finally influenced by our belief that the whole
> point of fashion is to make fashionable clothes available to everyone.
> Fashion is an inherent thing and should not be something which
> depends solely on beautiful and expensive.[53]

She decided Fashion should be mass-produced:

> I had the feeling this was my opportunity to prove I really meant
> what I had so often said. Also the money was good. We decided to
> go ahead. We accepted Mr James Cash Penney's kind invitation.[54]

Inventive Baptist

Quant appreciated America's marketing skills. Their Ginger Group
would become part of an international manufacturing and distribution
network through their American associations. Their union with
JCPenney linked them to one of the most successful retailing operations
of the 20th century. Penney had started his company as a dry goods
and clothing store in Wyoming in 1902. An honest and inventive
Baptist, he shared profits with managers and kept up with America's
changing demographics and retail trends. JCPenney is still adapting to
changing market forces today. In 2007 its slogan became 'Everyday
Matters', a message that works to inspire customers, whether visiting
stores or buying online. Shop workers are Associates and their policy is
to retain, develop and attract the best talent, 'becoming the preferred
choice for a retail career'. Penney's strategies point to advanced staff
development programmes. These continue the tradition of skilful

America loved the London Look. In 1957 Quant signed a contract with JCPenney to create clothes and underwear for the wholesale market. In a reverse arrangement, she was convinced by the informal 'preppy' style of American coordinates that separates were versatile and ideal for the young.

selling, used by other famous 20th-century US retailers Macy's, Lord and Taylor, Bloomingdale's, Neiman Marcus and F.W. Woolworth. In her biography, Quant discusses Fashion business practice as part of the book's lively overview of the Fashion world. She warns of the dangers of growing too quickly, and explains the importance, for a designer, of being able to work with others:

> A designer who is to succeed must have a team of people who believe in her so much that they are prepared to make a tremendous personal effort to carry out her ideas. A designer has to be able to talk convincingly to people as well as put down her ideas on paper. She has got to be able to persuade others to go along with her even at times against their own inclinations. And ... as often as possible ... she has got to be right.[55]

Quant learned so much about American retailing through her experiences with Penney's and the manufacturers Steinberg's that when they were invited to sell through the Puritan group of companies they were confident about practices and protocol. In 1965 after negotiating a deal which gave them the freedom to take their own models, who understood 'the look', they set off on a whistle-stop tour of the United States. With 30 outfits, they showed in 12 cities in 14 days. Sporting miniskirts and Vidal Sassoon's five-point geometric haircuts, the models ran and danced down the catwalk. It was a high point for 'Swinging' London's special relationship with America. When America took on Quant, it progressed the Modernist mission and altered ways in which Fashion would be consumed across continents. In *Fashion's World Cities* these shifts are charted in the section 'Urban Modernity and Urban Orders':

> The significance of designers like Mary Quant was that they showed that cutting-edge fashion could be very different from the Parisian model. In place of the wealthy, elite and mature couture customer Quant promoted the Chelsea Girl, a figure defined by her youth (and her skinny body shape), her casual confidence in the city, and her willingness to experiment with a rapid succession of new looks.[56]

Quant has said, 'Although at the start we made every mistake anybody could, the need was so strong that we couldn't fail.' When she and Plunket Greene opened Bazaar, their passion, to transform the way young people dressed swept many along with them. Her dissatisfaction with conservative, ageing and reactionary Fashion gave her the modernizing zeal to form a business with worldwide manufacturing potential. A copywriter at publishers Pan wrote for their 1967 edition of *Quant by Quant*:

> *Bazaar* – that riveting shop with the offbeat, uncompromising clothes – did more than give fashion a jolt: it uprooted it. Instead of wanting to be old enough to wear Mum's slinky black and pearls, suddenly young trend-setters couldn't wait to get into Mary Quant's mad, challenging gear.[57]

Other ingenious designers, part of this illuminating force, introduced youthful flattering styles to various clothes ranges. Its influence spread to haute couture and department stores. Marion Foale and Sally Tuffin, who dressed Audrey Hepburn for the London-based movie, *Two for the Road*, were inventive and influential in the more expensive end of the market. James Wedge's boutiques Countdown and Top Gear, in the King's Road and Bristol, were taken up with alacrity by the Fashion cognoscenti after an article appeared in *Woman* magazine. The revolutionary tone-setting Biba brought in well-designed clothes and accessories for a new object-of-desire-hungry demographic. Brighton Art College graduate Fashion illustrator Barbara Hulanicki opened a mail order clothing company with her husband, Stephen Fitz-Simon. Biba's Postal Boutique was overwhelmed with orders for a sleeveless gingham shift dress featured in the *Daily Mirror*. Early in her career, Hulanicki also became known for the outfits she designed for Cathy McGowan, presenter of the TV pop music show *Ready, Steady, Go*. Hulanicki and her husband ordered substantial numbers of units and introduced three or four new designs a week. Their Kensington store became an international shopping destination. Christopher Breward, considering the important signifiers of change in the social order, writes:

> the new breed of entrepreneurial retailer looked to the sartorial expertise of their clients for future directions. The divisive categories of service and deference which had formerly prevailed in the field of fashion shopping had become impossibly blurred as consumers and merchandisers defined new trends together.[58]

He reflects on the numerous, if unauthenticated, tales of retailers watching as customers dragged garments into other, new shapes which were then copied by manufacturers on the instructions of the shop owners. He thinks there was a 'wholesale hyping of London's fashion culture as being especially experimental'. With a generation of shoppers hungry for clothes to reflect less restricted lives, and more expansive wallets, to fail to publicize innovations in the capital would have been counterproductive to Fashion's progress. Breward tells of Quant's contribution to the change from distinction for the few, to delight for the many:

> she developed a signature style rooted in the bohemian ambience of Chelsea yet receptive to the desires of affluent young women for a look that echoed social and sexual freedoms.[59]

Ernestine Carter was the most influential Fashion writer in the late 1950s and 1960s. An Ivy League-educated American and curator of Architecture at the Museum of Modern Art in New York, she became a wartime intelligence officer with both US and British Information bureaux. A dearly held conviction that Fashion itself was a serious subject for study has been taken up by writers and curators on both sides of the Atlantic. Mary Blume, writing of Carter's days as Associate editor at the *Sunday Times*, maintained, 'Hers is the only English women's section that is regularly read by New York's fashion powers.' In typically iconoclastic style, Carter had insisted:

> It is given to the fortunate few to be in the right place, at the right time, with the right talent. In recent fashion there are three, Chanel, Dior and Mary Quant.[60]

In declaring Quant's inclusion in that select band, Carter suggests there are similarities between them. Chanel wanted to give distinction and an elegant freedom of movement to those who could afford couture. Dior, as a talented merchandiser, making money for textile magnate Boussac, had a commercial imperative in play. The questioning, rule-breaking Quant had a more ideological agenda than either Dior or Chanel. It depended on responding to the spirit of the age, working with it rather than merely exploiting it. Her Modernist drive inspired her to use new textiles, in new ways, replying to the desire for excitement and action she saw in young women around her. Carter spent the first five years of Bazaar's existence distrusting what she describes as the 'untidy Chelsea Look'. Strangely, coming out as a 'behaviourist' in her memoir *Tongue in Chic*, she thought what she saw was a sign of immorality. She was otherwise persuaded by Quant's dynamism and determination:

> But by 1960 Mary was inventing, no longer just reflecting what she saw on the King's Road. She was creating her own Look – a Look that jolted England out of it conventional attitude towards clothes. She was the first to express a mood that swept the world. That was news.[61]

Sporting miniskirts and Vidal Sassoon's five-point geometric haircuts, the models ran and danced down the catwalk. It was a high point for Swinging London's special relationship with America. When America took on Quant, it progressed the Modernist mission and altered ways in which Fashion would be consumed across continents.

Quant's design talents began to be used in every field of Fashion. The enterprise became Mary Quant Limited, a design company licensing manufacturers in Europe, Australia, Japan and the USA. Carter saw other Fashion careers develop. She spread the message of Britain's Fashion talent and recalls Jean Muir's 'steady progression' to successfully storm the 'bastions of the French *prêt à porter*', with collections made by leading couture ready-to-wear manufacturer Mendès. She writes of other British designers being put 'before trans-Atlantic eyes', of how she showed Tuffin and Foale's work to the American fashion artist Joe Eula. Her list of world-beating designers went from David Sassoon, Gerald McCann, John Bates and Bill Gibb to the 'strange compelling beauty' of Zandra Rhodes and Gina Fratini's 'happy' clothes.

Quant was joined by these inspired and energetic fellow spirits, whose careers transformed the way Fashion developed. As buyer for the 21 Shop at Woollands department store, Knightsbridge, in 1961, Vanessa Denza helped launch key young designers. She opened the Vanessa Frye boutique, Sloane Street (1966–70). In an interview with the V&A in 2006, she recalled the moment:

> There was a feeling that everything was possible. You were not laden with debt, you had time to go out and enjoy life and wear new clothes. Television was in its infancy and you stopped worrying about whether Paris said you had to have a short skirt or a long skirt. All that had gone out of the window.[62]

During the V&A interview, Denza identifies the players, responding to this outburst of youthful enthusiasm, in London at the time:

> The key people were Kiki Byrne, Mary Quant, Foale & Tuffin, Gerald McCann, Ossie Clark, Georgina Linhart, John Bates, Alice Pollock, and then a bit later Rosalind Yehuda. Her knitted clothes were just amazing, but she didn't come into it until about '66–'67 and she was not a Royal College graduate. But I would say she had the most enormous influence at that time. With commercial maturity the Swinging sixties revolution became institutionalised, complete with the trappings of business methods. Barbara Hulinicki followed closely behind. In 1964 she founded Biba – a store which went on to offer a complete fashion lifestyle experience, just as Topshop does on the British high street today.[63]

New world of retail

Denza sought out talent from the Royal College of Art and worked closely with young designers. Her '21' shop sold clothes that were 'simple, zany, not for squares', and she was known as the wunderkind of turnover, able to have an order of a thousand dresses delivered and within a week they would be sold out. Recalling it was 'Like a dam bursting', other retailers followed her lead, with Young Jaeger, Harrods' Way In and Miss Selfridge establishing themselves as household names. 'A whole new world of retail sprang up,' Felicity Green reported, writing of the explosion of buying and selling in Europe and America.

The charm and success of the sixties revolution would be bound to come to an end when it grew to include boutique chains such as Wallis, in King's Road, Vanessa Denza predicted. However, the democratization of Fashion, begun by first-wave designers and boutique owners, could not be halted. Fashion designers, influenced by changes in mood, brought their crusading zeal and egalitarian educations to the high street. Sylvia Ayton's freelance design work from 1959 to 1963 embraced BEA air hostess uniforms, clothing for B. Altman New York, Count Down and Pallisades stores, in London, and a project with the Costume Museum, Bath, England. She designed hats for the film *Freud*, in 1960, and opened the Fulham Road Clothes Shop with Zandra Rhodes in 1964. In 1969 she began as outerwear designer for the Wallis Fashion Group. Women wore her clothes, returning to Wallis season after season, gaining from new customer-led design considerations. Ayton describes how significant these became to the mass market, remembering her aims:

> to make thousands of women feel wonderful by providing garments that are not too boring, too safe, or too extreme but sharp, minimal, very functional, uncontrived, all very easy but with an element of surprise. I am a perfectionist. I care desperately about the shapes and proportions of my designs. I care about every detail, every stitch, button, and buckle.[64]

Her meticulousness meant shoppers could find clothes with appeal to individual personalities, and Wallis became the benchmark for other Fashion chains. During her time with the group Ayton focused on customers' lifestyles. Aware that Fashion is constantly evolving, she set out to interpret the changing needs of the women she was designing for while staying 'creative, experimental, and forward thinking'. She identified individual characteristics in society and responded to the results from her study:

> I design for a type of woman, not for an age group, and I become that woman as I design. I believe there are basically three types of women – the feminine woman, the classic woman, the fashion woman – and I feel she stays that type all of her life, whether she is 16 or 60.[65]

As the Youthquake rocked London, Paris fought back through a group of young designers trained in the couture tradition but open to ideas from Britain and America. Cardin, Courrèges and Saint Laurent set out to woo younger consumers. They launched ready-to-wear boutiques and negotiated concessions in department stores. Their space race creations became objects of desire, available from chic shops and concessions throughout France. The massive post-war baby boom market in the United States saw department stores making millions of dollars from imported London designs. Retailers realized the potential for the boutique concept. In New York home-grown ventures flourished, selling exclusive avant-garde designs to a sophisticated clientele.

Quant's record of events was probably written to make sure the zeitgeist was recorded from her point of view. As a guide for succeeding Fashion designers, it features high up on ex-journalist Luella Bartley's list and is used as a starting point for academic critiques of the times. Christopher Breward's investigations have led to some ambivalence in his interpretation of Quant's mission. His view seems to be that there was forgivable amateurism on the manufacturing and marketing front, and a knowing use of 'camaraderie' for covert customer research on the other. He proposes an alternative to be drawn from Quant's own account, which he quotes:

> I had always wanted the young to have a fashion of their own ... absolutely twentieth century fashion ... but I knew nothing about the fashion business. I didn't think of myself as a designer. I just knew that I wanted to concentrate on finding the right clothes for the young to wear and the right accessories to go with them.[66]

The 'throw-away crudeness' of Quant's stock is contrasted with the more noble aspirations behind the enterprise. Breward sees the Quant project representing 'a kind of freedom that was eminently marketable during that period' and, indeed, one containing the energy and prose-lytizing passion of an aesthetic movement:

> It was full of the possibilities of self-reinvention in a big city that was also in the process of transforming itself from a landscape of Victorian shadows and derelict bomb sites to an Americanized utopia (only partially realized) of glass office blocks and concrete

motorways. This sense of hope and change was further communicated through the avant-garde literature, theatre, and cinema of the
moment, but its most passionate advocates were the real young men
and women, like Plunkett-Green [*sic*] and Quant, who were prepared to invest their talents in the potential of the future.[67]

Alexander Plunket Greene was still proposing that he and Mary
Quant were innovators, experimenting with new ways with Fashion,
when he spoke to me in 1981. I speculated on whether it was more
than a sense of style, and business ability, which had kept the 'design
empire at the top for more than 20 years'. Tempted, like other

*The revolutionary tone-setting Biba, brought in well-designed clothes and
accessories for a new object-of-desire-hungry demographic. Brighton Art
College graduate Fashion illustrator Barbara Hulanicki opened a mail
order clothing company with her husband, Stephen Fitz-Simon. Biba's
Postal Boutique was overwhelmed with orders for a sleeveless gingham shift
dress featured in the* Daily Mirror.

journalists, to ask about the sixties, I was treated to a lively evocation of the times as our black cab sped between Chester and Manchester Airport:

> When we first began it was all duffle coats. There were still ration books, and apart from the basics there was no style. There seemed to be the need for a fashion revolution. In the Sixties and early Seventies, people never seemed to go back home. They were out at other people's bedsits, in discotheques or coffee bars.[68]

Dedicated Fashion executive as ever, he talked of the early eighties economic climate and ways of dealing with that particular downturn:

> Now we're in the midst of a recession we need sharp clothes rather than peasant looks to underpin an optimistic outlook.[69]

Mary Quant, in nostalgic mood, said she had begun designing clothes for students, friends and actors, and remembered that her parents were concerned with whether she would make a living or not. 'I designed with the supreme arrogance of youth but others felt the same,' she told me. She believed her behaviour was perfectly ordinary and that everyone else was very odd:

> When I was little I not only disliked – I resented the clothes I would have to have to wear when I grew up. I used to inherit clothes from my cousin and when I was 11, 12, and 13 it got worse.[70]

It was at this point that APG decided to move back into the present, realizing that the urge to rebel, to re-create, to invent, to make clothes which communicated style and meaning was what his wife had never lost:

> Mary and her team are like French couturiers. We don't take great whacks out of the business. Our first motive is a passionate interest in the goods.[71]

Forty years after *Time* magazine's 1966 'Swinging London' cover, the V&A put on Sixties Fashion. The exhibition featured Mary Quant, Ossie Clark, Pierre Cardin and Paco Rabanne, and categorized the age as a moment of 'innovation and pleasurable consumption'. Quant figures on 46 of the accompanying book's 123 pages. As the 'quintessential Swinging London designer', her clothes are written of as signifiers for the city's resurrection after its wartime desperation and destruction. Hailing its designer as prime mover, Christopher Breward believes that Quant's hessian dress signalled changes in the city beyond impressions carried by *Time* magazine's cartoon images:

> With its short skirt and deceptively simple line, utilizing an extended belt to form a halter-neck fastening with a large buckle worn high on the chest over a polo neck sweater, the ensemble points to the multi faceted version of fashionable femininity promoted by Quant and her generation.[72]

Christopher Breward reads the outfit as a political pamphlet, declaring it the bearer of messages beyond the language of seams, fastenings and belts:

> But stylistically it moved beyond comfort and practicality to suggest Bohemian revolt (in its emphatic use of black), graphic sophistication (in its play with textures, interesting shapes and bold accessorization) and schoolgirl innocence (the dress whose form tends to narrow the hips was worn with a schoolboy cap in matching linen material). It tells us much more about the lifestyles and aspirations of the King's Road habitués than *Time*'s stereotypes.[73]

Commentators and cultural historians see the sixties revolution as the beginning of the end for haute couture. Dick Hebdige felt it was made to seem 'tame' as designers like Quant, Cardin, Paco Rabanne, Courréges and Yves St Laurent developed a 'crossover field' of 'art into pop'. Quant, seeing that more advanced consumer and distribution-led trends were influential, was offering an informed overview by 1966:

> What ready-to-wear does today, the couturiers – even the Paris couturiers – confirm tomorrow. It has happened several times already. I think it will go on happening.[74]

176

It was *British Style Genius*'s intention to find out what makes British fashion and style 'so distinctive and influential'.[75] Mary Quant appeared in the first episode as the 'trail-blazing designer who broke the fashion mould by making clothes for young people'. British high streets have now reached a zenith of democratization, the programme makers claimed. Everyone had the opportunity to identify with the supermodel 'allure' of Kate Moss by buying from her 'collection' at Topshop. The directors thought they should mention that it all 'began with Quant', who was briefly interviewed. Before Quant there was no 'high end style at high street prices'. Only a small elite had access to 'style'. Then 'along came Quant'. Speaking to camera, she was cued to tell the story of the beginning of the revolution:

> There was nothing for young people. I made clothes which could move and could be quite unlike anything else on the market.[76]

So all-embracing was the social transformation in the sixties that we are still in its thrall. The link was made through this short interview with the changes begun by sixties visionaries and the rise and rise of high street Fashion. The scene shifted. In contrast to the lone reformer, filmed in middle distance in the centre of a monochrome set, Kate Moss and Phillip Green laughed together in a Topshop boardroom. Surrounded by post-Modern design and marketing professionals, they talked of scouring European flea markets for inspiration to draw in customers.

American writers Jay and Ellen Diamond's summary of the period covers all the bases:

> London emerged as a fashion capital with Mary Quant's unique designs. Using the Mod look of miniskirts to capture the youth market, her materials included denim, vinyl and coloured flannels all paired with tights.[77]

Quoting the journalist Katherine Betts in their *World of Fashion*, they conclude their assessment of the British Fashion iconoclast:

> When Mary Quant captured the attention of London in the 1960s she was not only introducing the miniskirt, she was responding to the rebellious nature of a new youth culture.[78]

As the 'Youthquake' rocked London, Paris fought back through a group of young designers trained in the couture tradition but open to ideas from Britain and America. Cardin, Courrèges and Saint Laurent set out to woo younger consumers. They launched ready-to-wear boutiques and negotiated concessions in department stores.

In 1967, Quant said, 'Good taste is death. Vulgarity is life.'[79] She was demonstrating the unstoppable rebelliousness which informs her life. Luella Bartley, at *Vogue*'s 90th anniversary celebration, waiting to meet her sixties idol, was 'fizzing with excitement' and anticipation. Claiming a loose affinity for her pretty frocks with Quant's unique creations, she said, 'All my clothes are based on that same groove of great music and street culture.' Quant's response to Bartley's work speaks of her own ideals and motivations:

> Well, I enjoy her stuff like mad. I'm a fan of hers. She's got that gutsy perversity that I like.[80]

178

In January 2009 the Post Office published a series of stamps celebrating 20th-century design. Mary Quant was recognized on a first-class stamp, with one of her most well-known dresses, the Banana Split in black. Choosing to launch the stamps in Carnaby Street, the centre of sixties Fashion, famous British designers were featured, among them Harry Beck (the London Underground map) and Sir Giles Gilbert Scott (the bright red telephone kiosk). In an interview with Jane Garvey from BBC Radio 4 *Woman's Hour*, Mary Quant was introduced as 'synonymous with British fashion, the swinging 60s and, most of all, the miniskirt'. She was thrilled to talk about her inclusion with Britain's other important 20th-century designers. The interview raised spectres of Britain's anti-Modernist attitudes and told of the early interest from America in Quant's label. Although Modernism was not embraced in Britain with open arms, as in America, Scandinavia and other parts of Europe, Mary Quant was a Modern designer whose work was recognized in the United States and then taken up widely at home and abroad. The interview held the key to understanding exactly what had happened and furthers my view of Quant's indisputable genius as a Fashion innovator. Describing the LBD chosen for the stamp's illustration, as if introducing it for the first time and talking of its structure, Quant as Fashion's doyenne comments:

> My favourite, favourite design and it's called Banana Split, because the zipper runs right from high up to the bottom of the hem. It went right up under the chin like a polo neck, even up to your ears and was zipped down. It has a sporty back to it and then it was possible to alter the feel. What we used to do, back then, we drew daisies on peoples' navels and unzipped it.

As one passionate about the ways of designing and making, which is the spell-binding heart of Fashion, Mary Quant began to talk in the language of clothes manufacturing. She spoke of shape, explaining how the dress had no waist seam, was fluted and fell 'well over the body and just clings to the hip top' and flared right out. She was inspired to say:

> So pleased they chose *that* dress. I regard it as a tremendous compliment because it was one of the early ones, which were mass-produced.

Shoppers thought that salesgirls working in Paraphernalia, with Vidal Sassoon next door, were the 'most sophisticated people in the world', who by just working there 'were practically sleeping with Mick Jagger'. Clothes with the Paraphernalia label might be made from plastic and paper and vinyl.

Asked if she could remember the first time she cared about clothes, she said she thought she was 'obviously a monstrous child', explaining that her clothes were inherited from a cousin, which she hated because, 'It wasn't me and that's when it started.' She remembered her mother, whom she described as beautiful and chic but not necessarily paying too much attention to Fashion. Quant thought she had been in disgrace when she cut up a bedspread to make clothes for herself, when she had been in bed with measles. Her incipient Modernism may have been being born when she felt her cousin's clothes were 'too fussy for me'. Complimented on the sharp outfit she was wearing when interviewed on Friday, 9 February 2009, she challenged Jane Garvey's idea that it was not necessary to always be involved with how one looked, saying, 'Do you ever not care? I suppose I care about it. I suppose I think about it, don't you? I see it as one of life's pleasures.' Attempting to explain Quant's 'look' for radio listeners, Garvey thought it 'masculine' with black pin-striped trousers, with waistcoat, deep purple shirt, black leather jacket. Quant brought her Fashion vocabulary back into play, to say how she might mix more formal fabrics with lush feminine ones, adding, 'I like the juxtaposition of the two things.' Asked whether she was saddened when women, reaching a certain age, give up on their image she replied, 'I believe in enjoying life,' but then remembered a time when she was less inclined to be immediately positive:

> I was at the heart of swinging London; in our shop in Chelsea when an American manufacturer came in and said he wanted to take our designs back to America and have the same thing there; planning to manufacture and produce in fantastic quantities. I felt slightly affronted. I thought this is for us, in Chelsea, for Art students, like me. But it didn't take long for me to realise we had anticipated a look and that this is something people want, even in America, people wanted to have our clothes.

Moving on to talk of celebrities from the sixties, and asked whether Paul McCartney had caused girls to faint, Mary Quant recalled that John Lennon had bought his cap from their shop Bazaar, and that the Beatles were frequent visitors. It was so likely that a Beatle might be mobbed that Paul McCartney went to their studio work room because it had become impossible for him to visit their more public shop. Amy Larocca, writing in the *New York* magazine in Spring 2003, noticed another revival of the mini dress. It had first landed, appearing as if from the heavens, when British entrepreneur Paul Young opened his 'spaceship-sleek boutique', Paraphernalia, on 67th Street and Madison Avenue in 1965. Until then stylish clothes were bought from reputable stores – Bonwit Teller, Lord & Taylor, Bergdorf Goodman. Paul Young, in interview, told her, 'Most stores treated young people like they were there to steal something':

Chic boutiques with design ambitions, clothes displayed like art in a gallery, cooler-than-thou young salesgirls, and rock and roll blaring from the speakers – shops that marketed clothes as part of a whole, deliriously amusing lifestyle – didn't exist.[81]

Shoppers thought that salesgirls working in Paraphernalia, with Vidal Sassoon next door, were the 'most sophisticated people in the world', who by just working there 'were practically sleeping with Mick Jagger'. Clothes with the Paraphernalia label might be made from plastic and paper and vinyl. They might glow in the dark, reflect light or grow when watered. Paraphernalia handled fast turnaround, part of the sixties Fashion revolution, with panache:

'If they thought of it Monday', says Andy Jassin, who worked for the boutique's manufacturer, 'it was in the store Friday.'[82]

Nothing in Paraphernalia cost more than $99, then, the price of a ticket to Puerto Rico. André Courrèges, Paco Rabanne and Pierre Cardin were fashioning dresses from white leather and plastic disks but 'most girls with the legs to pull it off were years from affording it'. Paul Young, the JCPenney import controller who helped Quant into the States, was passionate about America and retailing:

You have to figure out a way to make a name for yourself in such a big company and I realized pretty quickly that teenagers didn't have anywhere to go, and that we should focus on them.[83]

He felt there was a strong connection between music and fashion and 'nobody was exploring it':

Young opened a division of Puritan in 1965 and got to work. 'Carl Rosen said I could do the store if it would cost less than $10,000,' Young says. 'So I said sure, and then, of course, once it got rolling, it was too late to stop.' He imported Brits like Mary Quant and Ossie Clark but, most important, sought out young, untested American talent.[84]

As the 'quintessential Swinging London designer', her clothes are written of as signifiers for the city's resurrection after its wartime desperation and destruction. Hailing its designer as prime mover, Christopher Breward believes Quant's hessian dress signalled changes in the city beyond impressions carried by Time *magazine's cartoon images.*

He hired Joel Schumacher, a fashion-school graduate who was then decorating the windows at Bendel's and later went to Hollywood and directed *St. Elmo's Fire*, *Batman Forever* and *Bad Company*. There was also Betsey Johnson, a zany assistant in the art department of *Mademoiselle*, who charmed the staff with the little sweaters and T-shirt dresses she sewed at home. To keep up with the breakneck speed of change, 'Paraphernalia sold clothes that were – literally – perishable.' Marisa Berenson, Elsa Schiaparelli's granddaughter, was among the Manhattan night-time glitterati 'always out' and often found at Paraphernalia during the day. They were attracted by Paul Young's happenings and his international guest list:

> I thought it would be a good idea to have English models so I hired Patti Boyd, who was the girlfriend of George Harrison at the time. I also hired Jean Shrimpton, and then let her and Mary Quant collaborate on a line.[85]

They had a runway in the workroom and a rock-and-roll band. Anjelica Huston, Apollonia, Veruschka and Lauren Hutton showed the frocks. Models, then, worked only on photo shoots, not on catwalks. Berenson remembered:

> The opening of Paraphernalia was the only runway I ever walked, except maybe Halston, And it was really fun.[86]

Paraphernalia sold out completely in the first two weeks, and every day there was an event. Sometimes clothes would not be hanging from racks; they'd be shown only on video. They did everything they could to shake up the status quo. Schumacher tells of Betsey Johnson sticking neon bikinis into tennis-ball cans for packaging. There were dresses made from bright, transparent plastic disks that could be moved around and rearranged. Johnson recollects:

> There will never be another chunk of time of such pure genius, from the invention of pantyhose to landing on the moon to the Pill to the drugs. And it was the first and last time that fashion really, really changed.[87]

The 'bold optimism of that period has an obvious hold on designers' imaginations', Larocca believes. In Spring 2003 Dolce & Gabbana had revived Paraphernalia's silver textiles; Prada had gone 'Twiggy-short and accessorized with geometric plastic jewelry and flat silver sandals'. At Louis Vuitton, Marc Jacobs showed 'bright floral dresses – in rubber'. Larocca discovered that the designer and vintage collector, Anna Sui, 'still dreams about the pleated minidress – black and pale-pink crêpe' that she didn't buy in spite of its 'perfection'. Ellin Salzmann, former Bergdorf Goodman fashion director, believes the 'hottest thing she's ever owned was a white Paraphernalia Mongolian lamb coat'. The store's success led to its downfall. The label became diluted and lost its meaning:

> Debauched socialites and outré Warholians were confronting their inevitable hangovers, and the world was moving on to an era that was far darker.[88]

Young started a Fashion consultancy; opened Escalade, 'Paraphernalia in reverse', bringing American fashion to Londoners. He lent Kenzo £2,000 to make his first store collection and, in liaison with a French company, brought Rei Kawakubo of Comme des Garçons to American and European markets. Schumacher went to Hollywood. Betsey Johnson launched Betsey, Bunky, and Nini on Lexington Avenue with two former Paraphernalia managers and then went into business for herself. Paraphernalia franchises were around until the late seventies, some time after the flagship closed. It was the end of an era for a stunning shopping concept, and for Betsey Johnson, speaking to Larrocca, the beginning of Fashion's move towards post-Modernism:

> 'The whole thing had ended!' Johnson says. 'Everybody was OD'ing.' She lets out a dramatic sigh. 'In the Seventies, everything had to be made of cotton and flowers. I guess it was all right that it ended the way it did. It couldn't have lasted.'[89]

Epochs come and go in Fashion, marked by dreamy scenes, sharp suits, even sharper intakes of breath at first sights of new beauty or shocking novelty. Looking for distinction or trying to free the masses, there are decisive moments when designers change our ways of seeing. There is no doubt that the amateur venture, begun by the Welsh teachers' daughter and the Duke of Bedford's kinsman, meant we would never wear or buy Fashion in the same way again.

Notes

1 British *Vogue*, December 2006.
2 Mary Quant, *Quant by Quant* (London: Pan, 1967), p. 7.
3 Ibid., p. 11.
4 Ibid., p. 17.
5 Ibid., p. 22.
6 Ibid., p. 23.
7 Ibid., p. 19.
8 Ibid., p. 47.
9 Ibid.
10 Ibid., p. 48.
11 Ibid., p. 78.
12 Ibid.
13 Ibid., pp. 78–9.
14 Ibid., p. 79.
15 Ibid., p. 80.
16 Ibid., p. 81.
17 Interview with Sylvia Ayton in 'Out of London, Paris and New York, 1965–1968', Victoria & Albert Museum website, http://www.vam.ac.uk/collections/fashion/features/1960s/exhibition/outoflondon/index.html (accessed 4 May 2009).
18 Valerie Steele, *Fifty Years of Fashion: New Look to Now* (New Haven: Yale University Press, 2006), p. 56.
19 Quant, *Quant*, p. 81.
20 Ibid., p 82.
21 Ibid.
22 Ibid., p. 81.
23 David Wynne Morgan, interview with author, December 2006.
24 Quant, *Quant*, p. 83.
25 Wynne Morgan, interview, 2006.
26 Quant, *Quant*, p. 86,
27 Ibid., p. 87.
28 Ibid., p. 88.
29 Wally Olins, *Corporate Identity: Making Business Strategy Visible through Design* (London: Thames & Hudson), p. 54.
30 Ibid.
31 Note that the Fashion designer Jasper Conran is the couple's son.
32 Quant, *Quant*, p. 95.
33 Ibid., p. 96.
34 Ibid., pp. 96–7.
35 Ibid., p. 132.
36 Ibid., p. 140.

37 Christopher Breward, *Fashion* (Oxford: Oxford University Press, 2003), p. 186.
38 Quant, *Quant*, p. 98.
39 Ibid., p. 100.
40 Ibid., pp. 100–1.
41 Interview with Felicity Green, '1960s Fashion Interviews', Victoria & Albert Museum website, http://www.vam.ac.uk/collections/fashion/features/1960s/interviews/green_interview/index.html (accessed 4 May 2009).
42 Ibid.
43 Ibid.
44 Quant, *Quant*, p. 110.
45 Ibid.
46 Ibid., p. 113.
47 Ibid.
48 Ibid.
49 Ibid., pp. 114–15.
50 Ibid., p. 115.
51 Ibid., p. 115–16.
52 Ibid., p. 119.
53 Ibid., p. 122.
54 Ibid.
55 Ibid.
56 David Gilbert, 'From Paris to Shanghai: The changing geography of fashion's world cities', in *Fashion's World Cities*, ed. Christopher Breward and David Gilbert (Oxford: Berg, 2006), p. 24.
57 Quoted from Frontispiece, *Quant by Quant.*
58 Breward, *Fashion*, p. 150.
59 Ibid., pp. 150–51.
60 Ernestine Carter, quoted at Mary Quant website, http://www.maryquant.co.uk/home.htm (accessed 4 May 2009).
61 Ernestine Carter, *With Tongue in Chic* (London: Michael Joseph, 1974), p. 159.
62 Interview with Vanessa Denza, '1960s Fashion Interviews', Victoria & Albert Museum website, http://www.vam.ac.uk/collections/fashion/features/1960s/interviews/denza_interview/index.html (accessed 4 May 2009).
63 Ibid.
64 Interview with Ayton, V&A website, 2006.
65 Ibid.
66 Quant, *Quant*, p. 48.
67 Breward, *Fashion*, p. 186.
68 Interview with author, 1981.
69 Ibid.
70 Ibid.

71 Ibid.

72 Breward, 'Introduction', *Swinging Sixties*, ed. Christopher Breward, David Gilbert and Jenny Lister (London: V&A, 2006), p. 14.

73 Ibid.

74 Quant, *Quant*.

75 From *British Style Genius*, TV documentary, BBC2, 7 October 2008.

76 Ibid.

77 Jay and Ellen Diamond, *The World of Fashion* (New York: Fairchild, 1999), p. 37.

78 Katherine Betts, US *Vogue*, July 1996, cited by Diamond and Diamond, *The World of Fashion*, p. 55.

79 Quoted at *Sixties Central* website, http://www.geocities.com/fashionavenue/Catwalk/1038/quant.html (accessed 4 May 2009).

80 Quant quoted in British *Vogue*, December 2006.

81 Amy Larocca, 'The house of mod, *New York* magazine, 10 February 2003, http://www.nymag.com/nymetro/shopping/fashion/spring03/n_8337/ (accessed 4 May 2009).

82 Ibid.

83 Ibid.

84 Ibid.

85 Ibid.

86 Ibid.

87 Ibid.

88 Ibid.

89 Ibid.

CHAPTER FIVE

Paul Smith and the global shopping game

Outside of the leisured classes, dress is never linked to the work experienced by the wearer, the whole problem of how clothes are functionalized is ignored ... The garment is always conceived, implicitly, as the particular signifier of a general signified that is exterior to it (epoch, country, social class).

Roland Barthes, *The Fashion System*

Using computerized product-handling systems, full-length cream cashmere coats were sold worldwide through Alexon boutiques in the 1980s. As essentials, from co-ordinated ranges, they would be back on pristine white rails, within days of sale, without the fabric touching the factory floor. Fashion retailing stays ahead by adopting new technologies, and a principal player in these consumerist transformations is Paul Smith. Ingenious at using ever more advanced techniques and technologies for the encouragement of Fashion, he has influenced designers worldwide. His biography is a marketing text in itself – *You Can Find Inspiration In Everything*, full of free give-away products: 'The Bunny', a Paul Smith comic book which includes a board game as time-line for the designer's life; a Friends of the Earth leaflet; a paper pattern for a Paul Smith 'coat of arms' jacket; and a poster picturing and listing all his possessions stored in offices in London and Nottingham. These indicators of the man's gift for promotion are less significant than the clues in the record of Sir Paul's life itself. His understanding of business potential is marked on every page of *You Can Find Inspiration In Everything*: 'We have a wealth of talent in Britain, a gold mine of ideas. There is an industry for clothes but not for fashion. My business is currently about 80 per cent export. The whole design problem in this country goes back to our history.' Paul Smith is a merchant tycoon in the tradition of Arthur Liberty and Terence Conran: British entrepreneurs, importing and exporting *marchandise du terroir*, selling everyone's *objets d'art* back to everyone else. He has re-invented retailing for the 21st century. His sees into our desires and into those of others beyond the British Isles:

> Our priorities are just different from those of the French or the Italians, for example. Here every guy's got a mortgage, a fridge, a colour tv. He likes his football, his cricket and the pub. The same guy in Italy, probably, has a beaten up car and lives at home with his mother until he's in his late twenties. He'll love food and clothes and has more money to spend on both different priorities.[1]

Investigation and enthusiasm are at the heart of Paul Smith's rolling progress. He constantly researches how Fashion is consumed across continents. His empire-building career has fuelled global shopping fervour since he opened his first Nottingham, UK, boutique, in 1967, and a love of novelty and travel inspires his research and observations:

> The French and Italians tend to buy, perhaps, one piece a year – one per season. One good investment piece to be worn with a host of accessories – ties, shirts. So they'll buy a good suit. In most provincial towns, here, you don't even have a good clothes shop.[2]

Creative consumers

Paul Smith's story is well documented. His passion for cycling, his obsessions with photography and collecting, his family history in drapery and retailing, are on record in print and on websites. His role in the promotion of Fashion is part of a very British continuum, which David Gilbert identified, in 'London on Tour', for the V&A's *Swinging Sixties* catalogue. Fashion had become more egalitarian and accessible through the deliberate moves of modernizing designers and retailers in the 1960s. Charting these changes, Gilbert sees them as staging posts on the route to 'fast fashion'. He indicates the moment when 'dresses became simply another look to be knocked out as cheaply as possible in the latest cut-price fabrics, Bri-nylon included' as one of the stops. Beginning with 'multinational firms, off-shore production and planned rapid turnovers in style', they seemed to mark a 'new kind of fashion order that was less controlled and hierarchical and more sensitive to the demands of actively creative consumers'. Recognizing that British and French designers had set out to make money by mass-producing their labels, Gilbert thinks that the most telling move in 1960s London was when Cardin introduced a 'diffusion range at the opening of Miss Selfridge, the first of a new wave of "boutique" chain stores'. He deals with the effect of London's 'Youthquake' and tracks it through more distant latitudes:

> Mod-culture of early 1960s Britain, the designation of cut, line or detail as 'Italian' or 'French', 'Roman' or 'Parisian' was vital in a grammar of style that marked out the fashion sophisticates and true group insiders. However, when popularized, exported to America by the Beatles (never a Mod group proper), these fashions signified simply 'London', just as the term 'Mod' lost its particular meaning crossing the North Atlantic, becoming a catch-all for all that was 'modern' about English popular culture.[3]

Writing of the 'greyness' of the north, Gilbert contrasts it with how 'the excitement of the metropolis' was heralded, leading to the importance of emerging youth cultures in other British cities being downplayed:

> Nottingham in particular saw the development of a strong boutique culture that for a time in the mid-1960s sustained an independent design culture, including Paul Smith's *Birdcage*.[4]

Retailer Paul Smith had always longed for adventure, the thrill of speed and the open road. His parents were very grounded and kept him down to earth. To satisfy his longings for excitement and forgetting his job as a warehouseman, he would dream of the Tour de France, and race across the British Midlands after work. He met his friend Richard Williams, sports writer at *The Guardian*, in Nottingham in 1966. Williams would often stop by Paul Smith's first shop, The Birdcage, to

By 2007 he had been honoured by the Royal Institute of British Architects, having reinstated important city centre buildings and personally supervised the design and setting up of 347 stores and concessions from Knightsbridge to Kyoto. With his operational headquarters firmly established in the city of Nottingham, the flagship store, which opened there in 2005, was the fulfilment of a dream.

examine a 'new batch of button-down shirts or turtleneck sweaters' on his way to cover news stories for the *Nottingham Evening Post*. Williams writes in *You Can Find Inspiration* of Smith's early recollections: ploys to survive testing cycling conditions, like having sheets of brown paper down a shirtfront to keep out the cold, in imitation of heroes like 'Anquetil or Coppi on the Alpe d'Huez':

> ... being among the first to wear the club's new racing shirt, the one that wasn't made of heavy scratchy wool but of silk rayon, designed without food pockets at the front or back because that, just then, was the fashion.[5]

In the section 'Round the Bend', Williams captures the spirit of a young man whose passion for a sport would one day transfer itself to selling objects of desire to the nations of the world:

> Cyclists were as obsessive about the details and the nuances as the people he would come to know later in his life, the ones who threaded red laces through their brown Hush Puppies, or spent decades searching for exactly the right kind of stone-coloured cotton raincoat.[6]

Also for the publication, the cyberpunk author William Gibson's '*a most benevolent marvel*' is translated into Japanese, French, Italian and German. He takes a rapid journey through trans-Atlantic men's apparel, from a Dickensian Petticoat Lane clothes exchange in London, through Moss Bros and Brooks Bros, Ivy League, Ralph Lauren, original Levi's, Oxfam shops to the Indian Raj and R. Newbold. Focusing in on the Nottingham draper's son, he pinpoints Smith's marketable eclecticism:

> Paul Smith's designs seem to emanate from some extraordinary and encyclopaedic awareness of the intensely codified nature of 'Britishness'. It is as though he possesses some inner equivalent of the Houndsditch Clothes Exchange – not a museum but a vast, endlessly recombinant jumble sale, in which all of the artefacts of his nation and culture constantly engage in a mutual exchange of code.[7]

William Gibson's contextualization makes him see Paul Smith's output as a synthesis of Anglo 'pared-down cockney cool' with American newness and discovery.

> To possess a Paul Smith garment is to possess far more, somehow, than the sum total of code embodied in that garment. There is a species of poetry at work here, the equivalent of the literary awareness of the weight of the absent word.[8]

Gibson also comments on the designer's understanding of global idiosyncrasies, which are key to Paul Smith's promotional and marketing stock in trade:

193

> The inhabitants of London and Tokyo, however, are consummate appreciators of 'secret brands'; they act out private dramas of relative consumer-status with a gravitas seldom seen elsewhere.[9]

He tells of the skills of the English and Japanese as traders, describing both nations as fanatics of 'pure information':

> Both the English and the Japanese are brilliant importers. If you want to know what it is that your own country produces that is genuinely excellent, look for what the most obsessively discerning residents of London and Tokyo choose to import.[10]

The relationship between Japan and Britain, as traders, was explored in *British Style Genius* on BBC2 in October 2008. It posed the notion that British style has acquired the status of a religion in Japan; that the country is the foundation of Paul Smith's empire and that he is 'worshipped as a god' there. Paul Smith, filmed lecturing a large group of students on his 86th visit to the country, is there 'to share the secret of his success with another generation'. Smith tells them:

> As with any field of fashion it's about today and tomorrow and you can't rest on your laurels, ever. You've just got to keep moving forward.[11]

We are told that Paul Smith is the most successful Fashion brand in Japan, with clothes that combine British tailoring with a 'dose of British eccentricity which the Japanese love'. The documentary, filmed in March 2008 while an exhibition of English tailoring was on show at the British Embassy in Tokyo, made links between Paul Smith's 'Englishness' and the traditions entrenched in the select premises of Savile Row. Michael Caine, the restaurant-owning London film actor, appeared to back the idea that all men want to look like 'sober, but not flashy', silver-screen heroes, preferably modelled on Ian Fleming's James Bond. In a slightly awkward link, Paul Smith remembered his earlier Nottingham contact with the world of men's apparel:

> I was quite close to all the local tailors in my hometown. I used to spend my lunch hours, probably driving them crazy, watching them cut out a suit or sewing a jacket.[12]

Kawakubo sticks with her original design impetus and is personally involved with the company's graphic design, advertising and shop interiors. Her vision is particularly evidenced in Comme des Garçons' flagship store in Aoyama, Tokyo, which features sensational blue dotted sloping glass exteriors.

In briefly shown shots of Tokyo streets, it was possible to catch sight of Burberry and Asquascutum shop fronts, as we learned that the Savile Row embassy exhibition was designed to promote English tailoring to the rest of the world. The *Style Genius* episode continued, suggesting that one Briton had already 'cornered the market', taking a more colourful and playful approach to the craft of tailoring. We discovered that Paul Smith had become the biggest-selling European Fashion brand in Japan, creating clothes with the 'hallmarks of high-end tailoring, like quality fabrics, attention to detail, presented and packaged with a distinctive character'. Fashion curator and academic Christopher Breward, contributing to the episode, explained Paul Smith's singularity:

> What Paul Smith is very good at is taking visual icons of Britishness
> from the flag, through to the floral print, through to the cricket
> jumper, recognising that they are stereotypes, playing with their
> stereotypical nature and bringing them into the realm of Fashion.
> So you're always aware that Paul Smith has a playful touch but a
> respectful touch as well.[13]

Playfulness is the hallmark of the post-Modern approach, and is
embedded in much of Paul Smith's output and central to his considerations. His diacritical techniques allow him to take particular and dis-
tinguishing features from haute couture or Savile Row and then to give
them a flippant edge for universal delight. William Gibson explains
this indisputably post-Modern talent in an adulatory passage on the
déclassé cuff:

> Paul Smith did this tiny, wonderfully perverse thing with his shirt
> cuffs. All of which for me, so far, had been barrel cuffs but with an
> extra hole on the button side, allowing them to be worn with
> cufflinks.[14]

So Smith is mixing the practical with the decorative, rendering his
shirts useful for leisure or industry, to be worn by workers or sybarites;
by those of independent means, salaried, cash-in-hand, officers or gentlemen. Gibson had been told that the 'so-called convertible' cuff design
was déclassé but admires the fact that Paul Smith's shirts have them.
They seem to be a 'sort of secret trademark' and a characteristic hidden
style option. This signature mark represents Paul Smith's quest to
employ the tropes of men's tailoring and dress for his own and others'
amusement. He adopts them with blithe disregard for any signs of
status he might be subverting. His promotional style is also transparent
and ingenuous. He sticks to tried and tested rules. If it is the charming,
quirky clothes and accessories that the Japanese love, he is happy to
retell the story of their genesis. He talks of how, when he was 24 years
of age, he used a small amount of savings to set up his own first shop
with his then wife, Pauline Denyer, and developed their 'classic with a
twist' collections. In a crazy taxi journey through the centre of Tokyo,
he is filmed explaining how he 'slowly broke down' resistance to his
eccentric ways, in Japan, by always being polite and reliable. He would
then deliver the *Monty Python* moment during presentations, with a

working train set in a briefcase and a rubber chicken. Any unofficial moment during his visit he is seen capturing ideas and images, from every source, in a country whose 'culture still provides him with inspiration'.

Elegant acquisition

When Paul Smith sold 40 per cent of shares in his eponymous company to Japan in 2006, he still retained the control needed to continue to make 'quirky acceptable by tweaking British style'. By 2007 he had been honoured by the Royal Institute of British Architects, having reinstated important city centre buildings and personally supervised the design and setting up of 347 stores and concessions from Knightsbridge to Kyoto. With his operational headquarters firmly established in the city of Nottingham, the flagship store, which opened there in 2005, was the fulfilment of a dream. A profile by Jess Cartner-Morley for *The Guardian* sees Sir Paul Smith as the 'grandee of British fashion', and his elegant acquisition is evoked as a suitable setting:

> Willoughby House is a Grade II listed town house, built in 1738 for the Honourable Rothwell Willoughby and now lovingly restored. It is also a few yards from 10 Byard Lane, the site of Smith's first store, a 12-foot-square windowless room where he started his business in 1970, opening on Saturdays only because of his weekday job.[15]

The Smith empire was divided up in 2006, showing a yearly profit from 13 lines of menswear, womenswear and childrenswear of $26 million (£15 million) in 2005. The sale of 40 per cent of the business was seen as surprising by the Fashion industry but had resulted from Pauline Denyer Smith wanting to relinquish her 25 per cent, as did John Morley, the managing director, whose 15 per cent was included in the deal. Itochu, Smith's principal licensee in Japan, now shares the company with Sir Paul. Although John Morley's shares were sold, his intention was to stay on with the company, while Denyer Smith wished to retire after 35 years. Sir Paul, as designer and chairman, was to retain the 60 per cent 'for the long term'. During London Fashion Week in 2006, Hamish Bowles, European Editor-at-large for *Vogue* US, said:

In menswear Smith has been pivotal. He made 'quirky' acceptable by taking mainstream British dressing and tweaking it, with colour and subtle variations.[16]

Paul Smith is one of Harvey Nichols's best-performing brands, and spokesman Richard Gray took the opportunity to explain its successful positioning and its universal appeal:

He has a sense of what men and women want. That sounds prosaic, but it's very rare and hugely valuable. The ideas are well executed, whether it's the perfect shirtwaist dress for women or the perfect single-breasted jacket for men.[17]

The Paul Smith global phenomenon results from his skills with publicity and marketing, which he is happy to share with colleagues or rivals. In *You Can Find Inspiration*, he talks of the importance of communicating with the Press and of working as part of a team:

I have been lucky with the press, but that is because there is a story to tell. It is very difficult for a lot of companies to find a story at all. If you are making something basic it is difficult to ring a fashion magazine and say 'I've got a grey crew-neck'. They would say, 'so what?' But if your grey crew neck is made from silk, by hand, you may find a way through the reeds to the sea yet again.[18]

Writing of the packaging and presentation imperatives necessary to selling Fashion, he leaves few critical Public Relations techniques out of his counsel:

Graphics are important as is the 'welcome' of your office receptionist, pleasant well-mannered people with a good telephone technique, and, most of all, a broad outlook.[19]

Paul Smith ethos

Absolutely on the button, that liberal civilized quality, found in successful Fashion people, is essential to the Paul Smith ethos. Fashion writers, publicists, advertisers, retailers, all have appetites for news and trends; love of change and development is a given in the professions. During his many flights abroad, he has observed pessimistic characteristics in fellow passengers, which would not be creatively valuable to Fashion:

> They are always worried about the time of their flight, that the food is weird. They should forget such things and just get on and enjoy travelling and try to learn something new.[20]

His understanding of people has influenced his perceptive selection of colleagues. Their Nottingham base is a model for the Industry. A skilled Design Development Manager liaises with Head of Design, collaborating with pattern-cutting managers, supervisors and administrators, pattern cutters, graders and sample machinists. As an example of how British-trained designers feed the industry, the study surrounding Heather Fairhurst, who works in a design development role at Paul Smith, is an ideal case in point. After graduating with a BA in Fashion Design in 1987, she became a boys' and menswear designer for the former Coats Viyella group. Offered an initial post as design assistant with Paul Smith, she decided to focus on technical roles from then on. She told author Helen Gowerek in 2006, 'I made a conscious decision not to design any more and I've never regretted it for a moment.' As Design Development Manager, she motivates and organizes a large and diverse team of people. Her challenging life involves travel to clothing factories in Italy, Portugal, Morocco and India, and she attends the Paris menswear fashion shows twice a year. Echoing Paul Smith's own delight in the Fashion process, Heather Fairhurst expresses these views:

> I enjoy being involved in the development of new collections, travelling, managing the department and motivating people. I really love being in contact with the product, doing fittings and seeing new prototypes. I get a real kick out of seeing patterns being developed. Paul Smith is a very open company: you're encouraged to be yourself, which improves your flow of creativity and helps you get a lot out of people.[21]

However, the spirit of Fashion is tied into the spirit of change and Kawakubo went for something else when she developed Dover Street Market, in London, in September 2004.

Jess Cartner-Morley touched on Smith's skill in motivating colleagues when she interviewed various cognoscenti during London Fashion Week in 2006. In conversation with Stacey Duguid, Executive fashion editor of *Elle*, who worked for Smith as a press officer, she uncovered more of his inspirational management style. She was told: 'Paul involves you in meetings no matter how junior you are. Everyone's opinion matters.' He brought style to our cities and high streets, with a collection of amusements for the advancing middle classes. Fashion shopping is a quest for happiness. There are continuing possibilities for pleasure and the chance to transform ourselves through the acquisition of Fashion. The urge towards this consummation is part of human endeavour. Maslow might usefully have included Fashion shopping as a direct route to self-actualization, in his hierarchy of needs. Watching an Audrey Hepburn film makes a start. The desire for very beautiful things, which David Denby spotted as central to the film *The Devil Wears Prada*, is at the heart of our acquisitiveness, assuaged when we shop. Suzy Menkes, *International Herald Tribune* Fashion editor, identifying the link between retailing Fashion and the influence of a label, believes it is key; at the heart of the Fashion design business and a connection well worth nurturing. A frequent visitor to London, she is an especially strong supporter of Paul Smith's strategies:

> If you go into his Notting Hill shop on a Saturday you will often find him selling shirts. This link between dressing and selling is the missing link for many designers – particularly, British designers.[22]

While Paul Smith was embracing a 'recombinant' post-Modernism and taking it to Japan; Japanese designers were defying prevailing ideas, moved by aesthetic, rather than commercial, compulsions to invent a style defined as anti-Fashion. Avant-garde sculptor and designer Rei Kawakubo instigated the movement. As an advertising stylist, Kawakubo could not find the looks she envisioned for photo shoots, so she began making the outfits for herself. In 1973 she started her own company, Comme des Garçons, subverting French style while questioning ideas of gender and status. At first its women's wear was sold in independent boutiques in Tokyo, and in 1978 menswear was introduced. By 1981 Kawakubo's ambition to become an international designer began to be realized, with a small collection shown at the Hotel Inter-Continental in Paris. Two other important Japanese designers were involved in the Paris circuit: Yohji Yamamoto, in 1981, and Issey Miyake, who had been showing there since 1973:

> At the beginning of the 1980s, the placement of Tokyo on the fashion map became even more pronounced when the three controversial avant-garde Japanese designers, Issey Miyake, Yohji Yamamoto and Rei Kawakubo of Comme des Garçons, rocked the Paris fashion world by introducing clothes that were creative and unconventional to say the least, and their designs were definitely not Western.[23]

The inventive genius Schiaparelli put on a spectacle, only loosely related to shopping, when she brought her aristocratic Italian vision to Paris in 1927. Michael Bracewell's star-struck overview, in the Independent on Sunday *in August 2004, sees her as an empress of Fashion.*

Making connections between the successful Japanese car market and Fashion in 2006, Akira Miura, Editor-at-large Japan edition *Women's Wear Daily*, expressed the idea that Hanae Mori, Yohji Yamamoto, Issey Miyake and Rei Kawakubo were the 'dazzling' designers who had encouraged 'the cloistered world of high fashion to look East'. A subtle Fashion invasion was taking off. Toyota introduced the Corona sedan to the US in 1965, just as Hanae Mori presented her first collection in New York. It was a critical and commercial success as her 'Japanese aesthetics' blended with Western forms and went on sale at important department stores. She opened boutiques in New York and Paris and became the first Asian to join the exclusive Chambre Syndicale de la Haute Couture. Her reputation opened minds to the groundbreaking work and international style of later Japanese designers Issey Miyake, Rei Kawakubo and Yohji Yamamoto, whose creativity left 'indelible impressions' and indicated that:

> Asia could be a wellspring of inspiration, not just a base for textile mills and clothing factories.[24]

Miyake's stunning creations, 'functional yet futuristic', were frequently sculpted from a single piece of cloth. His influence spread to become a brand stamped on 'luggage, home furnishings, even bicycles'. Yohji Yamamoto had been designing avant-garde clothing since his 'collection of elegant women's fashions based on men's garments' in the 1970s. He was approached by Paris fashion houses but stayed in Tokyo, where he mentors his daughter, Limi, whose work is featured in 21st-century Tokyo Collections. Writing of how Comme des Garçons became a global phenomenon in the 1980s, Akira Miura tells of how Rei Kawakubo brought her austere garments to the Paris catwalks in 1981, where they were seen as 'almost anti-fashion'. Together, the influence of Yamamoto and Kawakubo was so far-reaching that since then Fashion has been identified as either 'before' or 'after' Comme des Garçons. Kawakubo told Miura, in 2006, that after reviewing a substantial number of her earlier pieces there was much she would 'happily discard', which prompted the *WWD* journalist to conclude:

> In an industry where reinvention and change is the only constant, that very un-Japanese dissatisfaction with the status quo has been an indispensable trait for all four of Japan's great fashion iconoclasts.[25]

Kawakubo sticks with her original design impetus and is personally involved with the company's graphic design, advertising and shop interiors. Her vision is particularly evidenced in Comme des Garçons' flagship store in Aoyama, Tokyo, which features sensational blue dotted sloping glass exteriors. In line with major couture designers, CdG began selling scent in 1994 and is an established label on the Place Vendôme in Paris.

Kawakubo brought inventions, slick as the haiku, to the retail world. In 2004, she opened the first 'guerilla' store in Berlin. A shop or market is located in a less than fashionable area, using a small budget, and is run for just one year. Setting up a market as a temporary feature in this way often happens in Japanese towns or villages. Allying the concept to guerrilla warfare, when crack forces, hiding away in the hills, dramatically descend onto civilized spaces, Kawakubo brought excitement to shopping. These Fashion invasions have taken place in Athens, Beirut, The Hague, Helsinki, Hong Kong, Krakow, Reykjavik, Singapore, Stockholm and Warsaw.

The running of a simple store for a limited period is quite common in Japan, where they often fill up undeveloped space in city centres. However, the spirit of Fashion is tied into the spirit of change, and Kawakubo went for something else when she developed Dover Street Market, in London, in September 2004. Selling mostly Comme Des Garçons, she also invites other designers to take part. Paul Davies from Purple PR writes that DSM is a place 'where various creators from various fields gather together and encounter each other in an ongoing atmosphere of beautiful chaos':

> Disorder dominates, with interior spaces looking as if the builders left prematurely. Customers are encouraged to investigate every nook for hidden gems. Makeshift huts appear temporary yet contain the operational tools for certain floors. On other levels, invited designers host their designated spaces. And, in the biannual Tachiagari that launches each season, they join the store in reconfiguring the building.[26]

Fashion capitals

Fashion's World Cities, which investigates the idea of how cities gain importance through their trade in Fashion, came out of a project involving a group of international writers and academics. Their story follows the rise of Fashion, since its inception, as our towns and cities grew to house the emerging bourgeoisie in the 19th century. It tells of the working quarters of craftsmen and craftswomen, established to create garments for our post-peasant ancestors. People who had left the 'land' behind them were re-imagined as professionals, entrepreneurs, administrators and merchants. It pans in on these centres, examining them as staging posts on a network of global shopping routes. Starting with the premise that 'London's West End is a key location in national and global cultures of fashion', it suggests that the city's 18th- and 19th-century shops became 'a focus for generations of fashion producers and consumers'. They held the key to how the world displayed and promoted goods, allowing 'individuals [to] construct their social identities'. *Fashion's World Cities* crystallizes the notion that we incorporate a sense of a city into our commercial thinking. When innovative designers devise experiences as extensions to their salons or ateliers, they open up the world of haute couture to a wider demographic. The inventive genius Schiaparelli put on a spectacle, only loosely related to shopping, when she brought her aristocratic Italian vision to Paris in 1936. Michael Bracewell's star-struck overview, in the *Independent on Sunday* in August 2004, sees her as an empress of Fashion:

> The middle to late Thirties saw the imperial phase of Schiaparelli's career. Her salon on the Place Vendôme might be deemed the precursor of today's 'concept stores', such as Colette in the Rue Saint-Honoré. Part gallery, part shop, the interior replicated the landscape of Schiaparelli's principal imagery: the perfume salon featured an outsized bird-cage as well as furnishings embroidered with Schiaparelli's personal 'logo' – the Ursa Major astronomical constellation (which was also described by the moles on Schiaparelli's face).[27]

New York, Paris, London, Milan, Tokyo carry such strong individual identities that they can be used as effortless denotation for promotion. *Fashion's World Cities* recognizes that Fashion uses places to mark designers and their collections: *Liberty of London, Diorlywood, DKNY.* The 'idea of a fashion capital' began over two hundred years ago when Paris was promoted as a centre of style. So established is Paris as a city signifying Fashion that it can be used to represent elan across a spectrum of commodities, from Yves Saint Laurent's 'Parisienne' handbag to Vosges's chocolate drink 'Couture Cocoa la Parisienne'. Evocations from cinema, Fashion weeks, couture shows from the French capital's recent past, are used as markers and, it is said, it was here that the idea of shopping for pleasure began.

*Here was the space which witnessed the birth of the flâneur and the flâneuse
– the strollers, the sybarites, the voyeurs, aristocrats or bourgeoisie who wish
to be seen as life's onlookers.*

In Montmartre there is a magical place, where international shoppers
buy ribbon or buttons, which has been saved from extinction by a
Marxist philosopher. Making a 'Pilgrimage to Cathedrals of Commerce'
for the *New York Times*, Richard B. Woodward noticed 'a renewed vigor'
around the 19th-century shopping arcade, Passage des Panoramas.
Described as 'inner boulevards' in an illustrated guide from 1852, it
was once the place for *le tout Paris* to be:

> Lining both sides of these corridors, which get their light from
> above, are the most elegant shops, so that the arcade is a city, a
> world in miniature, in which customers will find everything they
> need[28]

Constructed in 1823 and opened to the public three years later, the arcades became popular with Parisians. Influencing every galleria and shopping mall since, they were soon superseded by the mid-19th-century department store. These developments led to the demise of *fin de siècle* arcades both in Paris and in other parts of Europe. Fortunately, as shopping became the sport du jour in the latter part of the 20th century, historic malls were re-evaluated. Explaining that the French did a sumptuous restoration on the Galerie Colbert at the start of this century's first decade, Woodward writes of the galleria's role in promoting French style to Parisians and Fashion tourists:

> It is now stocked with high-end fashion boutiques, including Nathalie Garçon and Jean-Paul Gaultier; fun places to eat and drink, Bistrot Vivienne, La Bougainville and the sybaritic À Priori Thé, one of the oldest wine stores in Paris, Legrand Filles & Fils, and an excellent photography gallery, Serge Plantureux.[29]

Here was the space which witnessed the birth of the *flâneur* and the *flâneuse*. These are the strollers, the sybarites, the voyeurs, aristocrats or bourgeoisie who wish to be seen as life's onlookers; those with time on their hands, ready to critique and be critiqued. A pursuit embraced by poseurs, those who like to appear en vogue, it is the greatest fun to be seen as a casual consumer of Fashion without actually buying. The arcades of Paris were the first places where this phenomenon was identified, from a theory developed and advanced by the German literary and cultural critic Walter Benjamin. For the 13 years before his death in 1940, he speculated around questions of Modernity, using the arcades and their promenaders as the demographic. He recognized an ambiguity as visitors were both indoors and walking on the street, and also in the way they presented themselves, observed and observing, in the *flânerie*. He believed what he saw gave him insights into aspects of Fashion, boredom, advertising, prostitution and progress. His project has inspired critical thinkers, and it legitimized the movement to preserve the arcades in the 1970s and 1980s:

> He is as responsible as any urban planner for their present adoration and recovery. In an irony that he might not have appreciated, and that could perhaps only have happened in Paris, this fierce Marxist critic of the bourgeoisie has made shopping here an intellectual pursuit and unquestionably fashionable again.[30]

Paris is one of the 21st-century Fashion capitals with a mark and identity prized by promoters of tourism and Fashion. Important cultural assets from Milan to Shanghai, Los Angeles to Mumbai, with histories which have become part of Fashion's narrative, through production and consumption, pick up on its éclat.

Angela McRobbie traced the careers of young designers in the 1980s and 1990s in *British Fashion Design: Rag Trade or Image Industry?* and saw having an outlet in Hong Kong as a sign of success for new graduates. When Hong Kong became part of China in 1997, returned from its British protectorate status, it was subject to scrutiny by the Fashion industry as a burgeoning Fashion capital. During its 2007 Fashion Week, the Hong Kong Trade Development Council announced how it had prepared for the event:

> The TDC has organised 65 missions and more than 2,600 VIPs for Hong Kong Fashion Week, along with 64 missions and more than 2,100 VIPs for World Boutique. These include buying representatives from Spain's El Corte Ingles, Mango and the Cortefiel Group, Australia's Cotton On, K Mart and Zip Fashion House, Canada's Marie Claire Boutiques and Le Château, and Japanese department store Mitsukoshi.[31]

Jay and Ellen Diamond, for *The World of Fashion* in 1999, considered that Hong Kong had made 'significant strides in bringing its own apparel collections to the world of fashion', but that 'it is their ability to produce garments at low prices that makes them an important part of the field'. Bringing their elegant pragmatism to their overview, they explain that credible, happening, labels like Armani, Calvin Klein and Liz Claiborne all have goods made in Hong Kong. They believe the reason for this success is that 'few countries can offer such expert tailoring at such modest costs':

> The fashion excitement is balanced by the unpredictable implications of Hong Kong's return to China in 1997. This transition from a government which believes in free enterprise to one that has a history of tight control on business, leaves many unanswered questions.[32]

They add that the stipulation set out between Hong Kong and China might mean that Hong Kong would not be able to function

Playing for Italian team AC Milan is seen as a trophy opportunity for an international footballer, and in 2009, via Madrid and Los Angeles, the Beckhams achieved this sporting prize and sensational shopping prospect.

autonomously, from China, even though the trading regulations are laid down for 50 years. They believe this commercial model will be closely watched by the Fashion industry. Hilary Hollingworth, Senior Fashion lecturer at Huddersfield University, after a research visit to the city, told me:

> Hong Kong is a fashion city in a rather different way to New York or London. It is important because so many Fashion people go there and go through it. Ideas come, not necessarily from the runway, but from the ambience and the fact that all fashion in the world is because of manufacturing. Yes, it's a well kept secret that it's a place of inspiration. In a department store we overheard two American buyers looking at Dorothy bags, which are very old-fashioned, talking about getting them made for the American market. It's significant that WGSN has an office there. With the numbers passing through and the Chinese market, combining with western

influences, it could be destined to become a fashion city in the same way as Paris, Milan or Rome.[33]

More than 400 Designer labels were seen at World Boutique, Hong Kong Fashion Week, for Fall/Winter 2007, which attracted over 1,500 exhibitors from 24 countries and regions. Showing collections from Toppy, Episode, Girdano, G2000 and Goldlion, there were new designers emerging as creative forces: William Tang, Lulu Cheung, Ben Yeung and Allan Chiu.

New York has played a lead role in promoting Fashion to all of the Americas. Its position on the edge of the Atlantic, as the first port of call for European, Russian and Scandinavian immigrants and visitors, makes it wonderfully urbane and exciting. Decisive moments in its history have led to its commanding place in Fashion's narrative. Norma Rantisi, in *Fashion's World Cities*, explains 'how New York stole Modern Fashion'. Influential rich merchants, in the elite 5th Avenue shopping precincts in the early 20th century, wanted to maintain an exclusive feel to the eastern half of that Midtown section. In 1916 they had a zoning system imposed by the City, so that:

> Manufacturers congregated in the western half of the Midtown area to benefit from the Midtown amenities and remain close to the stores, creating a space of production adjacent to – though separate from – the pre-eminent space of consumption in the city.[34]

Cultural powerhouse

A decisive move in Fashion's promotion was the setting up of *Women's Wear Daily*, an unparalleled source of information on market trends, which began in 1910 to report on workers' strikes. It has kept the Fashion industry up to date ever since. To deal with the aspirations of a growing bourgeoisie, more garment workers needed training. To educate new recruits, design and production courses were set up at the Pratt Institute in 1888 and at the Parsons School of Design in 1906. New York was indeed powerfully placed to become the city which 'stole modern fashion'. Buying offices were established, so manufacturers and buyers could liaise. By the late 1920s the consumer Press, *Vogue* and *Harper's*, were using photography and advertisements in their magazines:

cultivating a homogeneous (or 'mass') consumer market across the USA that could sustain large volumes of ready-to-wear production.[35]

Vogue's avowed intent, in the purposeful hands of editor Edna Woolman Chase, was to stamp the idea of the capital on women throughout the States by keeping them informed about 'what the smart women of New York were buying'. New York's smart set had more and more places to be seen, in their newly acquired, *Vogue*-approved, ensembles. As New York became a cultural powerhouse with the establishment of Carnegie Hall, the Metropolitan Museum of Art and the Guggenheim Foundation, there began a social calendar of unrivalled glamour. A vibrant department-store way of life in place at Macy's, Bendell's and Bloomingdales was also part of the scene. Although Paris regained its Fashion status after WWII, New York found itself with a 'set of industry relations that could produce and endorse uniquely local designs' and a heritage to challenge that of other capitals:

> As New York was becoming synonymous with style, the industry was establishing its place within the international fashion circuit.[36]

Up until the 1960s, American Fashion designers were treated as backroom assistants, lacking identities and labels, and therefore not used to promote products. Bill Blass and Ralph Lauren appeared out of the shadows:

> opening their own operations and capitalizing on their roles as fashion originators to distinguish themselves as well as their products to cater to new market demands.[37]

At this time image makers began to be employed to develop designers' profiles, using their lifestyles to promote the cult of personality through public appearances and 'exclusive' interviews in a flourishing consumer media. For Klein, what began as a designer-led signature label, promoted through a well-reported social life with other celebrities, became a multimillion-dollar organization with groundbreaking campaigns held across the world.

By the 1980s and 1990s, popular marketing tools included brand logos (such as CK or DKNY), multiple-page advertisements in the established magazines such as *Vogue* (at a price of no less than 6,000 dollars per page), and public ads, such as billboards in New York's Times Square.[38]

Calvin Klein Collection stores were opened in Paris, Seoul and Taipei, with an extraordinarily extravagant version – cK Calvin Klein stores – in Hong Kong, Milan and Kuwait City. Only one Collection store is now operated by CKI but the New York store, which serves as the company's flagship at 654 Madison Avenue, remains open still today. Partners maintain Calvin Klein Collection stores in Milan, Beijing and Dubai. Started in 1968 and now owned by Phillips-Van Heusen, the company gave its A/W 2006 collections a runway presentation in 8,600 square feet (800 m²) of showroom space, seating 600 people, at 205 West 39th Street, Times Square South, Calvin Klein's headquarters since 1978.

She surrounds herself with the talented 'whose job is to translate her themes, concepts and especially her taste into clothes that bear the Prada name'.

Christine Sorensen, in *Fashion Marketing*, describes Milan as 'the other fashion capital of Europe', having 'fewer well-known designers' than Paris but with a vivacious idiosyncratic retailing culture as stimulus for young designers. Milan's reputation as the city of prêt-à-porter rests on its influence in the development of 'fast fashion', as it capitalized on the concept of 'made in Italy'[39] to mean worth buying for the quality of its fabric and make. Simona Segre Reinach describes the zenith of this tendency as she examines the moment when ready-to-wear met with moda Italian. She revisited the centre of its evolution in the light of 'emerging cultures of fashion'. She realized with the global take-up of 'fast fashion', drawing on the 'very pace of transnational industry', that the city needed to be poised to react:

> Milan, being the city that hosted the rise of modern prêt-à-porter, is especially sensitive to this crisis.[40]

Milan's hold on Fashion rests on its ability to be seen as the principal shopping destination in the world. Ever since Manchester United manager Alex Ferguson was said to have thrown a boot at David Beckham's head, the British Press have been speculating on how his wife, ex-Spice Girl ('I'll Tell You What I Want') Victoria, would deal with being a bus ride away from Fashion's shopping nirvana. Playing for Italian team AC Milan is seen as a trophy opportunity for an international footballer, and in 2009, via Madrid and Los Angeles, the Beckhams achieved this sporting prize and sensational shopping prospect. Milan's commanding place in Fashion's story has been achieved through corporate zeal, drawing on creative spirits for its various resurgences. In 2005 Segre Reinach thought it no coincidence that

> the endangered Milan fashion industry is looking again at design, as an example of a sector that has been able to evolve and shape its own destiny rather than simply react to events.[41]

Milan has been able to gather its strengths in manufacturing and service industries 'ahead of other Italian cities'. It is a model for the Fashion industry, worldwide. Segre Reinach explains how it draws on its history as an industrial powerhouse and takes on new communication techniques. She delights in the Italian regional system, writing of specialized districts – Como for silk, Biella for wool, Carpi for knitwear, Castelgoffredo for hosiery and the Italian Marches for footwear:

> On the other hand, Milan was also the leading Italian centre for communications; commercial TV channels started up in Milan, the editorial staffs of the leading fashion press were in Milan, as were the numerous advertising agencies and PR studios.[42]

Political activist

As a world style leader, Prada holds the sceptre. Its current leader, Miuccia Prada, is a Milanese girl from a 'good middle-class background'. Her family were luxury luggage makers. Her companion Milanese – Armani, Versace, Krizia, Missoni and Coveri – have various other pedigrees. Her skills are located in interpretation and promotion. She surrounds herself with the talented 'whose job is to translate her themes, concepts and especially her taste into clothes that bear the Prada name'. Her extraordinary career did not take off in her home city:

> Only after having made their name in the United States, did Miuccia Prada and her husband Patrizio Bertelli also make their mark in Milan.[43]

Influential members of the Fashion Press walked out of her first Fashion shows in Milan. Her history as a political scientist and a CP member may have antagonized over-sensitive Italian cronisti. She was only able to woo her hometown back after New York had acclaimed her. Her intellectual approaches are picked up for this *Vogue* online snapshot:

> Miuccia Prada is a woman's designer. She designs clothes that take account of a woman's curves, at the same time communicating intelligence as well as a sense of fun.[44]

Segre Reinach believes that Prada, one-time political activist and mime artist, was surfing 'the wave of the crisis in prêt-à-porter' which she had 'astutely anticipated' even when it was 'still in the distance':

> At the end of the age of the democratization of fashion and the heroic times of the 'summons to show', Prada presented herself as a producer of elite, cerebral luxury.[45]

Milan has come up with a series of contingency plans, Machiavellian strategies to deal with a commercial world in a state of flux. It has admitted losing its supremacy and drawn up blueprints for change. Developing ways forward at its Milano di Moda conference in 2005, planners expressed intentions to alter the way Fashion would be transmitted, through the Fashion show, to the world. From then on, it was agreed, the shows would take place over fewer, but more action-packed, days 'to give journalists and buyers the time to travel between the increasingly numerous fashion weeks in the different cities throughout the world'. Importantly, the collections to be shown would be from the current season, 'so as not to give time for fast fashion protagonists to copy the models'.[46]

Carine Roitfeld, editor of French Vogue, *was asked to weave her magic over Prada's Avenue Montaigne Paris location. Known for her ability to 'mix street culture, and society, while avoiding the caricatures, which define both worlds', Roitfeld typifies the haute bourgeoisie who occupy, and who have always occupied, Paris.*

Fashion journalism

When in the 1980s Felicity Green wondered how she had been able to keep her 1960s readers en vogue without the help of stylists, Fashion PRs or specialist photographers, she could not have predicted how sophisticated the practice of Fashion journalism would become today. Fashion promoters now direct their communicators through hazardous trend oceans, briefing them on market research, designers' moods, manufacturing economics and new ventures. No self-respecting commentator would leave home without being fully briefed by agents and any number of useful guides. Concluding that the industry's communication chain has been totally refashioned as a result of the global digital revolution, authors Kathryn McKelvey and Janine Munslow, in *Fashion Forecasting*, explain how these technological marvels can be drawn on to develop the Fashion industry's full potential. They write of the numerous resources available to designers, publicists, stylists, visual merchandisers, marketing creatives, PR and Advertising professionals for campaigns and strategies. They recognize how influential continuing technological advances are to Fashion and its promotion, and provide ways to capitalize on them. They undertook research to assess 'the impact of emerging digital technologies on the existing prediction industry' and discovered services which are grasping 'the potential of the Internet as a hub for multidisciplinary design exchange and broadcast'.[47]

Movers and shakers like Miuccia Prada are constantly keeping up not just with change, but with those who are, noticeably, keeping up themselves. In 2009 she invited Alex White of *W* magazine to make over her Lower Broadway store in Manhattan. When the label held its Iconoclast party to show the results of the liaison, online *Fashion Week Daily*, headlining the piece 'Inside Prada's Bedroom', felt it was 'all about the clothes'

> Prada's Iconoclast party was less the celebrity-driven soirée of the past and more a celebration of true fashion, with *W*'s Alex White taking over as guest stylist for the store. The collage-like wall of the SoHo flagship was reminiscent of a Richard Prince painting. Piles of shoes were displayed on the top floor, resembling a boudoir in homage to their Spring collection of louche separates.[48]

Katie Grand, whose magazine *Love* had recently launched, when invited to re-style *Prada* in Bond Street, London, in 2009, took the whole cross-marketing, multimedia, mixed-genre commission to keep the Italian label on the international map as an opportunity to party. Writing a diary for *Times* online, she described her social whirl:

> Monday morning. Hang on. Where was I? *Prada,* designing its Bond Street store. In at 10am, moving mannequins, changing crocodile gloves to knitted gloves and white beaded sandals to men's lace-ups. My friend, the photographer David Sims, has made a film of skateboarding mannequins to be shown on screens in the store.[49]

Olivier Rizzo of *V* and *Arena Homme Plus*, given the store in Milan to re-stage, might have been more circumspect. He has a serious reputation in Fashion's communication field to maintain. Stylist, consultant and freelance fashion editor Rizzo has worked with photographers Willy Vanderperre, Mert Alas & Marcus Piggot, Steven Klein and Alasdair McLellan. His creations and re-creations are published in *Arena Homme Plus*, *L'Uomo Vogue*, *Vogue Hommes International*, *Numéro Homme*, *POP*, *i-D Magazine*, *V-Magazine*, *V-Man* and *Vogue Nippon*. Carine Roitfeld, editor of French *Vogue*, was asked to weave her magic over Prada's Avenue Montaigne Paris location. Known for her ability to 'mix street culture and society while avoiding the caricatures which define both worlds', Roitfeld typifies the haute bourgeoisie who occupy, and have always occupied, Paris. After her daughter was featured in Italian *Vogue Bambini*, photographed by Mario Testino, in 1990, Roitfeld began working with him, in partnership, doing advertising work as well as shoots for American and French *Vogue*. Roitfeld became consultant and Muse to Tom Ford at Gucci, and Yves Saint Laurent, for six years. She began editing French *Vogue* in 2001 and has contributed to the images of Gucci, Missoni, Versace, Yves Saint-Laurent and Calvin Klein. Jess Cartner-Morley, writing for *The Guardian*, uses her as a marker for a Fashion world stereotype:

> In the boarding-school atmosphere that pervades the fashion industry, Roitfeld was already the sexiest sixth-former, the one all the other girls wanted to be; now she has got everyone wondering whether she just might be the smartest, too.[50]

Although the entrepreneur Sir Philip Green was said to have lost £500 million from his Fashion retailing businesses in the global financial downturn by April 2009, his hopes were high for a new Topshop flagship store opening in New York around the same time. He was 'visibly excited' by the results of the conversion of the four-storey Lower Manhattan space, which had been beset with difficulties including fire, floods, building delays and complaints from neighbours. Doing a bit of a Paul Smith for the BBC, he told Greg Wood, 'The pillars here are the originals.' Clearly delighting in the suitability of the building for retailing, he quickly moved on from projecting himself as a conservationist to what he loves most – the selling opportunities:

> What's wonderful is to be able to restore a 100-year-old building. And as a retailer you've got a lot of height and light. Where would you ever believe that an escalator could become a creative part of the building?[51]

Wood was interested in the size of the risk being taken by Philip Green. Saying that the world's Fashion market was at its most competi-

Ahead of the opening, it was revealed that Sarah Brown, with her husband Prime Minister Gordon Brown, on his first state visit with newly installed President Barack Obama in Washington, took gifts for the family. Included in her presents were a Topshop dress each for Malia and Sasha.

tive – 'US shoppers are reining back their spending and clothing sales have spiralled downwards' – he suggested that other British retailers had 'come to grief in America'. Green told him:

> If I think of all the other British retailers who have been here, they haven't had enough differential – a reason to be here.[52]

Green learns from their experiences and plans for perhaps 12 or 15 more flagship stores in the US. The New York opening no doubt swelled online sales across the world, as global Media turned out to the give their seal of approval to the venture. Gina Kelly, Fashion Director at *17* magazine, thought that although the recession was hitting readers hard, 'girls still loved to shop'. Wood took a positive view of the launch. He saw the store's arrival as 'sound economics at work', developed by Green. The successful retailing giant's career had begun by importing Fashion's cause célèbre, the universal denim blue jean. His holding company, Arcadia, with assets Burton, Dorothy Perkins, Miss Selfridge and Wallis with Topshop and Topman, ran 2,500 UK shops with 30 outlets overseas in 2009. His belief, expressed on BBC Radio 4's *Straight to the Top* at the time of his New York adventure, was that the most important thing in Fashion retailing was getting the supply chain in order. Knowing customers want to see new things each time they shop, he told the BBC, 'Speed is more important than price.' Ahead of the opening, it was revealed that Sarah Brown, with her husband Prime Minister Gordon Brown, on his first state visit with newly installed President Barack Obama in Washington, took gifts for the family. Included in her presents were a Topshop dress each for Malia and Sasha, which a blogger on the *Mrs.O* site, dedicated to Michelle Obama, approved:

> Mrs Brown made her gifts personal by giving the girls Top Shop dresses (with matching necklaces) [which means she would have had her staff go to the trouble of finding the girls' sizes] and a selection of books by British authors.[53]

During the anniversary of the British department store Selfridges, in 2009, a publication celebrating a hundred years of *Art, Life and Shopping* carried an investigation, 'Why do we shop?', in the form of an interview between journalist Harriet Quick and psychotherapist Susie Orbach. Quick, playing with the idea of fantasy and transformation through Fashion, discovered:

> Daydreaming in this sense, is a way of placing oneself in the group
> or sub-group that you imagine you want to be in. In my day we
> had Biba and it was a way of breaking with convention to imagine,
> then buy and wear that kind of clothing. It is more complex now
> because the demand is to be so many people at once: one can be a
> cowgirl and sophisticate, diva and secretary.[54]

Quick decided to check on the archetypes which occur in Fashion.
She wondered about the 'romantic princess in a love story at Galliano,
the urban warrior at McQueen and Balenciaga, the goddess at Sophia
Kokasalaki and Versace, the coquette, the femme fatale' and so on. She
wanted to know what their perpetual attraction was. Why were they
so 'resilient despite our changing lives?'. Susie Orbach spoke of the
fairy tales which occur in various cultures, seeing them as the 'emotional edifice that drives romance and self-identity', and unsurprised
by their appropriation as 'decorative stories of designers'. She sees that
shopping for clothes is an emotional journey. Each excursion offers the
chance of new friendships for short or lasting relationships. Those who
sell Fashion in the amusement arcade of the shopping gallery, the
department store, the charity shop or online, understand these longings
and are prepared to share their secrets with us. Mary Portas, the Fashion
entrepreneur named 'Mary, Queen of Shops' for a British television
series, is now famous for showing small, independent, failing retailers
how to cut it. Her passion to encourage good practice, good service
and small designers in small boutiques was broadcast to an entranced
nation in 2007/8. Her outspoken dynamism had helped her turn
Harvey Nichols into a modern Fashion powerhouse in the 1980s. She
persuaded the store's owners to use younger designers, and organized
free publicity in the BBC's *Absolutely Fabulous* series in the 1990s, after
giving promising writer and star of the show Jennifer Saunders the run
of the store, for research, if she name-checked the business. Her persuasive powers are in demand, globally, to make sure Fashion retailing
is influential in world trade.

Renewed popularity

Reliably tasteful, with a loyal following, Jaeger's stylishness was picked
up by the Fashion Media to enjoy an interesting turnaround in its for-
tunes at the start of this century, its strategy to make clothes for its

Natalie Massenet became Britain's 98th richest woman through her on-line designer shopping website, Net-a-porter. *She has devised a way of shopping for the 'time poor, cash rich'. Certainly branded French, even Paris, possibly Milan, by its clever name,* Net-a-porter *sells every label worth reciting, from Adidas, by Stella McCartney, to Zac Posen and Zimmerman.*

targeted demographic, but with one clever maverick piece in each collection, paying off. Celebrating its 125th anniversary in 2009 with a limited edition collection inspired by past designs, chief executive Harold Tillman was reassuringly confident about the industry: 'Fashion always improves in a downturn.' Worn by Prime Minister's wife ex-PR supremo Sarah Brown, Jaeger is taking its renewed popularity, seriously and making appointments to secure its future. Belinda Earl, Group Chief Executive, commenting on design director Stuart Stockdale's arrival at Jaeger in 2008, said:

> Stuart's broad international experience in both design and wholesale will be invaluable in our drive for worldwide expansion and new product development. He has a wealth of varied experience including

with Romeo Gigli in Milan, J Crew in New York, Pringle in London, Holliday & Brown in Italy and Jean-Paul Gaultier in Paris.[55]

Fashion retailers take on the challenge of restoring health to the economy by being more amusing, creative and bold. As Paul Smith asserts, in his world they cannot rest on their laurels; they feel that being even globally successful, they cannot afford to stay the same. Natalie Massenet became Britain's 98th richest woman through her online designer shopping website, *Net-a-porter*. She has devised a way of shopping for the 'time poor, cash rich'. Certainly branded French, even Paris, possibly Milan, by its clever name, *Net-a-porter* sells every label worth reciting, from Adidas, by Stella McCartney, to Zac Posen and Zimmerman. Said to have discovered the e-commerce pot of gold, a niche market of Internet-savvy high spenders, she started her Fashion career as a journalist with *Tatler*. Beginning the business with three people and £850,000 in a room in Chelsea, she was always confident she had a winner: 'I never thought it wouldn't work. I never once thought it wouldn't be huge.' Taking on the challenge of riding economic storms by widening her customer base, she launched theOutnet. com in 2009. It is designed for 'fashionistas who like a bargain as much as a designer label'.[56]

As Natalie Massenet enlarged her already worldwide market by adjusting her price point and Philip Green used international diplomacy to promote his latest flagship in New York, Paul Smith engaged the services of the Design industry through his relationship with Design Museum director Deyan Sudjic. Creating 138 individual bag designs for every Paul Smith shop in Japan, he invited customers to get something 'very rare and special' to take on their international flights. Each design was limited to an edition of 10, on sale in Japan and on view in London. Sudjic praised them as a 'breath of fresh air', like 'an encyclopedia of design thinking'.[57]

Each buying and selling tycoon is determined to continue the retail revolution, to leave no market untapped, to invade each city and engage its populace in preparation for the parade. In Fashion retailing, the war is fought in high streets, on catwalks, in magazine editorials, on television, online, in window displays. So when the going gets tough, the tough mobilize their forces to do more than just sell an extra few million new lipsticks.

Notes

1 Robert Violette (ed.), *Paul Smith: You Can Find Inspiration in Everything* (London: Thames & Hudson, 2003), p. 131.
2 Ibid.
3 Christopher Breward, David Gilbert & Jenny Lister (eds.), *Swinging Sixties* (London: V&A, 2006), p. 105.
4 Ibid., p. 117.
5 Violette, *Paul Smith*, p. 123.
6 Ibid.
7 Ibid., p. 79.
8 Ibid.
9 Ibid., p. 81.
10 Ibid.
11 Quoted in UK TV series *British Style Genius*, BBC2, Autumn 2008.
12 Ibid.
13 Ibid.
14 Violette, *Paul Smith*, p. 82.
15 Jess Cartner-Morley: 'He made quirky acceptable by tweaking British style', *The Guardian* online, 10 February 2006, http://www.guardian.co.uk/uk/2006/feb/10/fashion.clothes (accessed 25 May 2009).
16 Ibid.
17 Ibid.
18 Violette, *Paul Smith*, p. 280
19 Ibid.
20 Ibid.
21 Helen Goworek, *Careers in Fashion and Textiles* (Oxford: Blackwell, 2006), p. 60.
22 Jess Cartner-Morley, *The Guardian*.
23 Yuniya Kawamura, 'Placing Tokyo on the fashion map', in *Fashion's World Cities*, ed. Christopher Breward & David Gilbert (Oxford: Berg, 2006), p. 58.
24 Akira Miura, 'Four dazzling Japanese designers inspired the cloistered world of high fashion to look East', *Time Asia*, 2006, http://www.time.com/time/asia/2006/heroes/bl_jap_designers.html (accessed 25 May 2009).
25 Ibid.
26 Paul Davies, Purple PR, e-mail to author, 14 May 2009.
27 Michael Bracewell, 'Dream lover', *Independent on Sunday*, 29 August 2004.
28 Richard B. Woodward, 'Pilgrimages to cathedrals of commerce', *New York Times* online, 11 March 2007, http://travel.nytimes.com/2007/03/11/travel/11culture.html (accessed 25 May 2009).
29 Ibid.
30 Ibid.

31 Press release, Hong King Trade Development Council, 2007, http://hkfashionweekfw.tdctrade.com/press_rel/jan15.ht

32 Jay Diamond and Ellen Diamond, *The World of Fashion* (New York: Fairchild Publications, 1999), p. 122.

33 Hilary Hollingworth, interview with author, 2007.

34 Norma Rantisi, 'How New York stole modern fashion', jn *Fashion's World Cities*, p. 112.

35 Ibid., p. 114.

36 Ibid., p. 118.

37 Ibid., p. 119.

38 Ibid.

39 Christine Sorensen, 'The fashion market and the marketing environment', *Fashion Marketing*, ed. Mike Easey (Oxford: Wiley-Blackwell, 2009), p. 27.

40 Segre Reinach, 'The city of prêt à porter', in *Fashion's World Cities*, p. 123.

41 Ibid., p.125

42 Ibid.

43 Ibid., p. 128.

44 Jo Craven, 'Miuccia Prada, biography', Vogue.com, http://www.vogue.co.uk/biographies/080420-miuccia-prada-biography.aspx (accessed 25 May 2009).

45 Reinach, p. 128.

46 Ibid., p. 130.

47 Kathryn McKelvey and Janine Munslow, *Fashion Forecasting* (Oxford: Wiley-Blackwell, 2008) p. 217.

48 Adam P. Schneider, 'Inside Prada's Bedroom', *Fashion Week Daily*, 14 February 2009, http://www.fashionweekdaily.com/parties/fullstory.sps?inewsid=662706 (accessed 25 May 2009).

49 'My week: Katie Grand', *Times* online, 22 February 2009, http://www.timesonline.co.uk/tol/life_and_style/court_and_social/article5780310.ece

50 Jess Cartner-Morley, 'Fashion's sharpest operator', 20 May 2009, *The Guardian* online, http://www.guardian.co.uk/lifeandstyle/2009/may/20/carine-roitfeld-french-vogue-fashion-interview (accessed 25 May 2009).

51 Greg Wood, 'Topshop takes American plunge', BBC online, 2 April 2009, http://news.bbc.co.uk/1/hi/business/7978055.stm (accessed 25 May 2009).

52 Ibid.

53 Mrs. A, blogger, 'Follow the fashion of Mrs O: What and who she's wearing', *Mrs.O* website, 16 March 2009, http://www.mrs-o.org/?p=4754 (accessed 25 May 2009).

54 Harriet Quick, 'Why do we shop?', *Art, Life and Shopping: Selfridges & Co 100, 1909–2009,* Condé Nast, 2009.

55 Leisa Barnett, 'Jaeger's new stock', Vogue.com, 4 November 2008, http://www.vogue.co.uk/news/daily/081104-jaeger-appoints-new-design-director.aspx (accessed 25 May 2009).

56 Natalie Massenet, quoted in *Sunday Times* 'Rich List', 26 April 2009.

57 E-mail to author, 22 May 2009.

CONCLUSION

Roland Barthes and the compassionate professionals

Everyone knows ... that the Fashion phenomenon is linked to a certain economic gap within societies, characterised generally by the need to sell an object (clothing) at a rate which is faster than its wearing out; and that in the renewal of Fashion models, in their organization and dissemination, there intervene elements for which psycho-sociology alone can account.

Roland Barthes, *The Fashion System*

Fashion's tactic to deal with society's rapid evolution is to evolve rapidly itself. Changes are driven by the seasons but they are managed by the Industry. When the creative world was devastated by the late 1980s AIDS epidemic and the economy was going through one of its cyclical downturns, Fashion's business brains were activated. Catwalk designers focused on prêt-à-porter and others, like Gucci, Yohji Yamaoto and Rei Kawakubo, delivered clothes to satisfy the aspirations of the nouveau riche, the new generation of upwardly mobile young professionals. Paul Smith is said to have provided them with the Filofax, the leather bound personal organizer as the 'ultimate accessory'. Ralph Lauren appeared, in America, to bring a fictional, elevated lifestyle to department stores. Here shoppers could fantasize about a mythical heritage, inspired by Hollywood, and buy into its narrative through the important signifier – the multivalent denim blue jean.

Ubiquitous, and full of meaning, jeans began as work-wear in Europe. The name 'jeans' comes from 'bleu de Gênes', the blue of Genoa, in Italy, and 'denim' from 'serge de Nîmes', the fabric from Nîmes, in France, from which soldiers' and workmen's trousers were made in the 17th and 18th centuries. While Karl Marx, political economist and first human interest journalist, was formulating his theories which saw new groups of middle-class city dwellers emerging, Levi Strauss was making jeans for the Wild West workforce in America. A Jewish immigrant merchant, Strauss patented the copper-riveted design, worn by cowboys, miners and railroad workers, in 1872. They became, in the words of Bill Blass, 'the most significant contribution America has made to fashion'[1] with their links to Hollywood westerns, and promotion through television advertising. *The Women*, a film from 1939, featured Norma Shearer, Rosalind Russell and Joan Crawford as three hard-headed, wealthy Manhattan wives in 'sexy versions' of jeans, waiting in a Nevada hotel for divorces to come through. Rabine and Kaiser in *Fashion's World Cities* see the most 'spectacular celebrity endorser' as Marilyn Monroe, appearing in a 1952 calendar wearing 'nothing but Levi's and a bikini top':

> Thirty years before women engaged in body building she bench presses free weights from an angle that emphasises the border between her bare midriff and the fly of her blue jeans, foreshadowing the role jeans would play in signifying and performing women's sexual and gender revolution a generation later.[2]

In *The Jeaning of America*, John Fiske recognized that jeans carried signifiers, which could represent meanings for both, groups and individuals. He writes of their chameleon qualities, their ability to be seen as unisexual, masculine or feminine:

> This semiotic richness of jeans means that they cannot have a single defined meaning but they are a resource bank of potential meaning.[3]

When jeans are assigned to specific labels, manufacturers are able to compete with other makes in the market place. The social identities that the designers define become the signature look of the clothes:

> Designer jeans, then, speak to market segmentation and social difference; they move away from the shared values, away from nature, toward culture and its complexities.[4]

In Europe, members of the aristocracy began wearing jeans to express a commonality with the people, when the vogue was taken up by

Princess Diana, wife of the Prince of Wales and a member of one of the oldest noble families in Britain. Cast in the exclusive roles they have inherited, they are merely striking a pose, not assuming a lifestyle; so they choose to wear designer or traditional jeans, as either offers opportunities to identify with many various others. They do not have to attempt to 'move upscale socially'. They are above bourgeois, not needing to take on city sophistication or to become part of a trend-following group. They do not need to leave their country estates or stop herding cattle or harvesting crops. For the rest of us, in Levi's, Lee Cooper or Wranglers, we express the values of the country, the communal, of work, the traditional, the unchanging; in Diesel, Donna

For the rest of us, in Levi's, Lee Cooper or Wranglers, we express the values of the country, the communal, of work, the traditional, the unchanging; in Deisel, Donna Karan or Calvin Klein we become socially distinctive, feminine, sometimes more masculine, leisured, contemporary and ephemeral.

Karan or Calvin Klein we become socially distinctive, feminine, some-times more masculine, leisured, contemporary and ephemeral. Fashion designers take these basics and adapt them to the lives and aspirations of their potential audiences and buyers. They have become part of Fashion's story, included in many collections, sometimes used to express a moment, but never as a defining trend. If jeans are included in a collection, it merely mirrors the tendency towards the shift away from a single Fashion movement to a more multifaceted approach.

Today we consume Fashion through an infinite number of images and ideas, expressed through a constantly expanding Media. Designers and forecasters play the part of wizards. They are in the front line of promotional campaigns, with exceptional talent for briefing their teams. They take hold of myriad influences, from catwalks in cities to visions in ballparks, making them marketable to specific demographics. Like mystics, they consult on the future. They use strategic branding to develop new products. They bring in ethnographic studies to identify surfacing tendencies. They examine statistical trends. It is crucial to have fingers on the pulse of these changing signifiers. Economic and social patterns in family life, housing, entertainment, finance and leisure are considered. Creative intelligence is vital to maintaining Fashion's power; every possible fresh approach is adopted:

> Many consultancies have developed their own patented mapping processes, or barometers, using scientific methods of plotting refer-ence points creating a more systematic approach to analysing infor-mation and synthesising the data into actionable forecasts.[5]

Charlotte Philby, previewing an exhibition celebrating the 'young at heart' held at the London Royal Albert Hall in Spring 2009, began by observing the pageant of style in an East London borough:

> In the doorway, three middle-aged bouncers survey the young crowd with clear bemusement; their sober crew-cuts and practical footwear in stark contrast to a hive of vertiginous quiffs, Native American-print T-shirts, skin-tight pink jeans, heavy Nordic cardigans and acid-bright animal prints – all unisex.[6]

Gaps appear between generations, as one fails to keep up, and ignorance of Fashion movements is glorified by the ill-informed. The democratizing process progressed simultaneously with the growth of the middle classes and has been accelerated by the rise and rise of image-making. We are no longer divided as either voyeurs, *flâneurs* or workers. We are becoming totally individualized through access to Art and entertainment. As we feast on ideas and pictures, beamed into our lives, we look for more and more ways of being closer to their origins. We want to visit China to witness new fashions developed every day and see the striking parades on the streets of Shanghai. We become aware of the 'global theatre' and long to view embryonic Fashion in Japan. Yuniya Kawamura's *Japanese Teens as Producers of Street Fashion*, for the Fashion Institute of Technology in New York, sees how mavericks influence catwalks and high streets:

> Street fashion in the fashionable districts of Tokyo, such as Harajuku and Shibuya, is independent of any mainstream fashion system and goes beyond the conventional model of fashion business with different marketing strategies and occupational categories.[7]

Earlier identities

Technology has often frightened human beings, and there is the fear that we are being damaged by too many on-screen interactions. Sociologists think we need to go back to a more sensuous connection with the universe. We need to go back to more intimate relationships with our tribes, our villages, our earlier identities. Others advise us not to be neurotically looking for the next terror. We should see the information revolution as liberating, rather than enslaving; leading to socialization, empowering us to research, investigate and interact. It is Fashion which embraces the opportunity to communicate with others. Through inventive professionals, it has spread its message far and wide. Most at ease with well-designed websites, Fashion's practitioners develop ways of linking one technology to another, engaging with all the digital and conventional Media. The Fashion house Chanel bought into the lives of the *Harry Potter* generation when they contemplated engaging Emma Watson, youthful witch Hermione, as the new face for their cosmetics and beauty products in 2009. Having dressed her for red carpet pre-mieres, Chanel identified with the rising star. It could appropriate the latest romantic themes of transformation and enchantment to its own prestigious label, magically linking its glamour to Hollywood, J.K. Rowling and back to Paris, through Watson's maternal grandmother.

De rigueur for Westwood

Fashion promotion has an absolutely fascinating history. Although Percy Savage lived during the years when publicity, and Public Relations, were regarded with energetic suspicion, he used his consider-able love of Fashion to inspire his own career in its service. When he died, aged 72, in 2008, Winston Cuthbert, writing in *The Independent*, celebrated his life:

> Percy Savage, an enigmatic, Zelig-like character, personified the world of fashion and spent a lifetime promoting it. Arriving in Paris from Australia in 1947, the year Christian Dior launched his New Look, Savage became a close friend of the great designer, who was to name Eau Sauvage after him.[8]

After altering the way Fashion was advertised and promoted in Paris by having Elizabeth Taylor wear Lanvin for a movie premiere, he moved to London in the 1960s, promoting Quant to America, and where among other innovations he was an instigator of London Fashion Week.

> By 1970 he had settled in England permanently and at the behest of powerful journalists including Ernestine Carter and Beatrix Miller, Savage set about elevating the profile of British fashion. His years at the forefront of fashion PR boosted the fortunes of, among others, Zandra Rhodes, Bruce Oldfield, Katharine Hamnett, Wendy Dagworthy and Vivienne Westwood.[9]

He began a golden age of Fashion PR, and his career was overlapped by Fashion PRs' Fashion PR Lynne Franks, who inspires countless current practitioners. Her creativity came from a love of the creators, the designers and their assistants, whose passionate commitment to

their crafts, and their mission encouraged her to devote extra energies
to the cause. She told Charlotte Cripps about her life in the seventies
and eighties, and of how she dressed for her designer friends' Fashion
shows and new collections. She became a Punk, to be de rigueur for
Westwood:

> I had straps off all my jackets and all my trousers and I'd be
> taking the Press down to her shop in the King's Road. I looked
> like this mid-thirties Jewish mother in Seditionaries. Then I co-
> coordinated London Fashion Week, working for all sorts of fashion
> designers – Katharine Hamnett, Body Map, John Galliano, Ghost,
> Vivienne Westwood – and every time one of my clients or friends
> did a show, I would change into another outfit, with the accessories
> and hair.[10]

Mark Borkovski accuses the PR profession of promoting fake celebrity and creating sound bites which confuse important issues. Quoting
from an interview with the *Independent*'s Ian Burrell, he cites Jennifer
Saunders's fictional hit *Absolutely Fabulous* as an example of PR's cynical
approaches:

> PR guru Edina Monsoon is challenged by her daughter, Saffron, to
> describe what she does. 'PR! I PR things. People. Places. Concepts.
> I make them fabulous. I make the crap into credible. I make the
> dull into … ,' stammers Eddie before running out of inspiration.
> 'Delicious!' says Patsy, helping her out.[11]

This is parody. Fashion PR is in a different league from the rest. The
promotion of fake celebrity is unnecessary. All our talented are either
professional creators or performers. We have endlessly changing content.
There is no need to engage with the five-letter word 'stunt'. We have
exhibitions, range launches, international catwalks, backstage dressing
rooms, shows, designer interviews. A willing Media and an eager clothing industry support Fashion's sovereignty. Unlike Advertising, Fashion
does not need Barthes or Freud or Ed Bernays to teach it how exploit
the unconscious. Fashion is worn, like billboards in the street, in cafés,
and in bars; discussed by animated fanatics on, and off, red carpets, at
concerts, openings and soirées. When PR writers engage with Fashion,

they know they are dealing with the most humane part of being human. They are taking on the imagined pleasures that others anticipate. They are empathizing with their peers, their brothers, their sisters. They are involved with the most pleasurable, the most erotic, the most entertaining; able to indulge passions and share fantasies. Helen Sharpe, for All Saints Menswear S/S 08, began a Press release:

> Disengaged and dispirited our own generation's new doomed youth finds itself marching in groups – in gangs – in communes – and finds an intense unity in their disparity. Nowhere do we see this more than under the benevolent benediction of the all-permissive FESTIVAL – where together we are united and exalted through new noise and bright light – each beat of the drum intensified by chemicals and elements.[12]

Fashion is in the vanguard when new ways of promotion are needed. Miss Dior Cherie fragrance was sold through a multimedia campaign. Samples of the scent appeared in glossies at the same time as Sofia Coppola's first-ever commercial, featuring the model Maryna Linchuk, was aired. In a life imitating Art, post-Modern extravaganza, Coppola directed Linchuk using a script which followed a day in the life of the model. She has a fitting at the Dior atelier, in Paris, and joyfully romps through the city streets. Sixties sex kitten Brigitte Bardot's song 'Moi, Je Joue' provides the backing track. In more of Fashion marketing's conjuring tricks. the Coppola commercials were scheduled in breaks between *Gossip Girl* and *Sex and the City* re-runs. Meanwhile, *Marie Claire* Editor-in-chief Joanna Coles headed up her magazine's first television partnership, *Running in Heels*, an innovative collaboration between magazine journalism and reality television, making all the right noises. The commercials and the shows are discussed next day in offices, colleges, shopping malls. Essential links are made between international Fashion groups, the film industry and developing websites, through the endlessly hypnotic medium of television. Competing for audiences and consumers, magazines, newspapers and the music business plan ways of staying in the game. Fashion stays à la mode by engaging with Art and Technology, and nowhere is this more in evidence than in the increasingly smart world of Fashion illustration.

There is an imaginative change in how Fashion is now drawn and represented:

> No longer is fashion the reserve of the elite – with the rise in popularity of designer labels among the masses, designers are targeting a sector of the market that has been previously untapped. Concept drawings have become accessible and consumer-focused with imagery deriving from popular culture, music videos, advertising, and popular magazines.[13]

Writing for his *Big Book of Fashion Illustration*, Martin Dawber tells of how 'illustrators are fully in tune' with the technology which has

As well as enlisting Emma Watson's new glamour, designer Christopher Bailey knows his task, as creative director of the international Fashion house Burberry, is to lead an inspired team making beautiful things, with which people achieve their dreams.

opened doors to entirely new worlds, allowing creators more choice in media methods:

> Now there is an inspirational freedom of expression that challenges each and every illustrator to roll the dice and, by rising to the challenge, push their work to the limit.[14]

Notions of chic

Realizing that the written garment is made by publicists and journalists, created through words, Roland Barthes was interested in the way sign systems produce not clothing, not women, but the abstract notion of Fashion. He saw any number of extra meanings in everyday gestures and images. His genius was to write about them in a kind of reverse poetry; to reconstitute rather than condense. Arch *flâneur*, he was consumed with a passion for observation. Speaking of Fashion as a 'cross-subsidising organism', he was enchanted by its vivacity, seeing it as a living thing. He thought it could do two things at once: extend everyone's access to clothes, while making each wearer feel distinctive. He writes of modern democracy as if it were a universal given. In mid-20th-century Paris it may have felt quite near. Now, in spite of inflexible state systems, Fashion is able to fulfil Barthes' predictions. His vision was being progressed, as he wrote, through designers like André Courrèges and Coco Chanel, who had returned to couture in 1954. She was taking her house on to international acclaim, while dressing elegant, professional women whose aspirations she understood. Barthes saw her role in Fashion's story, and wrote about her for *Marie Claire* in September 1967, styling his essay as a contest between Chanel and Courrèges, which he was refereeing as a philosopher. He introduced Chanel as a designer who values classical order – its 'reason, nature, permanence, the desire to charm and not to surprise' He set the two Parisian designers up as binary opposites, suggesting that the polar extreme of classicism would be futurism. He looked ahead to the millennium, saying, Courrèges 'dresses women from the year 2000 who are already the young girls of today'.

> Mixing, as in all legends, the person's character with the style of the works produced, Courrèges is credited with the mythical

qualities of the absolute innovator: young, tempestuous, galvanic, virulent, mad on sport (and the most abrupt of these – rugby), keen on rhythm (the presentation of his outfits is accompanied by jerky music), rash to the point of being contradictory as he invents an evening dress which is not a dress (but a pair of shorts).[15]

In the essay he deals with the notion of 'chic' believing that the word carries a hidden sense which 'ties seduction to long life'. He uses this thought to play with ideas of the class system and dandyism, implying that 'chic' cannot stand the look of 'newness'. He tells of how the dandy Beau Brummel would have a servant wear his clothes to age them a little. He writes of Chanel's suits imitating the clothing men wear in the marketplace, describing the woman she dressed as 'not the idle young girl but the young woman confronting the world of work which is itself kept discreet, evasive'. Barthes' journalism is not meant to inform *Marie Claire* readers, but to question their assumptions about the two designers. Chanel should be seen as 'the most social' because she wanted to resist 'the vulgarities of petty bourgeois clothing'; Courrèges as the bringer of Fashion to 'a new social class' – 'youth' – one not yet defined by 'sociologists'. Barthes knew that civilized communities' views of gender were changing. Popular and traditional influences on women were altering how women were perceived. When he wrote of the faces of Garbo and Hepburn, he was recognizing Hollywood's access to our creative unconsciousnesses. Not closely involved with the promotion or production of Fashion, he had to invent back-stories to support his theories. He thought there was something significant hidden in the process of garment manufacturing, and devised a pseudo-scientific language, 'utilitarian or decorative quantum', to cover his mystification. His constant research, by watching, provided him with many insights into our behaviour. He thought Fashion was a suitable field for academics to investigate, and laid down rules for separating it from the study of dress.

As a follower of the semiotician Saussure, Barthes believed information, and especially images, could be broken down into elements and analysed for extra meaning. He hit on Fashion as an especially rich field in which to test his hypothesis. He wondered why Fashion journalists would build extra stories into their presentation of Fashion. He failed to admit, or realize, that the journalists in question would be feeding

We want to visit China to witness new fashions developed every day and see the striking parades on the streets of Shanghai. We become aware of the 'global theatre' and long to view embryonic Fashion in Japan.

their own desire to communicate, creatively, with their readers: that they would know which Fashion they wanted to track on any particular day. He thought clothes themselves must contain signs which could only be interpreted in a certain way. He supposed there was an immutable link between the concept chosen by the writer – say, spring, youth, this season – and the specific Fashion item, the accessory, the shoes, the colour. Barthes gave his followers the opportunity to recognize the signifiers of post-Modernism. He was working in a century which had barely left the traditional behind. Only the privileged 'leisured' could think of what they might wear for separate activities; 'dress is never linked to the work experienced by the wearer, the whole problem of how clothes are functionalized is ignored'. Before

238

Vivienne Westwood, and wives and girlfriends of footballers, took the signifiers of upper-middle-class dress and subverted them, for fun, it was simpler for everyone, including Barthes, to read the signs. He believed clothes were conceived as an indication of the times, as pointers of a nationality or state, or influenced by social class. All these things are relevant to his argument, but missing from his considerations is the language of the designers themselves.

Exit detail

Fashion designers are more closely involved with human beings than are architects. They are concerned with the roles the wearers of their clothes will enact. Their creative process surrounds how people feel. They plan lives for their wearers quite separately from thinking of marketing campaigns. They may know something of their customers from market research, but they work as artists, like playwrights or script editors. They envisage how a person will behave wearing the clothes. In their imaginations they are seeing the lives others lead. The scenarios, with costumes, that they put together include 'exit detail'. They envisage how a person will feel wearing the clothes. Christian Dior may have wanted to make money for his patron, the fabrics giant Marcel Boussac, but in his mind's eye his clothes were for 'flower women'. Schiaparelli spent some of her working life fighting for copyright protection, but she designed clothes which fed creative imaginations, so everyone wanted a piece of the action. Mary Quant was so impressed with the youthful people around her, whether doctors' or dockers' daughters, that she researched fabrics to make their lives easier and more eventful. Sylvia Ayton designed for the fantasy worlds her high street customers inhabited. Vivienne Westwood believes her clothes enhance the beauty in each woman who wears them. Paul Smith cares whether an Englishman might be foregoing the purchase of white goods to buy a new suit. As well as enlisting Emma Watson's new glamour, designer Christopher Bailey knows that his task as Creative Director of the international Fashion house Burberry is to lead an inspired team making beautiful things with which people achieve their dreams:

> We have to deal with so many issues and yet Fashion is seen as frivolous. We put in lots of hours and we have to think globally.

239

> It's not just incredible clothes it's also exhausting. Everyone is dedicated to their craft dealing in beautiful, aspirational ideas.[16]

Anna Sui's designs are thought of as cute. Thematic and whimsical, her clothes are made for a loyal fan base who see themselves as 'hip' and 'exuberant'. From Detroit and trained at Parsons School of Design, New York, Sui has a style which is neither 'household name' nor 'dewy upstart', which means she is able to design for those same friends and colleagues who have been with her from the start. Her clothing label is supported through the 14 global fragrance and cosmetics licences that she operates in 42 store franchises in China, Japan, Taiwan and Kuwait. Journalists enjoy her creativity. She mixes vintage styles with diverse passions and, like Westwood, she researches her influences so thoroughly that stylists and editors look to her for directions. Marc Jacobs likes to think his followers, even if they are behaving like single-minded materialists, can be made to look like cultivated lovers of society:

> The world would be a better place if people just engaged in sex and didn't worry about it. But what I prefer is that even if someone feels hedonistic, they don't look it. Curiosity about sex is much more interesting to me than domination. Like, Britney and Paris and Pamela might be someone's definition of sexy, but they're not mine. My clothes are not hot. Never. Never …[17]

Natalie Massenet investigated her market and set up the technology to make *Net-a-porter*, the designer Internet shopping site, into a 'huge' success. She had venture capital, all the skills and contacts from her days in glossy magazine journalism and a world-class distribution network. She could not fail. It is not witchcraft or rocket science. Yet the alchemy achieved by the designers whose labels she sells is what gives her the unique selling point. Magic is created when her clients are connected to the stars they adore. They know, when the clothing arrives, that the feelings are mutual. If your particular devil is a curva-ceous, successful, professional woman, it could be her outfit is courtesy of ex-Communist Party member and mime artist Miuccia Prada. The psycho-sociology which Barthes could not quite pin down is the simpatico Fashion designers feel with humanity.

Notes

1 Linda Watson, 'Bill Blass: Fashion designer to New York society', *The Independent*, 15 June 2002, http://www.independent.co.uk/news/obituaries/bill-blass-645359.html (accessed 30 May 2009). 'Once described as the designer "who is able to charm the clothes right on to a woman's back", Bill Blass was known as much for his social skills as his designing ability. Blass reinvented himself from Indiana resident to urbane New Yorker. "The really smart woman should be like a man," Blass told *Women's Wear Daily* in 1964: "By age 30, she should have decided what's best for her type. A man knows instinctively ... a woman should follow suit. She should be a little like an actress, always playing up to herself."'

2 Leslie W. Rabine and Susan Kaiser, 'Sewing machines and dream machines', *Fashion's World Cities*, ed. Christopher Breward and David Gilbert (Oxford: Berg, 2006), p. 245.

3 John Fiske, 'The jeaning of America', *Understanding Popular Culture* (London: Routledge, 1989), p. 5.

4 Ibid., p. 8.

5 Kathryn McKelvey and Janine Munslow, *Fashion Forecasting* (Oxford: Wiley-Blackwell, 2008), p. 7.

6 Charlotte Philby, 'Unordinary people: A celebration of British youth culture', *The Independent*, 18 April 2009, http://www.independent.co.uk/arts-entertainment/features/unordinary-people-a-celebration-of-British-youth-culture-1668559.html (accessed 30 May 2009).

7 Yuniya Kawamura, 'Japanese Teens as Producers of Street Fashion', for the Fashion Institute of Technology, *Current Sociology*, 54:5 (1 September 2006), pp. 784–801.

8 Winston Cuthbert, 'Percy Savage: Doyen of fashion PR', *The Independent*, 15 August 2008, http://www.independent.co.uk/news/obituaries/percy-savage-doyen-of-fashion-pr-897506.html

9 Ibid.

10 Charlotte Cripps, 'My greatest mistake – Lynne Franks, former PR', *The Independent*, 11 March 2004.

11 Ian Burrell, 'Confessions of a stunt man: Mark Borkowski on the fame game', *The Independent*, 28 July 2008, http://www.independent.co.uk/news/media/confessions-of-a-stuntman-mark-borkowski-on-the-fame-game-878504.html (accessed 30 May 2009).

12 Press release, e-mail to author, Spring 2008.

13 Front flap, Martin Dawber, *Imagemakers: Cutting Edge Fashion Illustration* (London: Mitchell Beazley, 2004).

14 Martin Dawber, *The Big Book of Fashion Illustration* (London: Batsford, 2007), p. 9.

15 Roland Barthes, *The Language of Fashion*, trans. Andy Stafford (Oxford: Berg, 2006), pp. 105–6.

16 Christopher Bailey in conversation with Colin McDowell at the doctorate ceremony for McDowell, Huddersfield University, 5 December 2008.

17 Marc Jacobs, quoted by Amy Larocca, 'Lost and found', *New York* magazine online, 12 August 2005, http://nymag.com/nymetro/shopping/fashion /12544/ (accessed 30 May 2009).

BIBLIOGRAPHY

Arnold, Rebecca, *Fashion Desire and Anxiety: Image and Morality in the 20th Century* (New Brunswick, NJ: Rutgers University Press, 2001)

Arnold, Rebecca, 'Vivienne Westwood's *Anglomania*', in *The Englishness of English Dress*, ed. Christopher Breward, Becky Conekin and Caroline Cox (Oxford: Berg, 2002)

Barthes, Roland, *The Fashion System*, trans. Matthew Ward and Richard Howard (New York: Hill and Wang, 1983)

Barthes, Roland, *Mythologies*, (trans. Annette Lavers, 1972) (London: Vintage, 2000)

Barthes, Roland, *The Language of Fashion*, trans. Andy Stafford, ed. Andy Stafford and Michael Carter, (Oxford, New York: Berg, 2006)

Blum, Dilys E., *Shocking! The Art & Fashion of Elsa Schiaparelli* (Philadelphia: Philadelphia Museum of Art, 2003)

Breward, Christopher, *Fashion* (Oxford: Oxford University Press, 2003)

Breward, Christopher, David Gilbert and Jenny Lister (eds.), *Swinging Sixties* (London: V&A, 2006)

Church Gibson, Pamela, 'New stars, new fashions and the female audience: Cinema, consumption and cities 1953–1966', in *Fashion's World Cities*, ed. Christopher Breward and David Gilbert (Oxford: Berg, 2006)

Cosgrave, Bronwyn, *Made for Each Other: Fashion and the Academy Awards* (London: Bloomsbury, 2007)

Dawber, Martin, front flap, *Imagemakers: Cutting Edge Fashion Illustration* (London: Mitchell Beazley, 2004)

Dawber, Martin, *The Big Book of Fashion Illustration* (London: Batsford, 2007)

Diamond, Jay, and Ellen Diamond, *The World of Fashion* (New York: Fairchild Publications, 1999)

Drake, Nicholas, *The Fifties in Vogue* (London: Heinemann, 1987)

Fiske, John, 'The jeaning of America', in *Understanding Popular Culture* (London: Routledge, 1989)

Frankel, Susannah, 'Vivienne Westwood', in *Visionaries: Interviews with Fashion Designers* (London: V&A Publications, 2005)

Gallico, Paul, *Mrs 'Arris Goes to Paris* (New York City: International Polygonics, 1989)

Goworek, Helen, *Careers in Fashion and Textiles* (Oxford: Blackwell, 2006)

Haskell, Molly, *From Reverence to Rape: The Treatment of Women in the Movies* (London, New English Library, 1975)

Howell, Georgina, *In Vogue: 75 Years of Style* (London: Condé Nast/ Random Century, 1991)

Kawamura, Yuniya, 'Japanese Teens as Producers of Street Fashion' for the Fashion Institute of Technology, *Current Sociology*, 4:5 (1 September 2006)

Kawamura Yuniya, 'Placing Tokyo on the fashion map', in *Fashion's World Cities*, ed. Christopher Breward and David Gilbert (Oxford: Berg, 2006)

Lapsley, Rob, and Michael Westlake 'From *Casablanca* to *Pretty Woman*: The politics of romance', in *Contemporary Film Theory*, ed. Antony Easthope (New York: Longman, 1993)

Ludot, Didier, *The Little Black Dress* (New York & Paris: Assouline, 2006)

Lynn, Eleri, 'Preface', *The Golden Age of Couture*, 2008 diary (London: V&A, 2007)

McKelvey, Kathryn and Janine Munslow, *Fashion Forecasting* (Oxford: Wiley-Blackwell, 2008)

McRobbie, Angela, *British Fashion Design: Rag Trade or Image Industry?* (London: Routledge, 1998)

Moseley, Rachel, *Growing Up with Audrey Hepburn* (Manchester: Manchester University Press, 2002)

Moseley, Rachel, 'Respectability sewn up: Dressmaking and film star style in the fifties and sixties', *European Journal of Cultural Studies*, 4 (4) (2001)

Paglia, Camille, *Sexual Persona, Art and Decadence from Nefertiti to Emily Dickinson* (London: Penguin, 1995)

Quant, Mary, *Quant by Quant* (London: Pan, 1967)

Quick, Harriet, 'Why do we shop?' in *Art, Life and Shopping: Selfridges & Co 100, 1909–2009* (Condé Nast, 2009)

Rabine, Leslie W. and Susan Kaiser, 'Sewing machines and dream machines', in *Fashion's World Cities*, ed. Christopher Breward and David Gilbert (Oxford: Berg, 2006)

Rantisi, Norma, 'How New York stole modern fashion', in *Fashion's World Cities*, ed. Christopher Breward and David Gilbert (Oxford: Berg, 2006)

Rocamora, Agnès, 'Paris, Capitale de la mode: Representing the fashion city in the media', in *Fashion's World Cities*, ed. Christopher Breward and David Gilbert (Oxford: Berg, 2006)

Scott, Linda M, *Fresh Lipstick: Redressing Fashion and Feminism* (London: Palgrave Macmillan, 2005)

Segre Reinach, 'The city of prêt à porter', in *Fashion's World Cities*, ed. Christopher Breward and David Gilbert (Oxford: Berg, 2006)

Sellers, Susan, 'How Long Has This Been Going On? *Harper's Bazaar, Funny Face* and the Construction of the Modernist Woman', *Visible Language*, 29 (Winter 1995)

Smith, Douglas '*Funny Face*: Humanism in Post-War French Photography and Philosophy', *French Cultural Studies*, 16 (1) (2005)

Sorensen, Christine, 'The fashion market and the marketing environment', *Fashion Marketing*, ed. Mike Easey (Oxford: Wiley-Blackwell, 2009)

Steele, Valerie, *The Red Dress* (New York: Rizzoli International Publications, 2001)

Steele, Valerie, *Fifty Years of Fashion: New Look to Now* (New Haven and London: Yale University Press, 2006)

Stutesman, Drake, 'Storytelling: Marlene Dietrich's face and John Frederics' hats', in *Fashioning Film Stars, Dress, Culture, Identity*, ed. Rachel Moseley (London: British Film Institute, 2005)

Taylor, Helen, *Scarlett's Women: 'Gone with the Wind' and Its Female Fans* (London: Virago, 1989)

Tungate, Mark, *Fashion Brands* (London: Kogan Page, 2005)

Vertrees, Alan, *Selznick's Vision* (Austin: Texas University Press, 1998)

Violette, Robert (ed.), *Paul Smith: You Can Find Inspiration in Everything* (London: Thames & Hudson, 2003)

Weisberger, Lauren, *The Devil Wears Prada* (London: HarperCollins, 2003)

Wilcox, Claire, *The Golden Age of Couture, Paris and London 1947–57* (London: V&A Publications, 2007)

Wilcox, Claire, *Vivienne Westwood* (London: V&A, 2008)

INDEX

Page numbers in *italics* refer to figures; n refers to Notes